ALSO BY CHARLES MURRAY

Losing Ground:
American Social Policy 1950–1980

In Pursuit
Of Happiness
and Good Government

CHARLES MURRAY

SIMON AND SCHUSTER

NEW YORK · LONDON · TORONTO · SYDNEY · TOKYO

SIMON AND SCHUSTER
Simon & Schuster Building
Rockefeller Center
1230 Avenue of the Americas
New York, New York 10020

10 9 8 7 6 5 4

Library of Congress Cataloging-in-Publication Data

Murray, Charles A.
  In pursuit : of happiness and good government /
Charles Murray.
    p.   cm.
Bibliography: p.
Includes index.
ISBN 0–671–61100–3
    1. United States—Social Policy—1980–   2. Happiness.
I. Title.
HN65.M87   1988   88–18115
361.6′1′0973–dc 19   CIP

Excerpts from the following copyrighted materials
have been reprinted with special permission:

"Images of Fear"—A *Harper's* Forum, *Harper's
Magazine*, May 1985, copyright © 1985 by the
Harper's Magazine Foundation.

Thinking About Crime by James Q. Wilson,
copyright © 1975, 1983 by Basic Books, Inc.

*Intrinsic Motivation and Self-Determination in
Human Behavior* by Edward L. Deci and
Richard M. Ryan, copyright © 1985 by Plenum
Press, a division of Plenum Publishing Corporation.

TO CATHERINE
This book especially

Contents

Prologue

THE ROOTS of this book go down twenty years. It was the spring of 1968 in Thailand, an insurgency was in progress in the northeastern part of the country, and the Thai and American governments were pouring resources into rural development—the Thai version of winning the hearts and minds of the people. Fresh out of the Peace Corps, I was leading the fieldwork for a case study of four villages. We wanted to interview villagers about the development projects in their communities and, more generally, about what they thought of the Thai officials in their district. We wouldn't try to force the villagers' responses into multiple-choice boxes; rather, we would just let them talk and then we would write down what they said, however they chose to say it.

After a few weeks in our first set of two villages, I was convinced the research was going to be a failure. The interviews were turning up only the most casual mentions of either the development projects or government officials. We weren't going to have enough data to analyze. So the Thai interviewers and I tried a variety of fixes. None worked. We were confident that the villagers were being candid with us, but probe as we might, the conversation kept veering away from the topics that were important to us. Instead, the villagers talked at

11

length about the affairs of the village. Sometimes it was about
the family next door, the price of kenaf, or the new bus service
into the market town. Often it was about governance—not the
governance of the nation or of the district, however, but governance of the village.

The accounts that unfolded were far different from the
ones I had expected. For while my two years in the Peace
Corps had taken me to many villages, I had always approached
them as a "change agent," as that role was called in those days.
We change agents had been enjoined to "consider the needs
of the people" and "encourage local participation," much as
change agents back in the States were calling for "maximum
feasible participation" in community development projects. But
my experience had been that villagers seemed never to get
anything done. Give a project to the village, and it would
bog down. Now, with the chance to sit back and just listen,
I was hearing about all the things that village headmen and
committees (*their* committees, home-grown) did when the
change agents weren't around. They ranged from major projects like building a reservoir to day-to-day functions like rec-
onciling marital disputes. Sometimes the mechanisms were
sophisticated: progressive taxation to finance repairs to a village
hall, renting a grader to make a road, designating one villager
to go away to learn brickmaking so he could teach the others.
Sometimes the mechanisms were simple. Not everything was
always done well. In one of the two villages, the main topic
of conversation was how to remove an incompetent headman.
But good or bad, the governance of the village's affairs was at
the center of interest.

As the interviews accumulated, I had to face the fact that
the villagers' concerns were anchored in things that we weren't
asking questions about. Then another thought hit me: *They
were right.* The conditions that made for a happy or unhappy
village had much more to do with the things they were interested in than with the things I was interested in.

My small epiphany had nothing to do with theories of social
change, just the simple truth that Alexis de Tocqueville had in
mind when he began his examination of American political
institutions, one hemisphere and more than a century removed.

"It is not by chance that I consider the township first," he wrote in *Democracy in America:*

> The township is the only association so well rooted in nature that wherever men assemble it forms itself. Communal society therefore exists among all peoples, whatever be their customs and laws. Man creates kingdoms and republics, but townships seem to spring directly from the hand of God.[1]

Had I read Tocqueville more thoroughly in my college days and remembered it better, I would have seen much more quickly how the villages worked and how effective "development" in them came about:

> It is in the township, the center of the ordinary business of life, that the desire for esteem [and] the pursuit of substantial interests . . . are concentrated; these passions, so often troublesome elements in society, take on a different character when exercised so close to home and, in a sense, within the family circle. . . . Daily duties performed or rights exercised keep municipal life constantly alive. There is a continual gentle political activity which keeps society on the move without turmoil.[2]

But it did not occur to me to consult my foggy memories of Tocqueville in trying to understand what I was observing. These were Thai villages in 1968, not New England townships in 1831.

The half-formed thoughts that came to me during the early stages of the research were brought more sharply into focus as the research proceeded. One of the next two villages we chose was a model village, the pride of the Mukdahan District. An energetic and engaging young Thai official had been imported into the community and had brought about a cascade of development projects—a fishpond, a new school building, a cotton-growing project, a rice cooperative, even a health clinic. This time, we were sure we would get material about our assigned topic, for in this village the official Thai government was very much a part of current village life.

We first occupied ourselves with trying to find how each individual project had affected the village. (Were there fish in the fishpond? How many people used the health clinic? How had these projects affected the villagers' lives?) Again, we ran into a problem. The villagers' answers about the effects of any individual project were short. But their discussions of the ways in which the life of the village had changed overall were spontaneous and subtle and deeply felt—and the news was not good. The energetic and engaging young official had taken over (with the best interests of the villagers at heart), and in so doing had supplanted the mechanisms by which the villagers ran their village and pursued their lives. The villagers said plainly and without qualification that the life in this model village had gotten worse, not better.

Well, you can't make an omelet without breaking eggs, right? It's too bad, but one of the costs of modernization is the breakdown of some quaint old-fashioned ways. They'll adapt to it after a while. Such were the assumptions I had brought to the work. But it was hard to listen to these villagers and be as confident as before. Again, it would have helped me to understand what had happened if I had remembered Tocqueville:

> The difficulty of establishing a township's independence rather augments than diminishes with the increase of enlightenment of nations. A very civilized society finds it hard to tolerate attempts at freedom in a local community; it is disgusted by its numerous blunders and is apt to despair of success before the experiment is finished.[3]

And again: "The institutions of a local community can hardly struggle against a strong and enterprising government."[4] And yet again: "If you take power and independence from a municipality, you may have docile subjects but you will not have citizens."[5]

I still did not see as acutely as Tocqueville, but I began to entertain a suspicion that within a few more weeks had become another small epiphany in that spring of 1968: Once again, *the villagers were right*. The things being lost in that village were at least as important as the things being added. The losses involved deterioration in the bedrock functions performed by any community, in Missouri or Brooklyn as in Northeast Thailand—settling neighbors' disputes, helping people in need, solving common problems. These in turn represented the bedrock resources for the individuals' pursuit of their private lives. The village had been doing a damned good job of filling those functions—not according to a romanticized Rousseauistic image of noble villagers, but by any standard for a civilized community. The conventional wisdom of development policy said that modernization must transfer functions and powers from communities to larger units. I began to ask myself a question that twenty years later I ask of contemporary America in this book: Are we really sure that's a good idea?

I did not subsequently try to stand athwart the bows of rural modernization yelling "Stop!" I continued to think (as I do today) that it is a good thing for villages to acquire fishponds and health clinics. When I returned to the United States, I continued to think (as I do today) that it is a good thing for hungry people to be fed, for the uneducated to be educated, for the disadvantaged to be given a helping hand. But two thoughts that I brought home from my experience in Thailand never completely left me.

The first was a notion that what I had seen in small rice-farming communities was relevant to complex American communities. The thought took a long time to mature; the reasons to resist were for a long time overwhelming. But I finally came to rest in the belief that Jeffersonian democracy is still the best way to run society, including the society in which we find ourselves today. Yes, I am aware that Jefferson himself said the earth is for the living, and that he chided those who "ascribe to the preceding age a wisdom more than human."[6] But it just may be that on certain fundamental questions of government, Jefferson and his colleagues were right more universally than they knew. In particular, they understood that the vitality of communities and the freedom of individuals are intertwined, not competitive.

But that conclusion came very late, as it does in this book. I reached it indirectly, by way of the second thought I brought home from Thailand: Whatever the best of all possible worlds may be, policy analysts have not been doing a very good job of deciding whether we are getting from here to there. By counting whether fishponds have fish and health clinics have patients—or, in America, by counting the number of people

under the poverty line or the number of people who receive
Medicaid benefits—policy analysts are not just failing to see
the forest for the trees. Ultimately, the trees we are counting
do not make up the forest of interest.

Policy analysts—and I include myself in the indictment—have
been in the position of the drunk in the old joke. You have
probably heard it: A man who has had too much to drink
is on his hands and knees under a streetlamp searching for
something. A passerby comes up and asks him what he is looking for. The drunk points to a nearby house and says that
he was unlocking his door and dropped his keys. But, the
passerby observes, the door is over there. "I know," the drunk
replies, "but the light's better over here."

We have looked where the light is, and for modern policy
analysis the light consists of quantitative analysis. I do not say
this altogether critically. Give a policy analyst variables that
can be expressed in numbers, and he has at hand a powerful
array of analytic tools to probe their meaning. The limitation—
and it has become more and more confining over the years—is
that so few of the interesting variables in the social sciences
can be expressed in numbers. The more complicated the constructs one wants to examine, the less likely that they can be
crammed within the quantitative paradigm. Concepts such as
"happiness" and "self-respect" and "the nature of man" (you
will be running up against all of these and more in the pages
that follow) force one to grapple with evidence that crosses
the disciplines of economics, sociology, political science, and
psychology, and for which hard data are hard to come by
and "proof" is usually impossible. And so it is with this book,
a queer mixture of hard data, soft data, thought experiments,
and speculations.

In such cases, and especially when a book has a controversial
point of view, the author should at least be obliged to provide
his readers with the equivalent of Informed Consent, telling
them in advance where the discussion is headed in both its text
and its subtext. In that spirit, this is the way I see *In Pursuit:*

Part 1, "The Happiness of the People," is a statement of
purpose and definition of terms. The question is how "success"
in social policy is to be measured. I argue that we have been
using inadequate measures, and propose that a better idea is

to use the pursuit of happiness as a framework for analyzing public policy. Then I discuss the concept of happiness in historical perspective and define how the word "happiness" will be used in the rest of the book. My objective in part 1 is to reach a common understanding about ultimate ends that readers from many perspectives can accept. Acknowledging this common understanding about ultimate ends doesn't imply anything about whether a specific policy will succeed or fail in achieving those ends—such issues remain suspended for many more chapters.

Part 2, "When There Is Bread," will, I hope, be for my readers what it was for me, an excursion into some fascinating topics. They include the uses of money in the pursuit of happiness, what "safety" means, the basis for self-respect, and my personal favorite, how people enjoy themselves. These are what I will call "enabling conditions," the raw material for pursuing happiness. My purpose is to explore each of them, sometimes drawing on recent empirical work, sometimes trying to tease out the implications of questions that don't have hard-and-fast answers (What is "enough" money? "Enough" safety?), but which lend themselves to more systematic exploration than one might have imagined.

My purpose is also to have fun with these questions, to play with them, and I hope that readers will relax and enjoy. You are not being led down a path that will suddenly leave you stranded in unacceptable company. On the contrary, as I point out in the text, a reader may with perfect consistency agree with the main points of part 2 and still disagree with just about everything I say in part 3.

That having been said, however, it is also true that part 2 presents what I believe to be evidence (even without subsequent interpretation) for fresh ways of looking at social policy, even if it doesn't logically compel one set of solutions. The subtext to part 2 is that old clichés about human lives (money can't buy happiness, the importance of self-respect, and so forth) examined closely not only are true but can powerfully influence one's thinking about policy.

Part 3, "Toward the Best of All Possible Worlds," begins with a proposition which must be true but rarely is acknowledged: Policy analysis is decisively affected by the analyst's conception of human nature. One may consider a government policy to be practical or impractical, safe or hazardous, only according to one's conception of what is good for humans, and that in turn has to be based on one's conclusions about the potentials and limitations of humans acting as social creatures. For decades, the dominant intellectual view in the United States seems to have been that humans acting in the private sphere tend to be uncaring or inept, whereas humans acting in the public sphere tend to serve (or can be made to serve) the common good. I associate myself with the view that humans acting privately tend to be resourceful and benign whereas humans acting publicly are resourceful and dangerous. After explaining the nature of that view and the reasons for it in the opening chapter of part 3, I analyze the policy implications of the preceding chapters from that perspective.

There is within part 3 a change of voice. For two chapters (9 and 10), I argue on behalf of new ways of evaluating results and designing solutions to specific social problems, saying in effect that there are better ways to conduct social policy than our current one even if you prefer reform in small doses. Significant improvements, I argue, would follow just by changing the frame of reference for perceiving what we are trying to accomplish. In chapters 11 and 12, I use successively broader strokes to present my reading of the implications of the material—implications not just for how we might best tackle specific social problems, but for the larger question, how society is to be organized so that it best serves "the happiness of the people." Chapter 13 closes the book by taking this line of thinking to its ultimate expression.

For many readers, this book will pose more questions than it offers answers. I will be satisfied with that. If we have learned nothing else from our problems in formulating good social policy in recent decades, it is that we need better questions about what we are doing and why. And I continue to hope that the longer the questions are pondered, the better the answers will become.

CHARLES MURRAY

Washington, D.C.
March 20, 1988

In Pursuit
Of Happiness
and Good Government

PART ONE

"THE
HAPPINESS OF THE
PEOPLE"

A good government implies two things; first,
fidelity to the object of government, which is
the happiness of the people; secondly, a knowledge of the means by which that object can be
best attained.

—JAMES MADISON

1

Measuring Success
in Social Policy

THIS BOOK is first about how people pursue happiness in their lives, and then about how government can help in that pursuit.

It is not a topic that is easy even to name, for "happiness" is an honorable word fallen on hard times. We have gotten used to happiness as a label for a momentary way of feeling, the state of mind that is the opposite of sad. Happiness is the promised reward of a dozen pop-psychology books on the airport book rack. It is a topic for bumper stickers and the comic strips—happiness as warm puppy. A book on public policy about "happiness"? Surely there is a sturdier contemporary term I might use instead. "Quality of life," perhaps: "This book is about personal quality of life, and what government can do to improve it." Or more respectable yet: "This book is about noneconomic indicators of perceived personal well-being, and their relationship to alternative policy options." But there's no getting around it. Happiness is in fact what we will be talking about.

WHAT IS THE CRITERION OF SUCCESS?

The first, natural question is why one might choose to discuss public affairs in terms of this most private and elusive of goals.

The pragmatic reason is that policy analysts are increasingly forced in that direction by events. The experience of the last half-century and more specifically of the last two decades must arouse in any thoughtful observer this question: *What constitutes "success" in social policy?*

For most of America's history, this was not a question that needed asking because there was no such thing as a "social policy" to succeed or fail. The government tried to be helpful to the economy in modest ways. It facilitated the settlement of the frontier. It adjudicated and arbitrated the competing interests of the several states. But, excepting slavery, the noneconomic institutions of American society remained largely outside federal purview until well into the twentieth century. As late as the 1930s, there was still no federal "policy" worthy of the label affecting the family, for example, or education, or religion, or voluntary associations. Some laws could be argued to have effects on such institutions (the child labor laws on the family, for example), but the notion that the federal government had a systematic relationship with the "success" of parents in raising their offspring, of schools in educating their students, or of poor people's efforts to become no longer poor would have struck most observers as perhaps theoretically true, but rather an odd way of looking at things.

Over a period of time from the New Deal through the 1970s, the nation acquired what we have come to call "social policy," with dozens of constituent elements—welfare programs, educational programs, health programs, job programs, criminal justice programs, and laws, regulations, and Supreme Court decisions involving everything from housing to transportation to employment to child care to abortion. Pick a topic of social concern or even of social interest, and by now a complex body of federal activity constitutes policy, intended to be an active force for good.

This brings us to the question of measuring success. For if the federal government seeks to do good in these arenas, there must be as well a measure of what "good" means. Whether you are a citizen or a policymaker, the same question arises with regard to any particular aspect of social policy: Are you for or against? Let's build more prisons. Yes or no? Let's dispense more food stamps. Yes or no?

For many years—certainly during my own training during the sixties and early seventies—social science faculties in our universities assumed a substratum of truths about why certain policies were good or bad things, and policy analysts did not have to think very hard about why the outcomes we analyzed were good or bad. We knew. Fighting poverty had to be good. Fighting racism had to be good. Fighting inequality had to be good. What other way of looking at good and bad might there be? And what other way of measuring progress might there be except to measure poverty, crime rates, school enrollment, unemployment?

By such measures, however, the policies didn't work out so well. In fact, by most such measures things got worse rather than better, and a fierce debate has raged about whether the policies themselves were at fault (a view that I share) or whether things would have been still worse without them. But even as the debate has continued, it has been increasingly difficult for policy analysts of any persuasion to avoid wondering whether we have been asking the right questions. Are we thinking about "progress" in the right way? *What constitutes "success" in social policy?*

Fighting poverty is good, yes. But if the poverty rate goes down while the proportion of children born to single women goes up, how are those two vectors to be combined so that we know whether, in the aggregate, we are headed up or down, forward or backward? Fighting racial discrimination is good, yes. But if the laws against discrimination in housing are made ever more stringent and actual segregation in housing increases, what are we to make of it? How are we to decide what course to navigate in the future?

Underlying these questions are others that ask not just how we are to add up conflicting indicators but rather the more far-reaching question, What's the point? What is the point of food stamps, anyway? What are they for? Suppose that we passed out food stamps so freely that no young man ever had to worry about whether a child that he caused to be conceived would be fed. *Would that really be a better world for children to be born into?* Or let us take food stamps writ large: Suppose that we made all material goods so freely available that parents could not ever again take satisfaction from the accomplishment of feeding, sheltering, and clothing their children. *Would that really be a better world in which to be a parent?* The immediate "point" of food stamps is simple—trying to help people have enough food to eat. But food stamps serve (and perhaps impede) other ends as well. What's the point? Ultimately, happiness is the point.

"The Pursuit of Happiness"

To make the case for happiness as something that a policy analyst can reasonably think about, there is no better place to start than with the stately and confident words of the Declaration of Independence. It is worth trying to read them as if for the first time: "We hold these truths to be self evident: that all men are created equal, that they are endowed by their creator with certain unalienable rights, that among these are life, liberty, and the pursuit of happiness—that to secure these rights, governments are instituted among men . . ."

"Happiness" was not Thomas Jefferson's idiosyncratic choice of words, nor was "pursuit of happiness" a rhetorical flourish to round out the clause. For the Founders, "happiness" was the obvious word to use because it was obvious to them that the pursuit of happiness is at the center of man's existence, and that to permit man to pursue happiness is the central justification of government—the "object of government," as James Madison wrote in the The Federalist No. 62.[1] James Wilson, who was later to become one of the chief architects of the Constitution, was voicing the general understanding of his contemporaries when he wrote in 1769 that the only reason men consent to have government is ". . . with a view to ensure and to increase the happiness of the governed, above what they could enjoy in an independent and unconnected state of nature," and then went on to assert that "the happiness of the society is the first law of every government."[2] John Adams calmly asserted that "Upon this point all speculative politicians will agree, that the happiness of society is the end of Government, as all divines and moral philosophers will agree that the happiness of the individual is the end of man."[3] Washington took happiness for his theme repeatedly, returning to it for the last time in his Farewell Address.[4] The concept of happiness and the word itself appear again and again in Revolutionary sermons, pamphlets, and tracts.[5]

What may annoy the modern reader approaching these texts is that these eighteenth-century writers never stipulated what they *meant* by happiness. The word appears in a sentence and then the writer or the speaker moves on. It is as if they were addressing people who would of course know what was meant by "happiness"—not only know, but agree. And so they did. They did not necessarily agree on the details. Some took their understanding from Aristotle and Aquinas, others from Locke, others from Burlamaqui or Hutcheson. But educated men were in broad agreement that happiness was a label for a ubiquitous concept, the concept of the good-that-one-seeks-as-an-end-in-itself-and-for-no-other-reason. The logic behind this concept is simple and highly intuitive, going roughly as follows.

Anything we enjoy—anything that is a "good" in some sense—we enjoy for itself, but we also enjoy it because of other goods to which it leads. I enjoy getting a new car, let us say. Perhaps I enjoy it for the thing-in-itself known as a New Car, but I also obviously value it for other things such as driving places. Or: I value friendship as a good-in-itself. But I also use friendship for other ends besides friendship. Friends may educate me, which is also a good; they may make me laugh, which is also a good; or they may loan me money when I need it, still a third good.

The same applies to political goods. An egalitarian may value equality as a good-in-itself, but he also values it for the other good things that equality facilitates. Ethical goods are subject to the same dualism (justice is a good-in-itself, but it also serves many other purposes).

What the men and women of the eighteenth century took for granted—and I will take for granted in this book—is that the mind must conceive a stopping point to the chain of questions about "What other ends does it serve?": an end at which there is no answer possible, an end that is reached when one is talking about the good-that-one-seeks-as-an-end-in-itself-and-for-no-other-reason. At this stage of the discussion, there is no need for us to try to decide what this ultimate good-in-itself consists of. We need only to agree that the concept of such a self-sufficient end-in-itself exists. To be discussed, it needs a label. That label is happiness.

HAPPINESS AND HIGHER GOALS

The use of happiness in this, its ancient and honored meaning, nonetheless continues to sound strange to contemporary ears. "Happiness" has become identified with self-absorption, the goal you seek if you are a young urban professional who doesn't give a damn about anything except your own pleasure. When "happiness" is proposed as the proper goal of life, the nearly reflexive response is that a major *problem* with contemporary America is that too many people are preoccupied with their own happiness and that too few understand that life has higher and more worthy purposes.

The most obvious response to this is semantic: *You can have no higher aspiration than happiness.* By definition (the traditional one), happiness is the only thing that is self-sufficiently good in itself and does not facilitate or lead to any other better thing. A "higher" goal would be another good. That other good, being good *as you define good*, would contribute to your happiness. (If you say that perhaps not—that it is possible for something to be good that nonetheless does not contribute to your happiness—then you find yourself entangled in self-contradictions. Somewhere along the line, you are shifting the definition either of "good" or of "happiness.")

But such semantic responses are not sufficient, for they seem to imply that a Mother Teresa's understanding of the highest good cannot be distinguished from an understanding of the highest good as a new BMW. Let me add therefore another common understanding from the eighteenth-century tradition. It was taken for granted that any thoughtful person thinks about what "the good" means, and especially about what the highest good means. It was also taken for granted that thoughtful people strive to live their lives (albeit with the frailties and inconstancies of humans) according to that understanding. The pursuit of happiness is not just something that human beings "do," it is the *duty* of a human being functioning as a human being, on a par with the duty to preserve one's integrity.

Let me take this thought further. To imagine a human being not pursuing happiness is a kind of contradiction in terms. To be fully human is to seek the best ends one knows, and to be fully human is also to apply one's human intelligence as best one can to the question, What *is* the good? I will be returning to this densely packed thought in the next chapter, but as starting points: Happiness is something that a Mother Teresa is striving to achieve. And anyone whose *highest* good *really is* a new BMW is not thinking in recognizably human ways. (If that seems harsh, note the italics.) For those who put their signatures to the Declaration, a society in which people were able to pursue happiness was no more and no less than a society in which people were able to go about the business of being human beings as wisely and fully as they could. The job of government was to enable them to do so.[6] People can have no higher calling, nor can governments.

My assertion, and the linchpin of this book, is that what was true then is true now. The longer one thinks about why one is in favor of or opposed to any particular measure to help people, the more one is driven to employ that most un-twentieth-century concept, happiness. The purpose of government is to facilitate the pursuit of happiness of its citizens.

UNDERSTANDINGS

As I set out to explore this strange but useful concept called "the pursuit of happiness," two understandings:

NO EQUATIONS

First, I will not be suggesting that we try to assess the "happiness yield" of a given policy. If catalytic converters are proposed as a way of reducing air pollution then air pollution remains the immediate problem at which they are directed and we had better do a hardheaded job of deciding whether catalytic converters are a good way to achieve that immediate goal. Nor shall I be trying to quantify a "happiness index" by which we may measure progress or retrogression. My goal is to make use of the idea of happiness, not trivialize it.

Rather, as I will be arguing in the chapters that follow, the concept of happiness gives us a new place to stand in assessing social policy. New places to stand offer new perspectives and can give better leverage on old problems. I will be arguing that the pursuit-of-happiness criterion gives us a valuable *way of thinking* about solutions, even when that way of thinking does not necessarily point us toward "the" solution.

NO ROSE GARDENS

I will be discussing the *pursuit* of happiness as it relates to social policy rather than the *achievement* of happiness. Only the former can be a "right." The latter is not within the gift of any government.

It is equally obvious, however, that the concept of "ability to pursue happiness" is not met simply by dubbing someone free to do so. You cannot pursue happiness effectively if you are starving or suffering other severe deprivations. You may meet misfortune with fortitude; you may extract from your situation what contentment is possible; but you may not reasonably be said to be "free to pursue happiness" under such conditions. "Pursuit" requires that certain conditions prevail, and part 2 explores the conditions that are most immediately relevant to government policies.

But neither does "enabled to pursue happiness" translate into a high probability of achieving whatever you set out to achieve. "Not that I would not, if I could," writes William James, "be both handsome and fat and well dressed, and a great athlete, and make a million a year, be a wit, a *bon-vivant,* and a lady-killer, as well as a philosopher; a philanthropist, statesman, warrior, and African explorer, as well as a 'tone-poet' and saint. But the thing is simply impossible."[7] Similarly, you cannot reasonably ask that you be enabled to achieve any particular sort of happiness you might prefer. "Ability to pursue happiness" will be treated as meaning that no one and no external objective condition controlled by government will prevent you from living a life that provides you with happiness. It may not be the most satisfying life you can imagine in its detail. Others with no greater merit than you (as you see it) may lead lives that you would prefer to live. But you will have the wherewithal for realizing deep and meaningful satisfactions in life. If you reach the end of your life unhappy, it will be your fault, or the fault of natural tragedies beyond the power of society to prevent.

And with that, we have cleared away enough underbrush to begin. Just as war is too important to be left to generals, so is happiness too important to be left to philosophers. It is a word with content that bridges widely varying political views. It lends itself to thinking about, puzzling over, playing with. Doing so can profoundly affect how we conceive of good laws, social justice, and some very practical improvements in the quality of American life.

2

Coming to Terms
with Happiness

MY OBJECTIVE is to provide a new backdrop against which to measure the wisdom or utility of specific government policies. I propose to use the concept of the pursuit of happiness for that purpose, considering the constituent conditions that enable us to pursue happiness and then asking how these conditions may be met.

This is easily said and not even very controversial as long as "happiness" has not yet been defined except as the good-that-one-seeks-as-an-end-in-itself-and-for-no-other-reason. The task in this chapter is to fill in the concept of happiness with enough content to permit us to talk about the pursuit of happiness more specifically.

HAPPINESS FROM ARISTOTLE TO THE SELF-ANCHORING CANTRIL SCALE

There is a curiously common assumption that everyone has his own idiosyncratic notion of what constitutes happiness. One contemporary scholar writing a book on the causes of human misery begins with a casual aside that "On the score of happiness, it is difficult to say anything more than that its sources seem infinitely various, and that disputes about tastes are notoriously hard to resolve."[1] To illustrate his point, he mentions "the happiness to be had by making other people miserable," apparently assuming that distinctions between sadism and other forms of human pleasure are arbitrary inventions.[2] Or there is the friend who, when told that I was writing a book dealing with the pursuit of happiness, assumed that I must necessarily get bogged down in what he viewed as the California school of happiness, sitting on the beach waiting for the perfect wave.

The assumption that definitions of happiness are idiosyncratic is curious because the oddball definitions are always the other fellow's. It is as if everyone recognizes the degraded concept of "happiness-as-feeling-good" that dominates popular usage, and assumes that that's how everyone else looks at it, while at the same time harboring (perhaps even a little guiltily) a private inner understanding of happiness that is close to the classical understanding.

In practice, the level of agreement about what constitutes happiness is remarkably broad—an assertion you may put to the test by turning to the end of this chapter and seeing whether you can tolerate the working definition I employ. If you can, you may skip this chapter without loss except the pleasure of knowing what good company you are in. The purpose of this chapter is not to persuade you of a particular understanding of happiness but to indicate, briefly and nontechnically, how recent has been the retreat from a common intellectual understanding of human happiness. For centuries, there was a mainstream tradition in the West about the meaning of happiness which I will call Aristotelian. In the eighteenth century, an alternative (which I will call Lockean) began to develop that nonetheless maintained an undercurrent of agreement about how men achieve happiness. It was not until the twentieth century that social science dispensed with the intellectual content of both traditions and began to define happiness by the responses to questionnaire items.*

---

* The terms "Aristotelian" and "Lockean" denote the same distinction as the terms "eudaemonian" and "hedonic" that are sometimes used in the literature on happiness.

THE ARISTOTELIAN MAINSTREAM

"We adopt Aristotelianism as our framework," writes a historian of the idea of happiness, "because it is the most complete and elaborate theory, because it asks the most questions, considers the most alternatives, and combines this amplitude with serious attention to consistency and proof." And, he adds, it also is unquestionably the most influential of the understandings of happiness, dominating the Western tradition until the eighteenth century and continuing to stand as the point of reference against which any alternative must be assessed.[3]

Aristotle's disquisition on happiness is found in the *Nicomachean Ethics*. He begins by developing the concept of happiness as the ultimate good-in-itself that proved to be such a unifying bedrock for subsequent writers. Every activity, he writes, has a good that is its own particular end. In medicine, the good to be achieved is health; in strategy, the good is victory; in architecture, the good is a building, and so on.[4] In modern idiom, everything we do can be said to be "good for" something.

Aristotle uses this commonsensical beginning to ask, Why seek any particular good? Why build the building, cure the disease, or win the victory? Any particular activity permits two answers: One engages in the activity for the sake of the thing-itself, yes, for there is something intrinsically satisfying in any good thing, but one pursues it as well for the sake of something else. Happiness is the word for that state of affairs which is the final object of these other goods. It is unique because it is the *only* good that we always choose as an end in itself and never for the sake of something else. "Honor, pleasure, intelligence, and all virtue we choose partly for themselves," Aristotle writes, "for we would choose each of them even if no further advantage would accrue from them—but we also choose them partly for the sake of happiness, because we assume that it is through them that we will be happy. On the other hand, no one chooses happiness for the sake of honor, pleasure, and the like, nor as a means to anything at all."[5]

To call the highest good "happiness" is "perhaps a little trite," Aristotle acknowledges, and he proceeds to specify its content more exactly. To do so, he invokes a characteristic of

man that today is sure to provoke an argument. He asserts that
man is distinctively rational. The unique proper function of
man, Aristotle argues, the one that sets him apart from all other
creatures, is delineated by human intelligence. Happiness cannot be understood, nor can it exist, without reference to behavior ordered by intelligence—that is, without reference to
rationality—any more than the proper function of a harpist
can be understood without reference to the playing of a harp.
"The proper function of man, then, consists in an activity of
the soul in conformity with a rational principle or, at least,
not without it."[6]

For Aristotle, "conformity with a rational principle" means
something far more complex (and realistic) than an icy, mathematical calculation of odds. There are instead two forms of
wisdom, "theoretical wisdom" and "practical wisdom."* Scientific knowledge advances by means of theoretical wisdom, but
the achievement of happiness is bound up much more closely
with practical wisdom, or, as Aristotle defined it, "the capacity
of deliberating well about what is good and advantageous for
oneself."[7] Such deliberation is not a scientific process. Indeed,
it could not be, for every actor and every situation is different
from every other, and every action is interpreted differently
and redounds differently depending upon the peculiarities of
persons and circumstances. General laws of behavior thus must
always be interpreted according to the particular situation.
The quality that permits these interpretations to be made
rightly and then acted upon appropriately is practical wisdom.
When a statesman makes a decision—Pericles is for Aristotle the
embodiment of the ideal—he must call upon his store of practical wisdom. So also must businessmen in making investments
for the future, a parent in dealing with his children, a young
woman in choosing a husband. None of these judgments can
be made adequately through scientific reasoning alone; all
must be informed as well by the broader, more diffuse wisdom
that is equally, but differently, part of man's unique gift of
rationality.

---

* The Greek abstract noun is *phronesis* and is translated as "pru-
dence" in some translations of the *Ethics*.

The more highly developed one's practical wisdom, the better the effects of one's actions for oneself and for mankind—a thought that leads to another key aspect of Aristotle's presentation, the link between thought and action. Aristotle's point does not demand that a man necessarily act on every conclusion or intention that forms in his mind. (He may know that rain is predicted and wish not to get wet, and yet still not carry his umbrella to the office.) But a man who *typically* divorces intention from action has in some profound sense shut himself off from human society, for a society cannot function at all if its members systematically fail to base their actions on their judgment. As philosopher Alasdair MacIntyre observes, "Were anyone systematically inconsistent in this way, he or she would soon become unintelligible to those around them. We should not know how to respond to them, for we could no longer hope to identify either what they were doing or what they meant by what they said or both."[8]

To repeat: The more highly developed one's practical wisdom, the "better" the effects of one's actions for oneself and for mankind. To be "better" in this way is also to be more virtuous—practical wisdom, Aristotle concludes, is both a virtue in itself and also the progenitor of virtuous behavior. And, to return to our original theme, practical wisdom facilitates happiness. It allows one to "deliberate well about what is good and advantageous for oneself," as well as to fulfill that most human of functions, the exercise of intelligence. For Aristotle, intelligence (or rationality), virtue, and happiness are all interlocked. In this passage from the chapter in which he initially defines happiness, he puts the relationship this way:

In other words, the function of the harpist is to play the harp; the function of the harpist who has high standards is to play it well. On these assumptions, if we take the proper function of man to be a certain kind of life, and if this kind of life is an activity of the soul and consists in actions performed in conjunction with the rational element, and if a man of high standards is he who performs these actions well and properly, and if a function is well performed when it is performed in accordance with the excellence appropriate to it; we reach the conclusion that the good of man is an activity of the soul in conformity with excellence or virtue, and if there are several virtues, in conformity with the best and most complete.[9]

It would be unfair to leave Aristotle's view of happiness at such an abstract level, however. Happiness as he envisions it is not at all austere or abstract. On the contrary, it is consistent with what "is commonly said about it" by ordinary people, Aristotle writes. It is pleasurable, for example, in that "the sensation of pleasure belongs to the soul, and each man derives pleasure from what he is said to love."[10] Elsewhere (see especially bk. 10), Aristotle clarifies the nature of pleasure and, as might be expected, he emphatically rejects an identity of pleasure and happiness: That happiness is pleasurable does not mean that pleasures constitute happiness. But the happy man enjoys himself, and the happier he is, the more he enjoys himself.

Aristotle adds that at least some resources (money, for example) are also necessary for happiness, and such things as personal attractiveness and good birth are helpful. But happiness as Aristotle develops the concept is not something to be reserved only to the rich or the brilliant. Even if the highest happiness is reserved to the wise, "it can attach, through some form of study or application, to anyone who is not handicapped by some incapacity for goodness."[11] In this context, Aristotle makes another point that is especially relevant: Just because you are not enjoying the most ideal happiness you can imagine for yourself does not mean you cannot be happy. Misfortunes may occur in the life of any person, no matter how wise and virtuous, but "if, as we said, the activities determine a man's life, no supremely happy man can ever become miserable, for he will never do what is hateful and base." He will act in the ways that bring happiness, "just as a good shoemaker makes the best shoe he can from the leather available."[12]

The prescriptions that flow from Aristotle's analysis sound familiar to modern ears. If your parents taught you that lasting satisfaction comes from developing your talents to their fullest, doing your job as well as you can, raising a family, and contributing to your community, your parents were teaching you an Aristotelian course. By the same token, Aristotle has been viewed by modern critics as a defender of bourgeois values. Thus Bertrand Russell writes with unconcealed disdain that

> Those who neither fall below nor rise above the level of decent, well-behaved citizens will find in the *Ethics* a systematic account of the principles by which they hold that their conduct should be regulated. The book appeals to the respectable middle-aged, and has been used by them, especially since the seventeenth century, to repress the ardours and enthusiasms of the young. But to a man with any depth of feeling it cannot but be repulsive. . . .[13]

Readers of Aristotle might well respond that in his evocation of courage as well as wisdom, justice as well as honor, he is calling forth not just "decency" or "respectability" but the very best that humans have in them. For that matter, it is not such a bad thing (or perhaps, such a common one) to be a decent, well-behaved citizen. It is easy to understand the resilience of the Aristotelian vision of happiness if only because it so closely corresponds to the evolving views of so many people who grow older, into "respectable middle age," and try to figure out what is making them happy or unhappy. Aristotle's view has, as a social scientist might say, a good deal of face validity.

This underlying correspondence between Aristotle's philosophy and everyday experience may account for why the Aristotelian framework was without serious competition for nearly two millennia. The advent of Christianity provided a religious branch of thinking about human happiness over which this book—after all a book about social policy and not a history of theories of happiness—must skip. It may be noted in passing, however, that in this area as in many others, Christian and especially Catholic theology owe much to Aristotle. For Aquinas, writing his *Treatise on Happiness*, Aristotle did not even need a name. He was simply and without peer The Philosopher.

THE LOCKEAN REVISION

An indispensable underpinning of the Aristotelian view of happiness was that all pleasures are not created equal; some are inherently superior to others. It is impossible for a person to make himself truly happy by stringing together episodes of sex, feasting, circuses, and idle good times. Beginning with the eighteenth century, an influential line of British philosophers discarded the underlying premise that pleasures can be ranked.*

The individual took center stage. An individual human being has inviolate rights, makes private decisions, and whether those decisions are "right" or "wrong" is a question that can be answered only by the individual who makes them. And so with happiness. It is not necessary, they argued, to assign a hierarchy of virtue or goodness to human activities. It is sufficient to say that human beings pursue their self-interest as they perceive it, including their understanding of such things as pleasure and happiness. *How* they perceive these things is not subject to validation by an outside party.

John Locke, writing at the end of the seventeenth century, was the first to voice this radically different approach to happiness. Happiness, he wrote, is sensible pleasure. Its lowest form is "so much ease from all pain, and so much present pleasure, as without which anyone cannot be content." Its highest form is not any particular type of activity nor is it even categorizable by its virtue or lack of it. Rather, the highest form of happiness is simply "the utmost pleasure we are capable of."[15] Happiness is as happiness does; therefore no outside agent—such as a king, for example—has the right to interfere with the individual's pursuit of those pleasures and satisfactions that have the most utility for his particular notions of what makes him happy as long as he harms no one else in that pursuit.

The theoretical gap between the Aristotelian and the Lockean view of happiness yawns wide. But if one asks whether the Lockean view of happiness really did represent a major change in the way men viewed the question that concerns us—How are men to pursue happiness?—the differences between the British philosophers and the Aristotelians are far less clear. The same writers who propounded a radically new view of man's

---

* I have not tried to include the French *philosophes,* deciding that the purposes of this brief survey are adequately met by summarizing the British line. This decision is more a matter of space than principle; still, as has been said, "The propagandists of the Enlightenment were French, but its patron saints and pioneers were British."[14]

natural rights, who overturned prevailing ideas about the rights
of kings and aristocrats over common men, tended to give descriptions of private virtue and its connection with happiness
that correspond quite closely to the Aristotelian one.*

To understand how these theoretical differences were
bridged, it first must be remembered that Locke's value-
stripped statement that happiness consisted of sensible pleasure was modified by his successors. The Scottish moral philosophers who followed—most prominently David Hume, Francis
Hutcheson, and Adam Smith—saw more in the human animal
than Locke had admitted; they saw as well "benevolence,"
which constituted for them the basis of the social order. For
Hutcheson in particular, the "moral sense" enabled and indeed
compelled thoughtful men to take pleasure—to find happiness—
in acts that Aristotle would have found entirely suitable.
Hutcheson, writing of the meaning of obligation and self-
interest, argues that men are so powerfully driven by their
nature "to be pleased and happy when we reflect upon our
having done virtuous actions and to be uneasy when we
are conscious of having acted otherwise" that self-interest inherently will tend to coincide with virtuous behavior.[17] Similarly, David Hume writes that "whatever contradictions may
vulgarly be supposed between the selfish and social sentiments"
are no greater than those between selfish and any other sentiments. "Selfish" has any attraction only because the things that
are selfishly sought are attractive. What is most attractive to
men? What gives the most relish to the objects of their selfish
pursuits? Hume sees "benevolence or humanity" as the ones
that perceptive men will naturally choose.[18]

---

* The argument that follows should not be construed as meaning
that the distinction is unimportant. Indeed, some hold that it is decisive—Alasdair MacIntyre, for example, argues powerfully that the
shift from the Aristotelian to the Enlightenment framework effectively destroyed our capacity to use moral language and to be
guided by moral reasoning.[16] My limited assertion here is that
someone who absorbs the full context of Locke or Hume (for example) and tries to seek happiness according to the philosophies
they express will not behave very differently from the person who
has been steeped in Aristotelian ethics, despite the very different internal rationales they may hold for their behavior.

We need not exclude even Locke from this line of thought. Locke was, after all, a Calvinist, and Calvinists were not notably permissive in their attitude toward what constitutes right behavior and suitable pleasure. Locke's writings include clear statements that only the shortsighted are content with pleasures of the senses. When he wrote that "the highest perfection of intellectual nature lies in a careful and constant pursuit of true and solid happiness," Locke meant happiness in Christianity and in just society.[19] Locke's epistemology permitted men to call themselves happy if they felt pleasure, whatever its sources. But the sources of pleasure that actually worked were limited.

Much the same points may be made about the utilitarians, identified primarily with Jeremy Bentham and John Stuart Mill, who followed in the nineteenth century.* The utilitarians, building on the Lockean tradition, saw happiness as a favorable balance of pleasure over pain in which Aristotelian considerations of higher pleasures versus lower pleasures need play no part. "Nature has placed mankind under the governance of two sovereign masters, pain and pleasure," Bentham wrote in a famous passage. "They govern us in all we do, in all we say, in all we think."[20] It is an uncompromising rejection of Aristotelian distinctions and moral precepts.

But then Bentham constrains his notion of the pursuit of happiness *in practice* to the point that one wonders whether it might not be easier to be a Calvinist than a Utilitarian. Bentham asserts that happiness (an excess of pleasure over pain) must be maximized for the community, not for any one member of it.[21] That his own happiness is his first concern does not free him from a moral obligation to act in ways that promote the greatest happiness for the greatest number. How is he to fulfill this moral obligation? Bentham proposes his "hedonistic calculus," which considers seven factors of pleasure and pain. One must choose the moral act by considering all seven and deciding whether a given action is a net plus or a net minus—an excruciatingly rigorous demand on an individual's moral

---

* Once again, I do not intend to blur major differences, this time between Lockean and Utilitarian ethics, but instead am referring specifically to the practical understanding of how happiness is achieved.

sense. Disregarding the practicalities of actually implementing Bentham's dictum, it is an understanding of "happiness as pleasure" that, if adhered to, seems likely to evoke the same middle-class morality that so offended Russell about Aristotle's *Ethics*.

John Stuart Mill went much further, identifying himself with man's capacity for rational action as a fundamental source of true enjoyment and happiness. "It is quite compatible with the principle of utility to recognize the fact that some *kinds* of pleasures are more desirable and more valuable than others," he wrote. "No intelligent human being would consent to be a fool, no person of feeling and conscience would be selfish and base," no matter how convinced they might be that doing so would yield them a greater amount of pleasure.[22] Shortly thereafter, he adds:

It is better to be a human being dissatisfied than a pig satisfied; better to be Socrates dissatisfied than a fool satisfied. And if the fool, or the pig, are of a different opinion, it is because they know only their side of the question.[23]

Thus, briefly, some reasons for arguing that in the evolution of the concept of happiness an array of philosophers espoused quite different conceptual views of happiness that nonetheless had very similar behavioral implications. To borrow from V. J. McGill's formulation in *The Idea of Happiness:* in Aristotle, virtue is the substance of happiness; in the post-Lockean revision, it is instrumental.[24]

The concept of happiness as employed by the Founding Fathers in general and Thomas Jefferson in particular reveals this easy coexistence of intellectually alien traditions. Jefferson was a good Lockean in his view of happiness as the constant pursuit of men. Indeed, he went beyond Locke, viewing the pursuit of happiness not just as something that men naturally did as a consequence of their human essence, but as an end of man ordained by natural law (or by God). A desire for happiness was itself part of man's essence.[25] But he also was drawn to the "moral sense" philosophy of Francis Hutcheson, and argued that "the essence of virtue is doing good to others."[26] Finally, bringing himself full circle back to a Lockean perspective, Jefferson rejected the public arena as a suitable place for virtue to manifest itself, putting it instead in the private sphere of effort and reward.[27] As historian John Diggins summarized it, Jefferson "made happiness the end of life, virtue the basis of happiness, and utility the criterion of virtue."[28] In less elaborated ways, the other Founders shared this rough compromise between theoretical options and real ones in the pursuit of happiness: Men may do what they will to pursue their vision of happiness, as long as they do not harm others, but thoughtful men will behave as virtuous gentlemen.

THE SOCIOLOGISTS' ALTERNATIVE, "AVOWED HAPPINESS"

As the nineteenth century drew to a close, people stopped talking about "happiness" as a philosophical construct. Howard Mumford Jones associated the demise of happiness with William James. No matter what tradition you endorsed, he argued, James left you adrift. With *Pragmatism*, James had dismantled the notion of happiness as a life lived in correspondence to immutable reason. With *Varieties of Religious Experience*, he had cast doubt on happiness grounded in theology. "And if happiness means the acceptance of things on the basis of right reason," Mumford Jones wrote, "the place of rationality in consciousness is so considerably shrunken by a study of James's *The Principles of Psychology* . . . that Locke seems for a time to be a mere museum piece."[29] Modern man was upon us.

William James is not the only suspect in the case, but whether it was he or Freud or the quantum physicists who did in the classical concept of happiness is not the issue. Happiness as defined by Aristotle or the Enlightenment or the utilitarians depended on man's being a recognizably rational, purposive creature. In the late nineteenth century, that assumption became intellectually untenable. By the time that the twentieth century dawned, the pursuit of happiness had become for the intellectuals a matter of healthy psychological adaptation. The man in the street might still be under the impression he was pursuing an Aristotelian ideal (not identified as such) of the virtuous life. But the scientific view had changed. For the twentieth century, Howard Mumford Jones gloomily concludes, "the problem of happiness is the problem of adjustment between the primitive subliminal urges of our hidden selves and the drab and practical necessities of every day."[30]

If the pursuit of happiness is in reality the pursuit of adjustment, then happiness is a matter of whatever feels good, and the pursuit of happiness is the pursuit of good adjustment—the therapeutic ethic, as Daniel Patrick Moynihan has termed it in a related context.[31] Twentieth-century social scientists have accordingly been reluctant to treat happiness as a construct which may be predefined. Instead, they have worked from the notion of "avowed happiness." If people say they're happy, the moderns have said, let us assume they are reporting accurately and then try to ascertain what "avowedly happy people" have in common.

The technique can be as uncomplicated as the one used by Norman Bradburn in his pioneering survey for the National Opinion Research Center in 1961. His interviewers asked simply, "Taking all things together, how would you say things are these days—would you say you are very happy, pretty happy, or not too happy these days?"[32] Another important study asked "How do you feel about your life as a whole?" and gave the respondent an opportunity to circle one of seven points on a scale ranging from "delighted" to "terrible."[33] Another technique has been to let the respondent define the extremes, then place himself at a point on that continuum. The best-known of these is called the "self-anchoring striving scale" developed by sociologist Hadley Cantril in a cross-national study.[34] Or the investigator may obtain more specific ratings on a variety of scales ("boring" to "interesting," "lonely" to "friendly," and so forth) and sum them to obtain a composite measure as Angus Campbell and his colleagues did in the "Semantic Differential Happiness Scale" used in the landmark assessment of American quality of life sponsored by the Russell Sage Foundation.[35]

I will not attempt a systematic survey of the outcomes of these studies, which in any case has been done quite well elsewhere.*[36] Still, two general points about the modern social

---

* This is not the place for a detailed methodological discussion of survey research techniques, their strengths and limitations. But my

science literature regarding happiness are pertinent to my use of the concept of happiness.

The first point is that social scientists have not found happiness to be a particularly variegated phenomenon. In all cases, the concept of "satisfaction" plays a central role in describing happiness. In some studies (Cantril, Campbell et al.), satisfaction is treated as the chief operational component of "happiness." An argument still rages about the elements of satisfaction (for example: Is satisfaction a function of the gap between aspiration and achievement? Or of the gap between aspiration and expectation?), but satisfaction itself, understood much the same way you probably think of the word, is indispensable.[37]

The second point is that momentary pleasures don't seem to be very relevant to happiness. Social scientists have avoided making value judgments about worthy and unworthy types of happiness so that they could measure what people really thought as opposed to what they were supposed to think. But this open-mindedness has yet to reveal a widely held (or even narrowly held) notion of happiness grounded in hedonism. Listening either to evangelists or to the evening news, one gets the impression that living for the moment is a prevalent idea of the good life, but the surveys have found hardly anyone who says he adopts it for himself. Very few people actually seem to attach much importance to the fleeting pleasures of the flesh in deciding whether or not they are happy.

---

reservations about the "avowed happiness" studies are apparent. My reasons, briefly, are as follows: The main problem with using happiness as a self-defined construct is that it has tended to produce reports of *correlates* without offering much leverage for getting into the black box of explanation. Suppose, for example, that one relates educational level to avowed happiness. Any result—a strong positive correlation, a strong negative correlation, or weak correlation—is "interesting," but only insofar as it prompts subsequent questions, complete with hypotheses to be tested, about why those results were obtained. The literature remains quite tentative in this regard. "Happiness" is an example of a construct that may be *informed* by the kinds of data that social scientists are able to obtain from surveys, but cannot very usefully be *defined* by such data.

A Working Definition of Happiness

Thus some of the reasons that a highly specific definition of happiness is not necessary to a discussion of the pursuit of happiness. Whatever their starting points, and regardless of theoretical differences, people who think about what makes a life a happy one end up with much in common. If you apply your own definition, it is almost certain that it will share enough of the core characteristics I have just discussed to permit common understanding.

For the record, the working definition I will employ is *lasting and justified satisfaction with one's life as a whole.* The definition is not original; indeed, minor variants of it have been used by so many that scholarly credit for it is difficult to assign.[38] The definition in effect says that when you decide how happy you are, you are thinking of aspects of your life that tend to *define* your life (not just bits and pieces of it) and you base your assessment of your own happiness on long-range satisfactions with the way things have gone. The pursuit of happiness will refer to an individual's everyday efforts to plan and conduct his life so that it yields lasting and justified satisfaction.

This is a prosaic definition with one barb, however: the word "justified." "Justified" is un-Lockean, implying that not all kinds of satisfactions are equal. "Justified" suggests that such things as objective right and objective wrong exist, that such a thing as virtue exists.

One must distinguish at this point between the specifics that you, the reader, or I, the author, attach to the meaning of "justified" and the level of agreement necessary to continue the discussion. Perhaps you are a religious person and interpret the concepts of right, wrong, and virtue according to a specific code that you believe to be universally applicable. Or perhaps you are willing to accept the notion that such a thing as virtuous behavior exists, but insist that it must be defined differently for different cultures and different times. In either case, we may put such specifics aside. In the context of this book, "justified" with regard to happiness says that it is not enough to feel good; you must have a plausible reason for feeling good. As philosopher Wladyslaw Tatarkiewicz writes, "The man who is satisfied is not only emotionally gratified but also *regards* his satisfaction as justified."[39] Happiness is more than a feeling.

To this extent, I am insisting that if reason is surrendered, happiness cannot be justified. Remember Mill's comment: Better to be a human being dissatisfied than a pig satisfied, regardless of the pig's view. Put in another context: If someone who is a drug addict says that by remaining in a permanent drugged state he can achieve a life of perpetual ecstasy, and that this is a valid way of being happy, the "justified" requirement says he is wrong. He is not happy, whatever he may think. He has surrendered reason. He has surrendered an indispensable element that makes him human.

Seen from one perspective, this assertion does not entail a great intellectual leap. Who wants to live the life of a drug addict? But it does require a dogmatic statement: It is true not just of me (that I could not be happy as a drug addict), *it is true of all people, even those who insist they are happy being drug addicts.* And as soon as we make such a statement, all sorts of thoughts intervene. What if one were poor? What if one lived in a ghetto? What if one had no education and no opportunity? Is it really appropriate for a person in the comfortable middle class to say that no one who lives in a euphoric stupor can be happy? I will be assuming that yes, it is appropriate and even essential to be dogmatic that life must be lived with self-awareness and self-judgment.

THE EXPERIENCE MACHINE TEST

I am not sure it is necessary to dwell on the foregoing point— perhaps it is self-evident—but it is so important to the rest of my argument that I refer you to philosopher Robert Nozick's device, the "experience machine," adapted here for my own purposes.[40]

Imagine a machine with electrodes that can be attached to your brain in such a way that it will make you feel exactly as if you were having whatever experience you wish. You want to write a great novel? The machine can give you exactly the sensations of writing a great novel. You want to make friends? Have an ideal marriage? The experience machine can do it for you, for a day or a lifetime.

You are not to worry about missing out on anything—you will have a huge library of possible experiences to choose from. If you wish, you may try a little of everything—two years a test pilot, two years a Talmudic scholar, two years the parent of loving children; whatever you wish. The main point is that while you are on the machine, your consciousness of what is happening will be indistinguishable from the real thing. You will think you are a concert pianist, or rock star if you prefer, and the experiences of a Vladimir Horowitz or of a Mick Jagger will not have been any more real than the ones you feel while floating in the tank, attached to the electrodes. All you have to do is ask to be plugged in. The test question: Would you choose the experience machine as a substitute for living the rest of your life in the real world?

Most people say no. Specifying why one would refuse is not easy, however. Every reason you may devise is irrational unless you hold an underlying, bedrock premise that what you *do* and *are* is anchored in something other than sensory input to your nerve endings. The stipulation that the satisfaction be "justified," while it will not involve any particular creed or set of values, does require this fundamental belief that the state of being human has some distinctive core—that a human being has a soul, if you will.

If you have any residual uncertainty about your stance, it may be useful to think of the judgment one would make for one's own child. Suppose that your child had a serious physical disability—was confined to a wheelchair, for example, and was therefore intrinsically prevented from ever having certain experiences.* Would you then choose a life on the experience

---

* At some point, presumably, a simulation of life would be preferable to the real thing. What is the equivalent of brain dead in deciding that it would be morally permissible to put someone on an experience machine?

machine for your child? (You could hook him up while he was asleep, so he would not have even the momentary anguish of knowing that his subsequent experiences would be fake.) I am assuming, and assuming that you agree, that the answer must be a horrified no.

PART TWO

WHEN
THERE IS
BREAD

It is quite true that man lives by bread alone—
when there is no bread. But what happens to
man's desires when there *is* plenty of bread and
when his belly is chronically filled?

—Abraham Maslow

Other things equal, human beings enjoy the exercise of their realized capacities (their innate
or trained abilities), and this enjoyment increases the more the capacity is realized, or the
greater its complexity.

—The Aristotelian Principle
as stated by John Rawls

3

Enabling Conditions
and Thresholds

To PURSUE HAPPINESS is to pursue the good we seek as an end in itself, that thing which, realized, expresses itself as justified satisfaction with life as a whole. The object of government is to provide a framework within which people—*all* people, of all temperaments and talents—can pursue happiness. The question remains: What does any of this have to do with practicalities, not social philosophy?

As a way of framing the question, I will use the notion of "enabling conditions." As the name implies, an enabling condition does not cause something to happen (governments do not make people happy), it permits something to happen (governments behave in ways that leave people able to be happy). And so with specific policies: Government policies affect the conditions that *enable* people to pursue happiness and thereby may be considered effective or ineffective, good or bad, efficient or inefficient. Why are food stamps good? One reason might be that food stamps are good because they keep people from starving. The very practical, down-to-earth proposition is that you can't pursue happiness if you're starving. Hardly anyone will disagree. Stated more formally as an enabling condition,

It is impossible to pursue happiness without a certain amount of material resources.

This seems self-evident—enough so, at any rate, that it makes sense to inquire how social policy interacts with this enabling condition. What does the policy called food stamps have to do with the enabling condition involving "enough" material resources to pursue happiness? And having asked that question, it then makes sense to ask (still sticking to the very practical issues involved) what "enough" might mean.

With material resources, I began with the most obvious of all enabling conditions. As soon as one pushes further, the room for disagreement increases. One quickly reaches possible "enabling conditions" that some will find marginal, irrelevant, or conceptually redundant with the conditions that have already been defined. I have no interest in pushing the limits. Anyone who wants to develop a definitionally taut, orthogonal set of enabling conditions for happiness is welcome to try to do so; I will not. The objective is not to set up an internally consistent intellectual system but to ask how some obviously important enabling conditions of happiness relate to day-to-day life and day-to-day social policy in the United States of America in the latter part of the twentieth century. For this task, we have an excellent conceptualization already available, and I draw upon it for organizing the succeeding chapters.

MASLOW'S NEEDS HIERARCHY

In 1943, psychologist Abraham Maslow published an article entitled "A Theory of Human Motivation," which argued that human needs fall into a few basic categories arranged in a hierarchy.[1] At the most primitive level, man needs to survive. Withhold food from a man, and food will be what he most wants; for him, utopia is a place with enough food. "Freedom, love, community feeling, respect, philosophy, all may be waved aside as fripperies which are useless since they fail to fill the stomach. Such a man may fairly be said to live by bread alone."[2]

When enough food is available, utopia stops being a place with enough food. Other needs surface. "A want that is satisfied is no longer a want. The organism is dominated and its behavior organized only by unsatisfied needs."[3] Maslow identified five categories of need and ranked them in this order:

• Physiological needs (food, water, shelter, sex).
• The need for safety (predictability, order, protection from physical harm).
• The need for intimacy (belongingness, friendship, relationships with spouse and children).
• The need for esteem (self-respect, recognition, and respect from others).
• The need for self-actualization (expressing one's capacities, fulfilling one's potential).

Maslow argued that these needs are met roughly in the order listed. People whose basic physiological needs have not been met are absorbed first in satisfying them, then in ensuring their safety, then in forming intimate relationships of love and friendship, then in attaining self-esteem, and finally in fulfilling their special potentialities. This order is not immutably fixed (and is not important to this discussion in any case). People trade elements of one good for elements of another, people value different goods differently, but such is the general sequence.

Maslow went on to become a major figure in psychology, with a controversial body of work that extends far beyond his original needs hierarchy. My use of Maslow is limited to this: He provides a useful way of organizing an unwieldy discussion. Taken together, his five categories are a capitulation of the enabling conditions for the pursuit of happiness—which is to say, if all of them were met, it is difficult to see how a person could claim that he was prevented by external conditions from pursuing happiness.

I have adapted them for purposes of this discussion under the chapter headings of material resources (corresponding to physiological needs), safety (safety needs), and self-respect (esteem needs). The discussion of self-actualization has been folded into a somewhat broader topic that embraces as well the concept of intrinsic rewards—taken together and dispensing with jargon, the label "enjoyment" is as good as any.

OMISSIONS

I have omitted a separate discussion of the need for "belongingness" and intimacy in this part of the book not because
social policy is irrelevant (quite the contrary), but for two
other reasons. First, some of the most important ways in which
social policy enables people to form intimate relationships with
others are through the other enabling conditions, especially
self-respect (self-respect being an enabling condition not only
for happiness in general but also for the development of relationships with others in particular). Second, I will be arguing
much later in the book that the formation of "little platoons"
(chap. 12) is the nexus within which the pursuit of happiness
is worked out. What Maslow calls the need for belongingness
is not just one of the needs, it is the key for meeting the others
as well.

Before leaving the list of enabling conditions, a few comments about two obvious missing ones. What about human
needs for freedom? Justice? Maslow argues that they are not
separate categories, but rather "preconditions for basic need
satisfactions."[4] It is perhaps an indication of the underlying
coherence of Maslow's system that, despite my own predispo-
sition to treat freedom as an enabling condition and the disposition of many other commentators on social policy to treat
justice as an independent enabling condition, it turns out to
be awkward to do so. Few of us wake up in the morning looking forward to the day because we are free or live in a just
society. We are much more likely to wake up looking forward
to the day (if we are so fortunate) because of other things that
freedom and justice have made possible—they are the enabling
conditions of the enabling conditions, if you will. In a book
about the felt satisfactions of life, freedom and justice seem to
be examples of things that from day to day are *good for* a wide
variety of other things and are better discussed in that context.

THE STRATEGY FOR THE DISCUSSION

For the next four chapters of this book about public policy, I ask that you temporarily forget about specific policies. In fact, the key to this enterprise is precisely *not* thinking about policies (which we will begin to do instead in part 3) and instead concentrating on *what it is we want to accomplish* regarding each of the enabling conditions, ignoring for the time being how to do so through government programs and largely ignoring even whether it is possible to accomplish such things through government programs. We have identified (I am asking you to agree) four extremely important enabling conditions for the pursuit of happiness: material resources, safety, self-respect, and "enjoyment." Perhaps public policy can contribute a great deal to the achievement of these conditions, perhaps not. We don't know yet, because we haven't yet thought about what the conditions consist of. When a person is living in a situation where the enabling conditions have been met—where he has "enough" material resources, safety, self-respect, and access to enjoyment to pursue happiness—what will be the characteristics of each of those states of affairs?

THRESHOLDS

My general strategy will be to superimpose upon the concept of "enabling condition" the concept of "threshold." To illustrate, consider the role of food as an element in the enabling condition "material resources." Has anyone been happy while starving? Only, one may assume, under the most extraordinary circumstances. Has anyone been happy while having only a Spartan diet, with little variety but adequate nutrition? Of course; it happens all the time. There is a *threshold* before which it is nearly impossible to pursue happiness, after which the pursuit of happiness becomes readily possible. The first question to ask of enabling conditions will be, Is there a threshold state and, if so, where does it lie? Is there such a thing as "enough" material resources to enable one to pursue happiness? "Enough" safety? "Enough" self-respect? "Enough" enjoyment?

An intuitive first response is that surely there is not such a thing as "enough" of these goods that can be defined concretely or generalized across all people. But that really amounts to saying that "threshold" can be a complex concept, not that thresholds do not exist. For example, continuing the food example, don't people who have a wide variety of foods tend to enjoy life more than people who must live on beans, other things being equal? The answer is probably "yes," if "enjoyment" is understood to mean "pleasure," and given the multitude of exceptions that are wiped away by that catchall, "other things being equal." But it is just as obvious that there are limits. At some point along the diet continuum from "beans and rice" to "every food in the world," the correlation between "access to amount and variety of food" to "ability to pursue happiness" drops to zero. Such a thing as a threshold exists, though we defer the question of where it is to be found.

Or consider the case of a person for whom good food provides the rewards that Bach provides for a music lover. Is his threshold the same as for the person who hardly notices what he is eating? In one sense the gourmet's threshold is different: The appreciation of food is for him a significant source of aesthetic enjoyment, whereas it is not for the indifferent eater. But in another sense his threshold is the same: If tomorrow the gourmet is told by his doctor to subsist on a few bland foods for his health, he can nonetheless continue to pursue happiness (even though he has been deprived of an important source of enjoyment), just as the indifferent eater can.

An examination of the threshold state and whether one exists will lead us to other kinds of analyses. For example, suppose there is a clear-cut threshold condition (a point below which happiness cannot be pursued and above which it can) but it differs widely among people. In this case, it becomes critically important that social policy maximize the ability of each person to put himself in a situation satisfactory to his own needs. Now, in contrast, imagine that there is no threshold condition for anyone, but instead everyone agrees that more is better: If you have two units of X, you are better able to pursue happiness than with one unit of X, and this holds true for all values of X. In such a case, social policy should be more concerned about pumping out an endless supply of this magic good and seeing that it is equitably distributed than with allowing people to seek their own level.

WHY NO MORE THAN ENABLE?

It may seem a minimalist approach to policy—just to "enable" people to do something (why not go further, and *help* them do it?), to worry just about reaching a "threshold" (why not go beyond, and supply a plenitude?). But the minimalism is intrinsic, not arbitrary. To understand the perspective of the chapters that follow, it is essential to understand first of all that when the topic is the pursuit of happiness, "enable" is as far as the government can go.

In the world of public policy that the television networks describe every evening on the news, governments face choices of how *much* to do, because the policies that get talked about the most are policies based on problems. A problem is shown— a flood in Pennsylvania, homelessness in Manhattan, traffic congestion in the skies, a scientific finding that a certain level of radon is dangerous—and always there is the question, What is the government going to do about it? Is it going to stand idly by? Reconsider its position? Invoke its powers? Propose new legislation? Increase the number of flight controllers? Issue new federal regulations?

Generally, the possible responses are characterized as choices among things to be done. The more primitive option—"doing something" versus "doing nothing"—is irrelevant for most issues. The fire department may choose to send one or two or three engines to a fire, based on an assessment of how many are needed to put out the fire. But the fire chief does not mull over each fire alarm, deciding whether to respond at all.

In such cases, it is appropriate to think in terms of the government "doing a little" versus "doing a lot." The public may debate whether the fire department should institute a fire prevention program or require fire drills or add paramedics to its fire-fighting teams. People may argue for a stripped-down fire department or an extensive one. Similarly, people may argue over the size of a road-building program, the scope of a Medicaid program, the eligibility rules for government-paid scholarships to colleges. In all such cases, governments have open to them the choice of doing a lot or a little.

But now consider the question, *"How much* should the government do to help people pursue happiness?" At first, it sounds reasonable: Surely the government has, in this case as well, choices to make about how much to do. Won't expanding the scholarship program (for example) do more to help people pursue happiness by expanding educational opportunity? But on reflection, that example does not refute the proposition that governments can only enable people to pursue happiness. An expanded scholarship program enables *more* people to pursue happiness (by expanding the number of people who are enabled to pursue happiness through access to education). But the "how much" question would have to be phrased in terms of the magnitude of aid available to a given individual: Does a government that provides full scholarships "do more" to help a given person pursue happiness than a government that provides half scholarships? If that's the case, does providing a personal tutor for each recipient do more than not providing a tutor? And if that's the case, does . . . But the point, a simple one, should be clear. People pursue happiness, governments *cannot.* The thing called "educational opportunity" always has to be transmuted by the individual who gets the opportunity into the process called "the pursuit of happiness." It can never be the thing-itself. And, while different people respond in different ways, it is intuitively obvious that at some point (for now, never mind where) the government will no longer be doing more to help people pursue happiness by providing them with ever more lavish educational services more tenderly provided. It will be doing less.

And so with all governmental functions in their relationship to the pursuit of happiness. If a government chooses to build a lot of roads, it may build a lot of roads. If it chooses to treat a lot of sick people, it may treat a lot of sick people. But if it chooses to "help people pursue happiness a lot," it can only go so far. It may not choose to pursue happiness on behalf of anyone. That must remain the quintessentially personal, undelegatable task of life. The government can "do as much as it can" to *enable,* but it can do no more than enable.

This is not necessarily equivalent to "government should do as little as possible." Rather, it is a question of choosing the things to do. Consider by way of analogy the work of a park ranger responsible for maintaining a hiking trail through a wilderness area. His work is curiously contradictory. The people who use his trail have certain expectations—they do not come prepared for a Special Forces survival course—and so if he does his job right, the footpaths will be maintained. Perhaps there will be a guardrail at a treacherous spot. But when the guidebook specifies that backpackers who take a certain trail should be on the lookout for grizzlies, he will do them no favors if he goes out and shoots the grizzlies. If a trail is rated as a rough and rocky climb, he will do them no favors by smoothing and paving the trail. And when it comes to the land off the trails, the whole point of his job is to protect it, not to alter it—which in turn can involve delicate tasks that require the ranger to expend a great deal of effort so that as little as possible is changed.

The park ranger's job is to prepare the wilderness so that it *enables* people to enjoy visiting a wilderness area—and there is no way in the world he can do an iota more than that. In describing the details of his job, the question is not *how much* is done, but choosing the things to be done and then determining whether those things are done *right*.

"Enabling" applies to any activity in which the doing is the thing. I could have evoked as appropriately the preparation of other kinds of facilities—a play perhaps, or a party. Sometimes the preparers have a lot of work to do (designing the set, preparing the lighting), sometimes their work consists of doing nothing with forethought (choosing the right mix of guests and then standing aside). The question is not how much the preparers do, but whether they do it right. Does the stage manager enable the actors to give a good performance, does the host enable the guests to have a good time? And that is what I will be asking about the human activity that is most thoroughly a case of "the doing is the thing," the pursuit of happiness: What does enabling consist of, and (in very general terms in this part of the book) how might these understandings affect what government does?

Often I will be suggesting that the things that are not done, the areas in which policy consists of deliberately refraining from action, are as critically important to enabling the pursuit of happiness as the things that policy actively tries to do. Or to return to the original analogy, I will be asking you to consider a world in which the fire department leaves certain types of fires unattended, not because it has too little equipment but because it would be a bad idea to put out the fire.

It is not such a radical thought—I am surrounded at this moment by hundreds of fires in my neighborhood that the fire department is ignoring and that everyone agrees the fire department should ignore. There's one a few feet away from me, keeping my coffee warm. In the case of fires, of course, we all know that fire departments are for putting out uncontrolled fires and there is no need to specify that fires in stoves and furnaces don't count. But the example calls attention to the peculiar problem facing this particular book on policy: In deciding what constitutes a good "policy for putting out fires," one first has to decide what fires one wants put out. In the case of fire departments, the decision rules are obvious; that's why we don't have to think about them. In the case of pursuing happiness, the decision rules are not so obvious. The purpose of the four chapters that follow is to think about decision rules *before* thinking about policy. This still leaves room for saying that governments should "do a lot" or "do a little"—but only once we have decided what needs to be done.

4

Material Resources

"POVERTY" HAS in recent years been to policy analysts what damnation is to a Baptist preacher. For more than two decades, progress or retrogression in social policy has been measured against this benchmark. Few goals have been more highly valued than to "bring people above the poverty line." To be below the poverty line has constituted proof that government help is needed.

There are three reasons for this preoccupation. One is that deficits in material resources are visible. We can see, paint, photograph, film, televise, and videotape sunken cheeks and tattered clothes. Deficits in the other enabling conditions are not so visible. Compounding this imbalance, deficits in any of the other enabling conditions may *manifest* themselves as poverty. Self-esteem again provides a good example. Large numbers of the homeless are dispirited in ways that are traceable to deficits in esteem (and in other enabling conditions besides poverty). It is often such deficits that created the homelessness. But the symptom is poverty—living in the streets, dressed in rags, begging for food—and the symptom can be alleviated by material resources.

This points to the second reason why money has taken on such a central place in social policy calculations: Material resources, alone among the enabling conditions, are fungible. I can use money to buy you a meal or a place to stay. I cannot use money to buy you esteem. Deficits in material resources are in this sense susceptible to "solutions" in ways that the other enabling conditions are not.

The third reason is that deficits in material resources suggest threats to survival. Without food, people starve to death. Without shelter, they perish of exposure. The state of being "in poverty" is loosely identified with a state of being at risk of life and health. The plight of the street people again provides an apt illustration. The street people *are* in the streets and *do* appear to be in danger of starving—and they are also "in poverty." The observer may point out that the street people constitute a small fraction of the people labeled "homeless," and that the homeless constitute a small fraction of the people under the poverty line. He may analyze the data on why people live in the streets, and point out that the reason why people live in the streets in Calcutta or Cairo (no way to make a decent living) applies to only a small fraction of street people in the United States. He may then conclude, with logic and evidence on his side, that the problem of street people and the poverty problem are separate, that the means for solving one are all but unrelated to solving the other. But for most of us the visceral link will remain. Poverty taken to its ultimate extreme means death.

These are some of the reasons why poverty has so preoccupied us. It is the generic stand-in for the social problems of our age. Solve the riddle of poverty, we have often seemed to hope, and the rest of our problems will solve themselves. As long as poverty exists, we have often seemed to despair, nothing else can compensate the poor for their condition. "Whatever progress has been charted on the graph of 'progress and poverty,' " Gertrude Himmelfarb writes in her history of the idea of poverty, "it is poverty that still strikes the eye and strikes at the heart. It is as if the modern sensibility can only register failure, not success, as if modernity has bequeathed to us a social conscience that is unappeasable and inconsolable."[1]

A continuing theme of this book will be that in fact most of the pains and damages that we associate with contemporary poverty in Western societies have little to do with a lack of material resources (beyond a certain point): that money *in itself, by itself* does not inspirit the dispirited homeless, make loving mothers of neglectful mothers, make a cheerful home of a dump. A few days later, even if the money continues to be provided, the dispiritedness and neglectfulness will be back and the home will be a dump with different furniture. The crucial qualifier, of course, is that phrase "beyond a certain point," for below that point money can make all the difference in the world. So the topic for now is material resources and an exploration of that "certain point." When the enabling condition is material resources, how much is enough?

I will present two talking points. The first is that, for purposes of opening up a wide range of ways to pursue happiness, "enough money" lies close to subsistence—not precisely at subsistence, but close. The second is that the first proposition can hold true, to a far greater degree than we commonly realize, for inhabitants of sophisticated Western societies.

WHAT IS "ENOUGH" MONEY?

The proposition that "enough money to pursue happiness" lies close to subsistence is a minor revision of the notion that money does not buy happiness. Combine this unoriginal proposition with the truth that you can't pursue happiness if you're starving, and the implication for the quantitative relationship of income to happiness is fully defined: If we have an accurate measure of happiness and an accurate measure of income, then the relationship of happiness to income should look something like figure 1.

Happiness is very low until subsistence is reached, rises very steeply immediately thereafter, but quickly levels off as subsistence is left behind. Or, as Maslow would argue, once the physiological needs are met, the next level of needs arises and determines the organism's state of satisfaction. How does this expectation compare with what is known about the relationship of wealth to happiness?

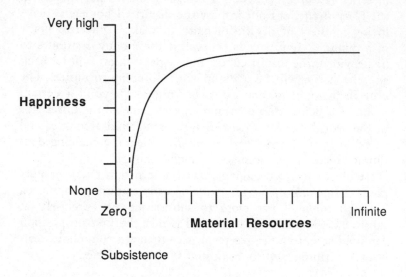

FIGURE I
ON MONEY BUYING HAPPINESS, THEORETICALLY . . .

HAPPINESS AND NATIONAL WEALTH

The answer depends on whether you look at the relationship of happiness to income *across* countries or *within* countries. If the question is "Are people in rich countries happier than people in poor countries?" the answer seems to be quite close to the expectation. Very poor countries in which much of the population is barely surviving—countries such as India, Bangladesh, and some parts of sub-Saharan Africa—show very low levels of avowed happiness. But this holds true only at the extremes (and even then with exceptions). Avowed happiness rises quickly with national wealth in the early stages, then much more slowly among the wealthier countries. Figure 2 gives a rough idea of the relationship, using happiness data from the Cantril and Gallup international surveys, both of which used a self-anchored scale that is claimed to have high cross-cultural validity.[2] National wealth is expressed as gross national product (GNP) per capita.

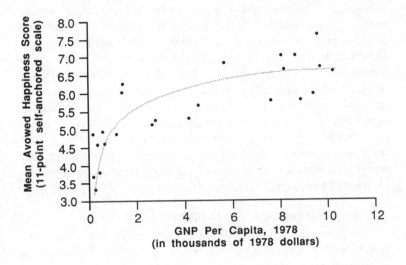

FIGURE 2
ON MONEY BUYING HAPPINESS, EMPIRICALLY . . .

SOURCE: The happiness data are from the Gallup world sample (1976) and the Hadley Cantril data (1965), as reported in Ruut Veenhoven, *Databook of Happiness* (Boston: D. Reidel, 1984), table e, p. 518. Per capita GNP data are taken from Charles Lewis Taylor and David A. Jodice, *World Handbook of Political and Social Indicators*, 3d ed., vol. 1 (New Haven, Conn.: Yale University Press, 1983), table 3.6, and from Bureau of the Census, *Statistical Abstract of the United States 1970* (Washington, D.C.: Government Printing Office, 1970), table 1254, p. 810. All per capita GNP are expressed in 1978 dollars. Note that a per capita GNP in 1978 of $9,770 in the United States translated into median family income of $17,640, or more than $30,000 in 1987 dollars.

These are not data to go to court with—sample sizes for some countries are only 300 people—but the general correspondence with the curvilinear "predicted" relationship in figure 1 is obvious. Very quickly, more money buys little more happiness.

Some argue that the relationship between national wealth and happiness is even weaker than figure 2 indicates. Political scientist Richard Easterlin, who has done the most rigorous work in this area, reached the conclusion that the relationship is nil: "[R]icher countries are not typically happier than poorer ones. . . . By and large, the evidence indicates no relation—positive or negative—between happiness and national income. Whether the people in a particular time or place are comparatively happy is seemingly independent of the average level of income."[3] The Gallup data suggest that this may overstate the case slightly—examined closely, those data show signs that happiness scores continue to increase, albeit slightly and irregularly, with wealth even after subsistence is left behind. But such uncertainties only tend to reinforce the proposition that national wealth has at most only a very tenuous relationship to avowed happiness.

HAPPINESS AND INDIVIDUAL WEALTH

The predicted relationship of wealth to avowed happiness fails to match reality, however, when we turn to the happiness of individuals *within* a given nation. This was the second of Easterlin's findings. People in poor Mexico and in affluent France may have similar mean avowed-happiness scores, but rich people in France are happier than poor people in France, as rich people in Mexico are happier than poor people in Mexico. In every country, Easterlin found, people with high income tended to report higher levels of happiness than people with low income.

The same relationship held true longitudinally within countries. The United States is a good example. As Easterlin pointed out, from the late 1940s to 1970, average real income in the United States increased by about 60 percent while reported levels of happiness in the United States were about the same in the late 1940s as they were in 1970, but in each survey richer people had higher happiness scores than poorer people. The same phenomenon continued through the 1970s. Table 1 gives the percentages of people who identified themselves as "very happy" in Gallup polls taken from 1948 to 1981, alongside the median family income in those years (expressed in constant 1987 dollars).

Perversely, the percentage of people reporting themselves

TABLE 1

YEAR	PERCENT RESPONDING "VERY HAPPY"	MEDIAN FAMILY INCOME (1987 DOLLARS)
1948	44%	$15,300
1956	54%	$20,400
1963	47%	$23,600
1970	43%	$29,400
1977	42%	$30,600
1981	46%	$28,500

SOURCES: *The Gallup Report*, no. 189 (June 1981): 40; Bureau of the Census, *Statistical Abstract of the United States 1982–83* (Washington, D.C.: Government Printing Office, 1982), table 714; Bureau of the Census, *Historical Statistics of the United States* (Washington, D.C.: Government Printing Office, 1975), table G179–88.

as happy dropped steadily from 1956 through 1977, as real income soared—then increased from the 1977 to the 1981 measures, as real income dropped. But at any given time *within* that period, rich people reported themselves as being happier than poor people. Table 2 shows the gradient, using Gallup's 1981 income categories.

The effect of income is not as great as some might have predicted. That more than a third of people with incomes under $5,000 reported themselves to be "very happy" is intriguing,

TABLE 2

FAMILY INCOME (1981 DOLLARS)	PERCENT RESPONDING "VERY HAPPY"
$25,000 & over	56%
$20,000–24,999	48%
$15,000–19,999	48%
$10,000–14,999	38%
$ 5,000–9,999	40%
Under $5,000	35%

SOURCE: *The Gallup Report*, no. 189 (June 1981): 38.

and it would be fascinating to find what happens to the relationship at higher income levels (Does it keep rising through $50,000? $100,000? $1,000,000?). But that a relationship exists is clear.

Putting the longitudinal and cross-sectional data together, one emerges with a paradoxical situation. You may think of it this way: Imagine a man with a real income of X dollars in 1950 and his son with precisely the same real income in 1970. On average, the son can be expected to be less happy with his income than the father was with his. To be *as* happy as the father, the son must make *more* money. Furthermore, there are no signs that the process will be any different for the son's son. Easterlin's gloomy conclusion was that "to an outside observer, economic growth appears to be producing an ever more affluent society, but to those involved in the process, affluence will always remain a distant, urgently sought, but never attained goal."[4] Two other researchers came up with a memorable phrase to describe the situation. We are caught, they said, on "a hedonic treadmill."[5]

This is all very well as a matter of aggregate statistics, but there is also the wisdom of Sophie Tucker to consider: "I've been poor, and I've been rich, and believe me, honey, rich is better." Perhaps the hedonic treadmill writ small works out to something like this: It is true that when you think back to the happy and unhappy times of your life, they do not necessarily match up with the amount of money you had at the time. Still, *other things being equal*, at this very moment in your life, you prefer your current income over any lesser amount and probably have a hankering for more.

The hedonic treadmill is not as depressing as it may seem at first glance. It is not irrational. We get caught on it for any number of understandable reasons, some of which are summarized in the note below.* And it is not even necessarily a

---

* The phenomenon called the hedonic treadmill is not necessarily irrational or mysterious. Economist Moses Abramovitz has discussed some of the reasons why the promised land of "all the money we need" keeps receding from us.[6] One explanation is habituation. A couple with children in the house save enough money to add a private bathroom for themselves. For a while, they luxuriate in their

frailty that we need to fight. Sophie Tucker was at least partly right. It may be true that people by and large are always going to seek more money and will always find as they succeed that money in and of itself is of limited value in increasing their happiness. People may still, quite reasonably, want to increase their income. If they can't buy happiness, they can make some other good use of the money.

The empirical findings about the relationship between money and happiness thus tell us little that is surprising or even particularly dismaying about human beings. They do, however, raise a fascinating question: What are the implications of the hedonic treadmill for good public policy?

---

new privacy. After a time, they don't notice it anymore. To recover the same sense of active pleasure, they have to do something new with still more money—buy a sailboat, move to a more exclusive neighborhood. It is not the use of one's luxuries one enjoys, according to the habituation argument, but the process of acquiring them and their (short-lived) novelty. Another alternative explanation is that increases in real income (as measured by the consumer price index) don't necessarily make the things that you want more affordable, if the rest of society is getting richer too. Affluence is commonly used to buy private space for example. But the number of spacious lots with beautiful ocean views is fixed, while the number of affluent customers expands. Real income may increase relative to the number of toasters one can afford, but the prices of the most valued luxury goods rise disproportionately and one is nearly as unable to afford them as before.[7] This point is perhaps even more vivid with regard to services. Western-style affluence brings with it laborsaving devices and some services, but only the very richest Americans enjoy the degree of true freedom from the bothersome daily "overhead" of existence—cooking, cleaning, washing, and the general bother of looking after oneself—as do large numbers of people with far lower incomes who live in countries where servants still work cheap. A final explanation is suggested by Stefan Linder in *The Harried Leisure Class:* It takes time and effort to reap satisfactions from the things we buy (a labor theory of leisure, as it were). As more things are acquired, the time we can give to each becomes more limited, and the satisfactions we obtain are accordingly diluted—thus Linder's hilarious image of the prosperous Scandinavian spending an evening at home, trying as best he can to read *The New York Times*, listen to the Italian opera, smoke his Havana cigar, sniff his French cognac, drink his demitasse of Brazilian coffee, and make love to his beautiful Swedish wife.[8]

THE ULTIMATE IRRELEVANCE OF
THE HEDONIC TREADMILL TO GOOD POLICY

The issue is how government *enables* people to pursue happiness. For the enabling condition called "material resources," the question therefore is: How may we characterize the state of affairs when everyone in a society has sufficient material resources to be able to pursue happiness? When will we be able to say, "The government of the United States has met its obligation to provide for the material needs of its citizens, and may now devote its attention to other matters"?

One internally consistent answer is "Never." The fact is that people with more money tend to be happier than people with less money at any given slice in time, no matter how much money the poorer people have. The appropriate conclusion, judging from these data, is that money does make a difference and that the only way to deal with the hedonic treadmill is to treat it as a fact of life and go on using the government to redistribute money from rich to poor, no matter how much money the "poor" have.

The logic is internally consistent. The only problem is that the conclusion is absurd. It is absurd first at the limit. No thinking person believes that more money means more happiness after a point. This assertion is no more controversial than saying that no thinking person believes that a person with five million dollars is likely to be happier than a person with four million dollars. The problem is to find the point after which increases in money no longer facilitate the pursuit of happiness.

We may cut down the range by asking questions of this sort: Suppose that at some time in the future the United States becomes so wealthy that the poorest families have the purchasing power of the current median (more than $30,000 in 1987), while the average income has tripled in the meantime. In that state of affluence, would you be prepared to argue that poor people are prevented from pursuing happiness because they have too little money? Or to put it another way, if all families in the United States had at least that much purchasing power, could we then forget about poverty as an issue for social policy and worry about other matters instead (even if the median had by that time increased to $100,000)?

In such a society, "poor" people—that is, people with only $30,000 in purchasing power—will doubtless still envy the rich people, that being human nature. And it will also be true that people with only $30,000 will be unable to purchase some desirable goods, and will feel that if only they made $40,000, or $50,000, or $100,000, *then* they would have what they need, and would be satisfied. But granting that these reactions will prevail, the question remains: In designing public policy, will changes in economics be the answer anymore, if our goal is to enable people to pursue happiness?

In answering the question, remember that we have defined out of existence all issues of safety nets and minimum income and the meaning of the poverty line. We are saying that the poorest people in the country are making the equivalent of $30,000 a year. So if we are to say that, yes, people are still prevented from pursuing happiness for economic reasons, the policy prescription that follows is (as far as I can tell) necessarily the egalitarian solution, whereby everyone makes roughly the same amount of money. That would succeed in changing the terms of the envy (people then could concentrate on envying other people their power, talent, beauty, and other unequally distributed gifts). Would it enhance the pursuit of happiness among the previously poor people?

In the egalitarian literature, there is a presumption that income leveling would have some such utilitarian effect, but these arguments have historically been put in terms of societies in which wealth exists side by side with abject poverty. It is an interesting question to put to the egalitarians, and one that is increasingly pertinent in a world of expanding wealth: Why, in pursuing happiness, is one person with enough money impeded by someone else's having more? As far as I can tell (the reader is invited to work through his own answers), the logic behind an answer ultimately has to hinge on some strange understandings of happiness—roughly on the order of, "my happiness is augmented by knowing that other people do not have more than I do." Presumably this logic is most attractive to those who see unequal incomes as ipso facto proof of social injustice, an argument that I will not try to contest here.

But if one is not attracted by the logic of the egalitarian solution, as I am not, then one is left without economic solutions for getting people off the hedonic treadmill. When we reach a state of prosperity in which poverty is defined as an income equivalent to $30,000 a year, the hedonic treadmill will remain, but policy solutions to the unequal happiness of the poorer members of society cannot be based on raising their income (I am arguing). Everything we know about how people have reacted in the past tells us that they are *not* going to be any happier when they are making $40,000, or $50,000, or $100,000, if the rest of society has continued to get still richer.

It may be objected that by assuming $30,000 as the floor I have fundamentally changed the terms of the issue. Currently, poor people in American society are genuinely in need of more material resources, whereas in my imaginary society the "poor" people who make $30,000 would not have such an objective deficit. This raises the fascinating question of where poverty begins, however. Macaulay, writing of Victorian England, chided his contemporaries for sentimentalizing about a Golden Age in the past when "noblemen were destitute of comforts the want of which would be intolerable to a modern footman."[9] A century later, we think of Victorian England as a swamp of Dickensian poverty. Would a $30,000 floor *really* be "enough material resources," whereas the current poverty line represents "not enough material resources"? Or has our current poverty line in fact already passed the threshold of enough?

Suppose, for example, that you put yourself in the position of a person in 1900. The same question is put to you, only slightly amended to fit the different moment in history: "Suppose that at some time in the future the United States becomes so wealthy that the poorest families have an income of the current (1900) average, while the average income has tripled in the meantime?" I suggest that no poor person in 1900 would have imagined that his material needs would not be met by the income of the average American at that time—which is to say, an average that made America at the turn of the century the promised land for poor people around the world.

The point is, of course, that we have already surpassed that millennial state of affairs from the vantage point of a poor person in 1900. The real purchasing power of families at the poverty line in the late 1980s (in 1987, $11,612 for a family of four) is much greater than the purchasing power of the average family in 1900.* Does this mean that people at the contemporary poverty line are living lives in which they can pursue happiness? Not necessarily. Rather, I am arguing that the *reason why* they cannot does not necessarily lie in money.

All this is far from demonstrating that people with near-subsistence incomes have "enough" material resources to pursue happiness. In fact, two points should be conceded. One is that providing more money to poor people probably will increase the felt-happiness of the people who get the money in the short term (for the same reasons discussed under the explanations for the hedonic treadmill). The second is that *if nothing else is done*, poor people who stay at the same near-subsistence income while the rest of the society gets richer will probably become more unhappy than they were before. But our topic is the pursuit of happiness. Once subsistence has been passed, what are the relative priorities to be attached to further augmenting income versus other steps (which may preclude augmenting income)? To explore this question, I ask you to join in a series of thought experiments.

THOUGHT EXPERIMENTS ABOUT BEING POOR

One of the great barriers to a discussion of poverty and social policy in the 1980s is that so few people who talk about poverty have ever been poor. The diminishing supply of the formerly-poor in policy-making and policy-influencing positions is a side effect of progress. The number of poor households dropped dramatically from the beginning of World War II through the end of the 1960s. Despite this happy cause, however, it is a troubling phenomenon. From the beginning of

---

* In 1987 dollars, the average annual earnings in 1900 for all occupations was about $6,000; in nonfarm occupations, about $6,700.[10] I acknowledge the incomparabilities—if a family that could afford domestic help in 1900 cannot now, but can afford a television, how does it all balance out? My point is simply that the contemporary poverty line represents a lot of raw purchasing power in historical terms.

American history through at least the 1950s, the new generation moving into positions of influence in politics, business,
journalism, and academia was bound to include a large admix-
ture of people who had grown up dirt-poor. People who had
grown up in more privileged surroundings did not have to
speculate about what being poor was like; someone sitting beside them, or at the head of the table, was likely to be able to
tell them. It was easy to acknowledge then, as it is not now,
that there is nothing so terrible about poverty per se. Poverty
is not equivalent to destitution. Being poor does not necessarily
mean being malnourished or ill-clothed. It does not automati-
cally mean joylessness or despair. To be poor is not necessarily
to be without dignity, it is not necessarily to be unhappy.
When large numbers of people who were running the country
had once been poor themselves, poverty could be kept in perspective.

Today, how many graduates of the Kennedy School of Government or of the Harvard Business School have ever been
really poor? How many have ever had close friends who were?
How many even have parents who were once poor? For those
who have never been poor and never even known any people
who were once poor, it is difficult to treat poverty as something
other than a mystery. It is even more difficult to be detached
about the importance of poverty, because to do so smacks of
a "let them eat cake" mentality. By the same token, however, it
is important that we who have never been poor be able to
think about the relationship of poverty to social policy in a
much more straightforward way than the nation's intellectuals
and policymakers have done for the past few decades. To that
end, I propose first a thought experiment based on the premise
that tomorrow you had to be poor. I do not mean "low-income"
by Western standards of affluence, but functioning near the
subsistence level, as a very large proportion of the world's
population still does.

In constructing this thought experiment, the first requirement
is to divorce yourself from certain reflexive assumptions. Do
not think what it would be like to be poor while living in a
community of rich people. I do not (yet) want to commingle
the notions of absolute poverty and relative poverty, so you

should imagine a community in which everyone else is as poor as you are; indeed, a world in which the existence of wealth is so far removed from daily life that it is not real.

The second requirement is to avoid constructing an imaginary person. The point is not to try to imagine yourself in the shoes of "a poor person" but to imagine what *you*, with your particular personality, experiences, strengths, and limitations (including your middle-class upbringing and values), would do if you were suddenly thrust into this position.

VERSION I:
BEING POOR IN A THAI VILLAGE

To do all this in the American context is difficult. Any scenario is filled with extraneous factors. Let me suggest one that I used as a way of passing the time when I was a researcher driving on the back roads of rural Thailand many years ago. What if, I would muse, I had to live for the rest of my life in the next village I came to? (Perhaps a nuclear war would have broken out, thereby keeping me indefinitely in Thailand; any rationalization would do.)

In some ways, the prospect was grim. I had never been charmed by sleeping under mosquito netting nor by bathing with a few buckets of cloudy well water. When circumstances permitted, I liked to end a day's work in a village by driving back to an air-conditioned hotel and a cold beer. But if I were to have no choice . . .

As it happens, Thailand is an example of an attractive peasant culture. Survival itself is not a problem. The weather is always warm, so the requirements for clothes, fuel, and shelter are minimal. Village food is ample, if monotonous. But I would nonetheless be extremely poor, with an effective purchasing power of a few hundred dollars a year. The house I would live in would probably consist of a porch and one or two small, unlit, unfurnished rooms. The walls might be of wood, more probably of woven bamboo or leaf mats. I would have (in those years) no electricity and no running water. Perhaps I would have a bicycle or a transistor radio. Probably the nearest physician would be many kilometers away. In sum: If the criterion for measuring poverty is material goods, it would be difficult to find a community in deepest Appalachia or a neigh-borhood in the most depressed parts of South Chicago that even approaches the absolute material poverty of the average Thai village in which I would have to make my life.

On the other hand, as I thought about spending the next fifty years in a Thai village, I found myself thinking more about precisely what it is that I would lack (compared to my present life) that would cause me great pain. The more I thought about the question, the less likely it became that I would be unhappy.

Since I lacked any useful trade, maybe I could trade the Jeep for a few *rai* of land and become a farmer. Learning how to farm well enough to survive would occupy my time and at-tention for several years. After that, I might be able to im-prove my situation. One of the assets I would bring from my Western upbringing and schooling would be a haphazardly ac-quired understanding of cash crops, markets, and entrepreneu-rial possibilities, and perhaps I could parlay that, along with hard work, into some income and more land. It also was clear to me that I probably would enjoy this "career." I am not saying I would *choose* it, but rather that I could find satisfaction in learning how to be a competent rice farmer, even though it was not for me the most desired of all possible careers.

What about my personal life? Thais are among the world's most handsome and charming people, and it was easy to imag-ine falling in love with a woman from the village, marrying, and having a family with her. I could also anticipate the plea-sure of watching my children grow up, probably at closer hand than I would in the United States. The children would not get the same education they would in the States, but I would have it within my power to see that they would be edu-cated. A grade school is near every village. The priests in the local *wat* could teach them Buddhism. I could also become teacher to my children. A few basic textbooks in mathematics, science, and history; Plato and Shakespeare and the Bible; a dozen other well-chosen classics—all these could be acquired even in up-country Thailand. My children could reach adult-hood literate, thoughtful, and civilized.

My children would do well in other ways too. They would grow up in a "positive peer culture," as the experts say. Their Thai friends in the village would all be raised by their parents to be considerate, hardworking, pious, and honest—that's the way Thai villagers raise their children. My children would face few of the corrupting influences to be found in an American city.

Other personal pleasures? I knew I would find it easy to make friends, and that some would become close. I would have other good times, too—celebrations on special occasions, but more often informal gatherings and jokes and conversation. If I read less, I would also read better. I would have great personal freedom as long as my behavior did not actively interfere with the lives of my neighbors (the tolerance for eccentric behavior in a Thai village is remarkably high). What about the physical condition of poverty? After a few months, I suspect that I would hardly notice.

You may conclude that the thought experiment is a transparent setup. First I ask what it would be like to be poor, then I proceed to outline a near-idyllic environment in which to be poor. I assume that I have a legacy of educational experiences that would help me spend my time getting steadily less poor. And then I announce that poverty isn't so bad after all. But the point of the thought experiment is not to suggest that all kinds of poverty are tolerable, and even less that all peasant societies are pleasant places to live. When poverty means the inability to get enough food or shelter, it is every bit as bad as usually portrayed. When poverty means being forced to remain in that condition, with no way of improving one's situation, it is as bad as portrayed. When poverty is conjoined with oppression, be it a caste system or a hacienda system or a people's republic, it is as bad as portrayed. *My thought experiment is not a paean to peasant life, but a paean to communities of free people.* If poverty is defined in terms of money, everybody in the Thai village is poor. If poverty is defined as being unable to live a modest but decent existence, hardly anyone there is poor.

VERSION II:
BEING MADE SUDDENLY POOR IN THE UNITED STATES

Does this thought experiment fail when it is transported to the United States? Imagine the same Thai village set down intact on the outskirts of Los Angeles. Surely its inhabitants must be miserable, living in their huts and watching the rest of the world live in splendor.

At this point in the argument, however, we need no longer think in terms of thought experiments. The situation I described is one that has been faced by hundreds of thousands of immigrants to the United States, whether they came from Europe at the end of World War II or from Vietnam in the mid-1970s. Lawyers found themselves working as janitors, professors found themselves working on assembly lines. Sometimes they followed the same process I just described, working their way up and out. Many had to remain janitors and factory workers, because they came to America too late in life to retool their foreign-trained skills. But their children did not have to remain so, and they have not. A reading of their histories, in literature or in the oral testimony of their children, corroborates the pattern I described. Was a Latvian attorney forced to flee his country "happy" to have to work as a janitor? No. Was he prevented by his situation—specifically, by his poverty— from successfully pursuing happiness? Emphatically, no.

Let us continue the thought experiment nonetheless, with a slightly different twist. This time, you are given a choice. One choice is to be poor in rural Thailand, as I have described it, with just enough food and shelter and a few hundred dollars a year in cash: a little beyond bare subsistence, but not much. Or you may live in the United States, receive a free apartment, free food, free medical care, and a cash grant, the package coming to a total that puts you well above the poverty line. There is, however, a catch: you are *required* to live in a particular apartment, and this apartment is located in a public housing project in one of the burned-out areas of the South Bronx. A condition of receiving the rest of the package is that you continue to live, and raise your children, in the South Bronx (you do not have the option of spending all of your waking hours in Manhattan, just as the village thought experiment did not give you the option of taking vacations in Bangkok). You still have all the assets you took to the Thai village—once again, it is essential that you not imagine what it is like for an Alabama sharecropper to be transplanted to the South Bronx, but what it would be like *for you*.

In some ways, you would have much more access to distractions. Unlike the situation in the Thai village, you would have television you could watch all day, taking you vicariously into other worlds (an inferior form of the Experience Machine). Or, for that matter, it would be much easier to get books than in a Thai village, and you would have much more money with which to buy them. You could, over time, fix up your apartment so that within its walls you would have an environment that looks and feels very like an apartment you could have elsewhere.

There is only one problem: You would have a terrible time once you opened your door to the outside world. How, for example, are you going to raise your children in the South Bronx so that they grow up to be the adults you want them to be? (No, you don't have the option of sending them to live elsewhere.) How are you going to take a walk in the park in the evening? There are many good people in the South Bronx with whom you could become friends, just as in the village. But how are you to find them? And once they are found, how are you to create a functioning, mutually reinforcing community?

I suggest that as you think of answers to those questions, you will find that, if you are to have much chance to be happy, the South Bronx needs to be changed in a way that the village did not—that, unlike the village as it stood, the South Bronx as it stands does not "work" as an environment for pursuing happiness. Let us ignore for the moment how these changes in environment could be brought about, by what combination of government's "doing things" and "refraining from doing things." The fact is that hardly any of those changes involve greater income for you personally, but rather changes in the surrounding environment. There is a question that crystallizes the roles of personal vs. environmental poverty in this situation: What is the dollar sum that would persuade you to move self and family to this public housing project in the South Bronx?

VERSION III:
POVERTY AND YOUR OWN CHILDREN

The purpose of the first two versions of the thought experiment was to suggest a different perspective on one's own priorities regarding the pursuit of happiness, and by extension to suggest that perhaps public policy ought to reflect a different set of priorities as well. It is easy in this case, however, to assume that what one wants for oneself is not applicable to others. Thus, for example, it could be said that the only reason the thought experiments work (if you grant even that much) is because the central character starts out with enormous advantages of knowledge and values—which in themselves reflect the advantages of having grown up with plenty of material resources.

To explore that possibility, I ask you to bear with me for one more thought experiment on this general topic, one I have found to be a touchstone.[11] This time, the question is not what kinds of material resources you (with your fully developed set of advantages) need for your pursuit of happiness, but what a small child, without any developed assets at all, needs for his pursuit of happiness—specifically, what your own child needs.

Imagine that you are the parent of a small child, living in contemporary America, and in some way you are able to know that tomorrow you and your spouse will die and your child will be made an orphan. You do not have the option of sending the child to live with a friend or relative. You must choose among other and far-from-perfect choices. The choices, I assure you, are not veiled representations of anything else; the experiment is set up not to be realistic, but to evoke something about how you think.

Suppose first this choice: You may put your child with an extremely poor couple according to the official definition of "poor"—which is to say, poverty that is measured exclusively in money. This couple has so little money that your child's clothes will often be secondhand and there will be not even small luxuries to brighten his life. Life will be a struggle, often a painful one. But you also know that the parents work hard, will make sure your child goes to school and studies, and will teach your child that integrity and responsibility are primary values. Or you may put your child with parents who will be as affectionate to your child as the first couple but who have never worked, are indifferent to your child's education, who think that integrity and responsibility (when they think of them at all) are meaningless words—but who have and will al-

ways have plenty of food and good clothes and amenities, provided by others.

Which couple do you choose? The answer is obvious to me
and I imagine to most readers: The first couple, of course. But
if you are among those who choose the first couple, stop and
consider what the answer means. This is *your own child* you
are talking about, whom you would never let go hungry even
if providing for your child meant going hungry yourself. And
yet you are choosing years of privation for that same child.
Why?

Perhaps I set up the thought experiment too starkly. Let us
repeat it, adding some ambiguity. This time, the first choice is
again the poor-but-virtuous couple just described. The second
couple is rich. They are, we shall say, the heirs to a great fortune. They will not beat your child or in any other way mal-
treat him or her. We may even assume affection on their part,
as we will with the other couples. But they have never worked
and never will, are indifferent to your child's education, and
think that integrity and responsibility (when they think of
them at all) are meaningless words. They do, however, possess
millions of dollars, more than enough to last for the life of your
child and of your child's children. Now, in whose care do you
place your child? The poor couple or the rich one?

This time, it seems likely that some people will choose the
rich couple—or more accurately, it is possible to think of ways
in which the decision might be tipped in that direction. For
example, a wealthy person who is indifferent to a child's education might nonetheless ship the child off to an expensive
boarding school at the earliest possible age. In that case, it is
conceivable that putting the child with the wealthy ne'er-do-
wells is preferable to the poor-but-virtuous couple, *if* they end
up providing the values of the poor family through the surrogate parenting provided by the boarding school—dubious, but
conceivable. One may imagine other ways in which the money
might be used to compensate for the inadequacies of the parents. But failing those very chancy possibilities, I suggest that
a great many parents on all sides of political fences will knowingly choose hunger and rags for their child rather than wealth.

Again, the question is Why? What catastrophes are going to

befall the child placed in the wealthy home? What is the awful fate? Would it be so terrible if he grew up to be thoughtlessly rich? The child will live a life of luxury and have enough money to buy himself out of almost any problem that might arise. Why not leave it at that? Or let me put the question positively: In deciding where to send the child, what is one trying to achieve by these calculations and predictions and hunches? What is the good one is trying to achieve? What is the criterion of success?

One may attach a variety of descriptors to the answer. Perhaps you want the child to become a reflective, responsible adult. To value honesty and integrity. To be able to identify sources of lasting satisfaction. Ultimately, if I keep pushing the question (Why is honesty good? Why is being reflective good?), you will give the answer that permits no follow-up: You want your child to be happy. You are trying to choose the guardians who will best enable your child to pursue happiness. And, forced to a choice, material resources come very low on your list of priorities.

REPRISE: A QUESTION OF PRIORITIES

We have begun with the most obvious of all the enabling conditions. How is policy to be arranged so that everyone has enough material resources to pursue happiness? Let me try to draw together the discussion in terms of the usual way of construing the problem, the problem reconstrued according to the pursuit-of-happiness criterion, and where this leaves us.

Construing Progress: The Usual Understanding. The contemporary intellectual basis for talking about public policy and material resources has been redistribution. Great inequalities in material resources exist. They are at the least morally suspect and, if they are morally permissible at all, must be justified.*

---

* I am adumbrating John Rawls's "difference principle," elaborated in *A Theory of Justice*, which holds that "social and economic inequalities . . . are just only if they result in compensating benefits for everyone, and in particular for the least advantaged members

A main function of public policy is to define a floor of material resources below which no one should be permitted to fall. The criteria for assessing public policy are the poverty line (progress consists of reducing the number of people who fall below it) and distribution (a widening gap between rich and poor is in itself seen as a problem, independently of other considerations).

One need not endorse the ethics of redistribution to be in favor of a redistributive solution to the problem of poverty, however. Probably everyone who is troubled by the problem of poverty in America has at one time or another thought something like this: "America is so rich that it can afford to give everyone a decent income. Let's do it and be done with it: Guarantee an adequate material base, then let people work out the other goods they need to be happy as best they can. Maybe it's not the ideal way, but at least I won't have to worry about poverty anymore." The underlying assumption in all such formulations, whether they are proposed enthusiastically from the left or reluctantly from the right, is that the way in which people provide for their material needs is more or less independent of the way in which they provide for their other needs.

Recasting the Role of Material Resources. In this chapter, I have limited the discussion to a narrow point: In deciding how to enhance the ability of people to pursue happiness, solutions that increase material resources beyond subsistence *independently of other considerations* are bound to fail. Money per se is not very important. It quickly becomes trivial. Depending on the other nonmonetary enabling conditions, poor people can

---

of society."[12] In the seventeen years since it appeared, Rawls's book has achieved remarkably broad international acceptance as the statement of the ethical basis for redistributive social democracy. In particular, Rawls's difference principle tends to be treated not as a proposition but as an inarguable moral precept. In some European countries, parliaments have been known to debate at length whether a given bill is sufficiently consistent with the difference principle. It is hardly less widely accepted by liberal intellectuals in the United States. In a recent discussion with the head of a major social science institute, I was interrupted by, "But it sounds as if you don't accept the difference principle!" in a tone as genuinely astonished as if I had rejected the law of gravity.

have a rich assortment of ways of pursuing happiness, or affluent people can have very few.

The thought experiments and the farfetched scenarios of
future general affluence were stratagems intended not to convince you of any particular policy implications, but rather to
induce you to entertain this possibility: When a policy trade-
off involves (for example) imposing material hardship in return
for some other policy good, *it is possible that imposing the material hardship is the right choice.* For example, regarding the
"orphaned child" scenario: *If* a policy leads to a society in which
there are more of the first kind of parents and fewer of the second, the sacrifices in material resources available to the children
involved might conceivably be worth it.

The discussion, with its steady use of the concept of "near-
subsistence" as "enough material resources to pursue happiness," has also been intended to point up how little our concept
of poverty has to do with subsistence. Thus, for example, if one
simply looks at the end result of how people live, a natural
observation of contemporary America might be that we have
large numbers of people who are living at a subsistence or sub-
subsistence level. But I have been using "subsistence" in its
original sense: enough food to be adequately nourished, plus
the most basic shelter and clothing. The traditional Salvation
Army shelter provides subsistence, for example. In Western
countries, and perhaps especially the United States, two problems tend to confuse the issue. One is that we have forgotten
what subsistence means, so that an apartment with cockroaches,
broken windows, and graffiti on the walls may be thought of
as barely "subsistence level," even if it also has running water,
electricity, heat, a television, and a pile of discarded fast-food
cartons in the corner. It might be an awful place to live (for
the reasons that the South Bronx can be an awful place to live),
but it bears very little resemblance to what "subsistence" means
to most of the world. Secondly, we tend to confuse the way in
which some poor people *use* their resources (which indeed can
often leave them in a near-subsistence state) with the raw purchasing power of the resources at their disposal. Take, for example, the apartment I just described and move a middle-class
person with middle-class habits and knowledge into it, given

exactly the same resources. Within days it would be still shabby but a different place. All of which is precisely the point of the thought experiments about Thailand and the South Bronx: Money has very little to do with living a poverty-stricken life. Similarly, "a subsistence income" has very little to do with what Americans think of as poverty.

That being the case, I am arguing that the job of designing good public policy must be reconstrued. We do not have the option of saying, "First we will provide for the material base, then worry about the other enabling conditions." The enabling conditions interact. The ways in which people go about achieving safety, self-respect, and self-fulfillment in their lives are inextricably bound up with each other and with the way in which people go about providing for their material well-being. We do not have the option of doing one good thing at a time.

In the discussion of the enabling conditions, I have put material resources first on the list only because that is where it has stood in the political debate. I am suggesting that properly it should be put last. This stance still leaves us with the problem of making sure that the basic material resources for pursuing happiness are available to all. Warmth, shelter, and food are still essential. Under present social policy, large numbers of people are cold, unsheltered, and hungry. But before we decide how these basics are to be provided, let us examine the framework within which they should be provided if the other nutrients of happiness are to be available as well.

5

Safety

A MAIN REASON why communities form in the first place is that we may be safe from the tigers beyond the compound. This elemental notion of safety—safety from predators who might otherwise do us physical harm—is behind Maslow's placement of safety as number two in the needs hierarchy. But safety and threats can take many forms. It is necessary to begin with a few words about the larger framework that relates safety and social policy to the pursuit of happiness.

Types of Threats, Types of Safety

Threats to safety can be roughly divided into those which are passive and those which are predatory. By "passive" I mean that no one is out to get you. There may be a bone in the fish, and you may choke on it, but no one put it there in an attempt to kill you. "Predatory" threats are ones created and pursued by some active, purposeful agent. Someone *is* out to get you.

We may then divide threats on a second dimension: avoidable and unavoidable. By "avoidable," I mean that you can anticipate the existence of a potential problem and act to forestall it. You know that fish have bones that are easy to choke on, therefore you take small bites and chew cautiously; perhaps you eat fish only when in the presence of someone who knows the Heimlich maneuver. By taking these precautions, you are unlikely to die of choking on a fish bone. Similarly, many threats that are created unintentionally by other people are highly avoidable, even though you technically shouldn't be put in a position of having to avoid them. If your neighbor digs a hole beside the sidewalk and neglects to cover it, he may legally be negligent. But if some sunny morning you fall into it, you have been careless—the threat is highly avoidable. An example of an extremely hard-to-avoid threat is that you will be hit by a meteorite, or that some food you currently eat will be found to be carcinogenic twenty years from now.

From a policy perspective, these threats have historically called for four responses. For the threats that fall under the generic heading of "acts of God," insurance was created— private initially, now increasingly governmental. The insurance function can, of course, be applied to any type of threat, including the most predatory and the most avoidable. One distinctive feature of insurance in all cases, however, is that it applies after the fact. It does not increase safety; it only cushions the consequences of failures in safety. Ironically, another distinctive feature of insurance is that it tends inherently to *decrease* safety for all threats that are avoidable: If I'm fully insured, I tend (ceteris paribus) to take fewer precautions to avoid the threat.

The second response is tort law, which applies to breaches of safety through negligence. In theory (disregarding some serious contemporary problems with application), tort law provides an economical way to deal with a wide variety of injuries and losses: the injured party is relieved, or at least cushioned, from the consequences of the act, and everyone is made safer because the threat of a civil action encourages prevention of a recurrence.

The third response is represented by the peculiar nature of actions that are both highly predatory and unavoidable by the individual, the worst of which tend to be those in which the most unmanageable force (the government) has run amok. Thus the appropriate response is governmental self-restraint—in the United States, constitutional limitations on what the government can do and the self-policing to make good on those limitations. (A second category of threat that fits the pure predatory-unavoidable category, but one that I will ignore here, is attack by a foreign power, for which the response is national defense.)

This leaves us with the fourth and final response to threats to safety, the police function. The police function is called into play for all highly predatory acts not sanctioned by the state. Even if the individual is completely able to defend himself, the police function applies.

Those who are of the opinion that the rest of the chapter should be devoted to the threat of nuclear war and its relationship to the pursuit of happiness, or to the threat of acid rain, have an arguable point. But they also are entering into some highly technical areas that would take us far afield.[1] The police function—protection of the individual against aggression by his fellow citizens—comes first to mind when most of us think of the degree to which we are at risk from day to day, and is the one on which I will be focusing for this discussion. In this context, the threats posed by crime seem most central to day-to-day life for most people, and the links between crime and the pursuit of happiness are archetypal.

What Is the Baseline?

It would seem that we can begin the discussion of the enabling condition called "safety" by assuming that a problem exists, one that public policy ought to do something to correct. Few if any other issues in contemporary social policy arouse more widespread public concern than crime in the streets and its first cousin, the illegal drug traffic that engenders so much street crime. But the topic is not whether the crime rate is "too high" in an abstract sense. Instead, we are inquiring into the nature of the condition called "safety" relative to the pursuit of happiness, which I will argue leads us to a quite different conception of what is broken and therefore needs fixing.

The difference first becomes apparent because of the lack

of a baseline. With material resources, a baseline is readily definable: enough food for good nutrition, enough clothing and shelter to ward off the elements. We may argue about how much more than those basics is appropriate in an advanced society, but the bare minimum is definable. Not so with safety. The crime statistics, for example, are usually put in terms of crime rates. But how many homicides per year per 100,000 people, or how many muggings per year per 100,000, is low enough to make you feel so safe that you will go about your daily business without taking precautions? It is unlikely that you can answer the question—that's not the way one thinks about "feeling safe."

Even more to the point, some people like risk while others don't, which makes it tricky to talk about "safety" as being a universal need. The issue of job security is probably a better example of this than crime. Some people are made uneasy, even frantic, by the prospect of job insecurity. For them, a secure union job or university tenure system, say, are the ideals. Others are bored by a secure job and become happy only after they have struck out on their own. In reality, both types of people want a certain degree of safety (most risk-takers want enough predictability to be able to assess the risks they might choose to take), but the level that constitutes "enough" is vastly different. Furthermore, for the risk-takers there can be "too much" safety: Force them to live in a society where they are not permitted to take such risks, and they will be miserable.

I am alluding to sources of human satisfaction that will come up again in different language under the discussions of self-respect and enjoyment. The point here is that the wide differences in personal taste for risk make it difficult to talk about a uniform "need for safety" with regard to any of the types of threats, including the threat of crime. When ten different people pick an acceptable crime rate, and all ten answers are different, how is a policymaker to choose the reasonable one?

Differences in the "baseline tolerance of risk" across people are only part of the problem. The degree of safety and risk we enjoy constantly changes for each of us as individuals, and so do our responses. For example, would I feel safe walking across New York's Central Park at noon? Yes, and I've done it often.

Would I feel safe walking across Central Park at midnight? I'm sure I wouldn't, and I'm not about to try. So is the city of New York meeting an appropriate standard of "enough safety," or not? Do I have a right to go wherever I please, whenever I please and expect the same degree of safety from crime, or does the standard of "enough safety" properly vary with time and place?

Such considerations illustrate the pervasive problem: In discussing whether safety is adequate, the great difficulty is answering the question, "Compared to what?" I begin that task by considering, then discarding, the notion that the number of crimes is the right measure.

Quantity of Crime Is Not Really the Problem

Two different issues tend to become mixed when people discuss the crime problem. One is the explosive increase in crime during the late 1960s and the slower but still troubling increases during the 1970s. The increases were real. In 1960, for example, 161 violent crimes were reported per 100,000 people.[2] In 1980, when reported crimes reached their peak, there were 581. This constituted more than a tripling of violent crime, large by any standard. For property crimes, the increase during the same twenty-year period was from 1,726 to 5,319, also a tripling. Hardly any community of any size was immune from this increase.

But while the increase is lamentable, a reduction in safety must be distinguished from having so little safety that one's quality of life is affected, and that, it must be remembered, is our topic: "enough safety" so that one may go about one's life seeking happiness without being deflected. Seen from this perspective, "enough safety" probably exists for the great bulk of the population despite the increase in crime.

The small Iowa town where I grew up illustrates the distinction to be drawn between an increase in crime and inadequate safety. Local crime has unquestionably increased in the last twenty-five years, and it is a topic of complaint. The increase in crime has even changed behavior: Once, few people bothered to lock their homes when they left the house to go shopping. Now, many do. Some, especially the elderly, think they are taking a risk when they go for a walk after dark, and are reluctant to do so. But there really isn't much of a threat. Months, even years, can go by without anything resembling the classic street mugging in which an ordinary citizen walking peacefully on an ordinary street is attacked. So while there has been an increase in the crime problem that has aroused some concern, safety remains at a level that ought to be adequate by any reasonable criterion.

Compare this situation with the one described by Claude Brown, who wrote in *Manchild in the Promised Land* about Harlem of the 1940s and 1950s, regarding Harlem in the 1980s:

> In any Harlem building, whether a tenement or a relatively luxurious high-rise, every door has at least three locks on it. Nobody opens a door without first finding out who's there. In the early evening, or even at midday, you see people—middle-aged men and women—lingering outside nice apartment houses, peeking in the lobbies. They seem to be casing the joint. They are actually trying to figure out who is in the lobby of *their* building. "Is this someone waiting to mug me? Should I risk going in, or should I wait for someone else to come?" If you live in Harlem, USA, you don't park your automobile two blocks from your apartment house because that gives potential muggers an opportunity to get a fix on you. You'd better find a parking space within a block of your house, because if you have to walk two blocks you're not going to make it. . . . In Harlem, elderly people walking their dogs in the morning cross the street when they see some young people coming. They try to act casual, but of course they aren't. They are very aware of those young people—you can almost feel the tension as the youngsters get closer. And what those elderly men and women have in the paper bags they're carrying is not just a pooper scooper—it's a gun. And if those youngsters cross that street, somebody's going to get hurt—you're going to hear it. Everybody knows this.[3]

The crime problem in the big city of which Brown writes is radically different from the crime problem facing most of the nation.

How many people are affected by this type of high-density

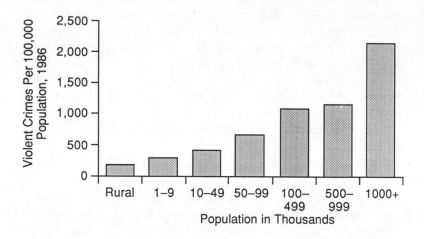

FIGURE 3
THE IMPORTANCE OF SIZE

SOURCE: Federal Bureau of Investigation, *Uniform Crime Reports
for the United States 1986* (Washington, D.C.: Government Printing Office, 1987), table 14.

crime? Surprisingly few. Consider first that the high crime
rates are concentrated in large cities. The larger the city, the
higher the rate. The striking relationship of crime to city size
is shown in figure 3.

The relevance of the graph lies in a fact that may come as a
surprise to many, that comparatively few Americans live in
the core cities where the crime problem is worst. In 1980, fully
one-half of the population of the United States lived in the
countryside or in a jurisdiction of fewer than 10,000 persons.
Only a quarter of the population lived in cities of 100,000 or
more (the ones that showed the big jump in crime rates in
fig. 3). Only 8 percent of the population lived in the cities of
a million or more persons that had the highest crime rates.[4] The
United States may be famous for its megalopolises, but most of
the people who may live in suburbs *near* large cities actually

have their residences, and spend most of their "vulnerable" time, in much smaller communities.

And these crime figures are for the city as a whole. The communities that Claude Brown describes are so different from anywhere else that they exist in a world of their own. Contemplate what happens when we append to the above figure, using the same scale, the violent crime rate of the 25th Precinct in New York, the East Harlem area that was part of Claude Brown's description (see fig. 4).

The image of urban danger that we carry in our minds is based on neighborhoods experiencing a rate of crime several

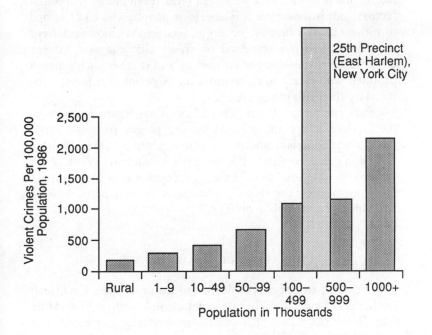

FIGURE 4
THE IMPORTANCE OF SIZE REVISITED

SOURCE: Data for the 25th Precinct are taken from unpublished statistics provided by the Crime Analysis Division of the New York City Police Department.

magnitudes worse than that which the great bulk of the American population ever encounters.* A very few places with a very small fraction of the population have a horrendous problem with crime and personal safety. But it is difficult to infer from the crime statistics for the nation as a whole that many other Americans are impeded from going about their daily business by a fear that they will be assaulted or robbed, or that their home will be burgled while they are away. If you use the crime statistics as the basis for analyzing the enabling condition called safety, "enough safety" already exists for almost everyone.

The policy implication seems to be that "If you live in a high-crime neighborhood, that's your business. If you don't like it, move somewhere else." But this conclusion is unsatisfactory, not just because it is cruel for people who can't afford to move but also because of a gut feeling that, however hard to define, there *is* a standard of safety that the government ought to be responsible for enforcing, and there *is* a widespread problem with safety in contemporary America that is not captured by the FBI's crime index.

Let us back away from "crime" as an aggregate measure of the level of safety and ask: What are people so upset about when they complain about the crime problem (even though they don't live in places like the 25th Precinct)? What is the "threshold of safety" that in their perception is not being met? I will argue that the threshold consists of two parts, labeled "lawfulness" and "public civility."

THE NEED FOR "LAWFULNESS"

The first half of the threshold has to do with what I will call lawfulness. Lawfulness is not coincidental with a low crime rate. Rather, it means that predatory behavior is treated in a reasonably *predictable and understandable* way that corre-

---

* It may be noted that, according to unpublished New York Police Department statistics, the 25th Precinct's violent crime rate in 1986 had *declined* by 31 percent since 1980. In 1980, the rate was 5,812 violent crimes per 100,000.

sponds with commonly shared principles of right and wrong within the community.

The police fill this function on the front lines by visibly *trying* to enforce lawfulness, as illustrated by a recent description in *The New York Times Magazine* of a homicide detective working long hours to solve the murder of a crack dealer. No one was sorry the crack dealer had been killed—not the police, not the people in the neighborhood. It had been what the police sometimes call "a community service homicide." Nonetheless, the detective was doggedly trying to find the killer. Why? In answer to the reporter's question, the detective recalled a resident of the neighborhood he had questioned that morning, a poor workingman in his fifties who himself had been burglarized many times.

> Now there's a guy . . . who's worked all his life, paid his taxes, lived an honest life and what does he get for it? He gets a neighborhood where he can't keep a lock on the door and he can't afford to leave. So you ask me where's the motivation in a case like this where the deceased is a crack dealer? What it's really about is that gentleman there in that apartment. What's he got back? What's he got back? But at least if he sees, here I am, the representative of the law, I'm going around, I'm talking to people, I'm working on this case, it's not as if it's completely gotten to the point where people are shooting each other in the streets and nobody cares, nobody even notices.[5]

The detective was recognizing, as William Tucker has written, that "the criminal justice system is more than just a method for dealing with criminals. It is also a public stage upon which the continuing drama of public morality is enacted."[6] Or to put it slightly differently, it is not enough that crime be dealt with *efficiently* or even *effectively*. It must also be dealt with *appropriately*. This perception of appropriateness begins with the police and extends through the courts and into the correctional system.

I use "lawful" to describe the appropriate process instead of the obvious alternative, "just." Justice is a very big and complicated concept, whereas what I have in mind is a simple-minded notion that goes something like this: In a lawful community, someone who does something everyone agrees is both illegal and harmful is sought by the police. If he is caught, he is prosecuted. If he is convicted, he suffers a penalty.

The hunt and the prosecution and the severity of the penalty will be in proportion to the crime and to the person. Major offenses will get more severe punishment than minor ones, repeat offenders will be treated as a greater menace than first-time offenders, and so on. But a penalty—and a penalty that is generally agreed to be meaningful—will be assessed. When the court is merciful, it is because of mitigating circumstances in the crime or the person, not because of a game in which the offender is awarded points for being clever. Lawfulness means a calling to accountability, a solemn truth-seeking process whereby a law-abiding community asserts its supremacy over outlaws.

For lawfulness to exist, it is not necessary that the police catch every lawbreaker. On the contrary, large numbers may go uncaught as long as they go uncaught for understandable reasons (it's hard to catch a good burglar). Nor is it necessary that every guilty person be found guilty (juries make mistakes). Nor need the punishments be severe (accountability is the critical concept, not vengeance). The only thing that is necessary, if I may put it colloquially, is that when someone who commits a crime is arrested for it, his neighbors' perception of the world leads them to say, "He is in big trouble." In such a case, lawfulness exists. If they say, "He'll probably walk," it doesn't.

LAWLESSNESS AND MIRANDA ET AL.

Seen in this context, much of the public discontent with the law enforcement and criminal justice systems in recent decades may be interpreted not as a reaction to the real danger of being mugged or murdered, but to the perception that the world isn't lawful anymore. The controversial Supreme Court decisions regarding admissible confessions (notably *Miranda*) and evidence (notably *Mapp*) offer excellent examples. Because I am touching on issues that attract passionate responses from all sides, let me emphasize some arguments that I am *not* making, one way or the other. I am not arguing that decisions such as

Miranda and *Mapp* have handcuffed the police. I am not arguing the constitutionality of such decisions. I am not even arguing the wisdom of such decisions. Rather, the proposition is that while such decisions increase what might be called "rulefulness" (*society* in the form of the police is held to tighter accountability for *its* observance of the rule of law), their effects have come to symbolize lawlessness. Such decisions shift the function of the justice system from a solemn truth-seeking process in which society sits in judgment to something that resembles an arcane game with lots of hidey-holes for those smart enough (and with enough money) to find them. Thus when a criminal gets off because of procedural errors in the arrest or the gathering of evidence, despite overwhelming evidence of guilt, the event mocks the community's supremacy over the outlaws and is also disquieting to one's sense of safety. People can do bad things with impunity even if they are caught.

The public's unease about *Miranda* and *Mapp* are only emblems of a broader perception of lawlessness. Many people (I include myself) take for granted, for example, that a defendant with a good lawyer can usually either get off altogether or strike a deal that is far better than the one he could have gotten without a good lawyer. Many people take for granted that if the government has enough interest in getting someone, it can eventually pin something on him or make him go broke in the process. More generally, many people take for granted that the final result of any given case depends heavily on who spends the most money on it. To the extent that "many people" is becoming "most people" and is heading toward "just about everyone," each of these opinions constitutes a troubling indictment of the perceived lawfulness of the system, and the underlying way in which it is troubling is not to be fixed by providing everyone with better lawyers.

Other aspects of the criminal justice system that have quite persuasive internal rationales affront our sense of lawfulness. Plea bargaining arrangements and the granting of immunity to a little fish in order to get a bigger fish make good sense in terms of efficiency, but such strategies are not lawful (in the sense I am using the term): people are supposed to get the appropriate penalty for what they did, not be punished for a lesser crime or go unpunished altogether because the criminal justice system finds it more convenient to do business that way. Similarly, it may make economic sense and may serve the ends of deterrence and rehabilitation to assign people to minimum-security or maximum-security prisons according to their personal characteristics instead of the gravity of their offenses, but it does not seem quite lawful to do so. Something is intuitively not lawful when the white-collar criminals (some of whom damaged the lives of thousands of people) all seem to end up in minimum-security camps in the woods instead of the penitentiary just because they are more tractable prisoners than the inner-city offender who is imprisoned for a much less serious offense.

The critical difference between lawfulness and lack of lawfulness is exemplified by the difference between a man who "gets away" with something because there is a reasonable doubt that he did it, and a man whose guilt is not in question but who gets away with it because of a technicality, whether it is a procedural technicality that leads the judge to throw out the case or a legal technicality that can be exploited by a sufficiently clever lawyer. In a lawful world, people may be presumed to be innocent until proven guilty because the existence of the doubt makes the likelihood of a miscarriage of justice tolerable—the system *probably* let a guilty man go free because prosecutors and jurors are not perfect and innocent people must be protected. When it is agreed that the system *certainly* let a guilty man get away, and everyone knows it, lawfulness has been undermined.

LAWFULNESS AND JUSTICE

One reason why I avoided the word "justice" in the preceding discussion is because justice is only incidental to the threshold of safety. This does not mean that people are indifferent to fairness and equity (part of the reason that minimum-security prisons for white-collar criminals are disquieting has to do with inequities), but that the elements of justice do not have a one-to-one correspondence with the elements of safety.

In a rough-and-ready way, justice to most of us means fairness—sauce for the goose is sauce for the gander, or, if you prefer Aristotle, justice consists of treating likes alike and unlikes unlike. Another commonplace notion of justice has to do with magnitude of the offense. Theft is always a crime, but stealing ten million dollars is in some sense worse than stealing ten dollars. Still a third common notion of justice has to do with culpability. A person who knows exactly what he is doing and who has no reasonable excuse for deciding to commit a crime is more culpable than a person of diminished mental capacity, or one who is youthful, or one who faces powerful temptations.

On all three of these justice-based grounds, a great deal of white-collar crime demands (if we are to do justice) more energetic investigation and prosecution than street crime. When it comes to lawfulness and the pursuit of happiness, however, our ideals of what should constitute good practice and the reality of what we want done by law-enforcement agencies depend crucially on where we live. Often, the resources of the police and prosecutor's office should be directed at a mentally borderline, poverty-stricken youth who steals ten dollars before they are turned to the educated, fully self-aware, affluent man who steals thousands. Not always, but often.

By way of illustration, suppose that two thieves live in your neighborhood. The first has figured out how to penetrate the computer codes of the nation's major banks and has programmed the computers, as they calculate the daily interest accruing to each savings account, to round down to the next penny and deposit the fractional leftover penny to an account of his own. No person in the country loses more than a few dollars a year to this gentleman, but his yearly income is millions of dollars. The second thief is seventeen years old, has grown up in a deprived environment, and a few times a week mugs someone—physically corners a person, threatens him or her with a knife, and robs that person of wallet or purse. If the victim refuses to give up wallet or purse, or if he has fewer than five dollars, the young thief stabs the victim with his knife. Both of these thieves live in your neighborhood. You may ask the police to arrest one or the other, but not both. Whom do you choose?

If we are interested in doing justice, the issue is cloudy. Maybe the size of the nonviolent theft makes the computer bandit the "worse" criminal; maybe the act of inflicting serious physical injury makes the young mugger the "worse" criminal. A long and inconclusive argument could be fought about which of the two ought to be arrested first if justice is the goal. But if the issue is which criminal is a threat to safety and thereby an impediment to the pursuit of happiness, the answer is un-equivocal.[7] No one's pursuit of happiness is impeded in any meaningful way by the computer thief, whereas the mugger poses an active threat to everyone in the neighborhood and vic-timizes even those whom he does not actually encounter by the fear he engenders.

This does not mean that the computer bandit should not be caught, prosecuted, and punished. To do so constitutes an im-portant law-enforcement function. When the computer bandit or fraudulent financier or other white-collar criminal visibly gets away with crime, he undermines the public's sense of law-fulness just as does the street mugger. At some distant remove, catching and punishing the computer bandit may even have something to do with safety (insofar as the deterioration of standards encourages people who are disposed to commit more hurtful crimes). But if the topic is safety, I suggest that *the only people who would choose to catch the computer bandit rather than the mugger* (if they have to choose one or the other) *are people who don't live in the neighborhood where the mugger is operating.* Indeed, the only reason any law-enforcement resources are devoted to computer bandits is that enough people who control the allocation of such resources do not live where the muggers do.*

I began by saying that justice has little to do with safety. A

---

* An important distinction must be emphasized. It is quite possible to go into a high-crime neighborhood and find people vocally up-set about rich white-collar criminals who get away with it. One may easily find people who (as a general principle) think that the police should catch the rich criminals instead of picking on poor folks who are just trying to scuffle a few bucks to get by. I am say-ing that these principles are discarded in the specific case. If the young mugger is operating on your block, threatening you, your spouse, and your children, and you control the disposition of police resources, you will first make sure that resources are being devoted to catching the young mugger.

more precise statement is that, conceiving of justice as treating likes alike and unlikes unlike, such a thing as local justice must be distinguished from global justice. In the global scheme of things, the computer bandit and the mugger are "likes"—they are both thieves of a sort, and to that extent should be treated the same. In the local scheme of things, they are "unlikes." One endangers his neighbor, the other does not. Justice is not forsaken—if the rich man's son takes to mugging, he should be treated the same as the poor man's son. But it is defined within the sphere that matters for the enjoyment of the good called safety.

LAWFULNESS AND COMPLEXITY: "LAW SUFFICIENTLY COMPLEX IS INDISTINGUISHABLE FROM NO LAW AT ALL"

So far, I have been arguing that the threshold condition of safety requires not that the government provide a particular level of safety, but that it embody a particular stance toward outlaws. But I have also limited the discussion to predatory crime and the criminal justice system. Frank Rizzo's observation that "a conservative is a liberal who has been mugged," and Tom Wolfe's recent codicil, "a liberal is a conservative who has been arrested," both capture a truth: Crime and the criminal justice system can decisively affect quality of life, but do so mostly to those who are forcibly brought into contact with them. Let me now broaden the issue of lawfulness to encompass the whole fabric of the legal system, and suggest that the problem of lawlessness has broader ramifications.

I refer specifically to the problem of predictability and understandability, of "knowing what will happen" in response to a behavior. In the case of criminal law, most of the laws themselves are fairly well understood—we know it is against the law to rob someone, and we know what robbery means—but the administration of the law is so Byzantine that only an insider can size up what is likely to happen to a specific person who is arrested for robbery. In the case of noncriminal laws and regulations, the problem is more immediate and has more pervasive effects on the lawfulness of the world around us.

Imagine, for example, that you are a responsible homeowner

who maintains your property carefully. But a person falls on your front steps and, lying there, announces that he has injured his back. At that moment, just how much money would you be willing to pay in return for a promise that the person lying on your sidewalk won't sue you? Knowing yourself to be morally blameless, do you really want your day in court in the American legal system that exists in 1988?

To the extent that a payoff sounds attractive, I am arguing that we have a problem with lawlessness interfering with the pursuit of happiness: *Even if the law "ought" to be on your side*, a rational person will fear being subjected to it. Science fiction novelist Arthur C. Clarke once observed that technology sufficiently advanced beyond the understanding of the observer is indistinguishable from magic. I am suggesting analogously that law sufficiently complex is indistinguishable from no law at all.

This form of lawlessness is most pervasively a problem in the areas of threat and safety that I put aside: tort law, governmental self-restraint, and the insurance function.[8] The tax code is an obvious example. Few citizens who make a good faith effort to observe the law *know*, when they get a letter from the IRS telling them that their return is being audited, that they will not have to pay a penalty. Their confidence is a function of how good they think their accountant is. It is not within their power (without taking a few years off to study the tax code) to fill out a tax return on their own and be sure that they have not broken the law. By the same token, it is not possible for many business executives to know for sure what their liability is. There is so much subjectivity, there are so many precedents available to judges who may exercise so much judicial discretion, that beyond a certain point all people can do, if they have the money, is to hire a good lawyer and hope for the best.

When I say that law sufficiently complex is indistinguishable from no law at all, I have a literal meaning in mind. If I live in a state where I cannot get a building permit for X except by paying a bribe, and my friend lives in a state where he cannot get a building permit for exactly the same X except by paying the same amount of money to a lawyer to represent him before the dispenser of building permits, what is the nature of the

difference? The detached observer may know that in the corrupt state, I am dependent on the whim of the bureaucrat, who
will probably sanction all sorts of bad building permits in return for a bribe. My friend lives in a state where it takes just
as much money to use the law, yes, but the law is there, in
black and white, and we may be confident that the law is sound
and wise, else it would not have been written that way, and the
dispenser of building permits is bound by that law, and will
only say yes to a legally suitable building. We may hope all that.
But similarly, the scientist may explain to the savage how the
transistor radio works. That doesn't make it any less like magic
to the savage.

To make matters worse, we know as a matter of fact that
the law can be bent and interpreted, that complexity in the
law is an open invitation to real lawlessness among those who
hold the keys to the kingdom. Thus the intimate relationship
between the amount of money one has and one's freedom from
(or vulnerability to) the letter of the law makes the difference
between the ability to pay for a good lawyer and the ability to
bribe the right bureaucrat more a matter of semantics than of
end result.

The Need for Public Civility

We return to the overall problem of safety. To repeat the
question: What are people so upset about when they talk about
"the crime problem"? What is the "threshold of safety" that
in their perception is not being met?

I have argued that one aspect of the need for safety is a need
for lawfulness. The other aspect is a need for public civility. The
proposition is that the threshold condition of safety requires
public civility that has very little to do with preventing "crime"
formally defined. Once more, a thought experiment is useful as
a way of recognizing commonly shared reactions.

Imagine that tomorrow you have been flown to New York
City, driven from La Guardia to East Harlem, and deposited on
a corner in that East Harlem precinct with the astronomical
crime rate shown in the earlier figure. You are to spend the

afternoon walking, shopping, eating, and generally going about your business in that neighborhood. Let us further imagine—since this is not a story about social differences—that you have adapted your dress and demeanor in such a way as not to stand out among the local inhabitants.

Are you, even so, nervous? Apprehensive? Do you suffer from a perceived lack of safety that is importantly affecting your quality of life? For most people, the answer is probably yes. But if crime is at issue, you shouldn't be. True, the crime rate in East Harlem is astronomical. But even that skyscraping bar on the chart represents only about 4,000 violent crimes per 100,000 persons per year. There are about 43,000 people in East Harlem and 365 days in a year. Your time of exposure is going to be about four hours. Even without a calculator, you as a rational person can figure out that you have a trivially small chance of being killed, raped, robbed, or assaulted during your afternoon in East Harlem. And you presumably are going to be very alert throughout your visit, thereby narrowing still further the odds that someone will get a crack at you. So what are you really apprehensive about?

What you may realistically be apprehensive about is another set of problems altogether that fall under the rubrics of being hassled and offended. Hassling includes panhandlers asking for change and being abusive if you do not make a contribution; small knots of teenage males hanging out on the streets and making you detour around them; being accosted by men if you are female and/or by hookers if you are male. Being offended might mean walking past a drunk sitting on the curb, stepping through litter, seeing obscene graffiti. These are unpleasant, anxiety-provoking, and potentially dangerous aspects of a visit to an inner city some of which you *are* likely to encounter on your walk, of which you *are* properly apprehensive, and which you *cannot* avoid by preventive action. Neither can they be avoided by the residents. They are part of the daily reality of the street.

These unpleasantnesses do not usually represent crimes, although some of the behaviors are technically illegal. They are not usually physically dangerous in and of themselves. Rather, they represent offenses against standards of public civility commonly shared in other neighborhoods, and they arouse (with reason) the kind of apprehension produced for a subway rider by the masses of scrawled graffiti, an apprehension, as Nathan Glazer has said, based on the "inescapable knowledge that the environment he must endure for an hour or more a day is uncontrolled and uncontrollable, and that anyone can invade it to do whatever damage and mischief the mind suggests."[9]

James Q. Wilson has written the best analysis of why breakdowns in civility and good order are important, evoking broken windows as the emblem.[10] He points out that if a window in a building is broken and is left unrepaired, the unvarying result, observed by sociologists and police officers alike, is that all the rest of the windows will soon be broken. "One unrepaired broken window is a signal that no one cares, and so breaking more windows costs nothing."[11] He suggests that unrepaired behavior, as it were, leads to the same kind of sequence; that a "stable neighborhood of families who care for their homes, mind each other's children, and confidently frown on unwanted intruders can change in a few years, or even a few months, to an inhospitable and frightening jungle." He traces the events—the minor changes whereby enforcement of the minimum standards of civility and order deteriorates: "A piece of property is abandoned, weeds grow up, a window is smashed. Adults stop scolding rowdy children; the children, emboldened, become more rowdy. Families move out." Wilson's description of what happens next deserves quotation at length:

At this point it is not inevitable that serious crime will flourish or violent attacks on strangers will occur. But many residents will think that crime, especially violent crime, is on the rise, and they will modify their behavior accordingly. They will use the streets less often, and when on the streets will stay apart from their fellows, moving with averted eyes, silent lips, and hurried steps. "Don't get involved." For some residents, this growing atomization will matter little, because the neighborhood is not their "home" but "the place where they live." Their interests are elsewhere; they are cosmopolitans. But it will matter greatly to other people, whose lives derive meaning and satisfaction from local attachments rather than from worldly affairs; for them, the neighborhood will cease to exist except for a few reliable friends whom they arrange to meet. Such an area is vulnerable to criminal invasion. . . . [I]t is more likely that here, rather than in places where people are confident they can regulate public behavior by informal controls, drugs will change hands, prostitutes will solicit, and cars will be stripped. Drunks will be robbed by boys who do it as a lark, and the prostitutes' customers will be robbed by men who do it purposefully and perhaps violently. Muggings will occur.[12]

Wilson's treatment is not theoretical, but a summary of what has happened recently in urban America, and he does not exaggerate the speed of the sequence. The burned-out South Bronx seems to have been a symbol of urban hopelessness for so long that it is startling to hear a teacher in a South Bronx elementary school reminisce that during the mid-1960s, the competition for places in the middle-class apartment building across the street from the school was so intense that you had to pay an under-the-table fee to get one. By the beginning of the seventies, the building was derelict.

In proposing that the threshold state for safety consists of enforcing community standards of civility, I hasten to add that such standards will vary across communities. In a neighborhood in Newark, New Jersey, George Kelling, a colleague of Wilson's, observed how a cop on the beat enforced that community's rules: "Drunks and addicts could sit on the stoops, but could not lie down. People could drink on side streets, but not at the main intersection. Bottles had to be in paper bags. Talking to, bothering, or begging from people at the bus stop was strictly forbidden."[13] These standards might not be demanding enough for Scarsdale, but they were appropriate to the neighborhood where they were being enforced: "Another neighborhood might have different rules, but these, everybody understood, were the rules for *this* neighborhood. If someone violated them, the regulars not only turned to Kelly [the beat cop] for help but also ridiculed the violator."[14]

Historically, every American community of any size had at least one such neighborhood where people who had the loosest requirements for public civility gravitated—skid row, or a lower-*class* neighborhood (to be distinguished from lower-*income* neighborhoods, which could be among the most prim and proper anywhere). Everywhere else, the minimum standards were broadly accepted and enforcement was wanted. The difference today is that the public behaviors once confined to skid row are permitted in low-income neighborhoods. This does not mean that some communities of Americans no longer object to drunks or drug addicts or mentally disturbed people sprawled out on the streets. (The reason that drunks can be found passed out on the street in East Harlem is not, I submit, because the residents of East Harlem are evenly divided between those who do and those who don't approve of drunks lying on the sidewalk.) Rather, it means that what is considered acceptable enforcement of this community standard has changed.

Without attempting a tight definition: The underlying requirement for civility in the normal range of neighborhoods seems to be that public places, especially the streets and sidewalks, be neutral ground, not used for business, not used for unsavory displays, not used for social turf, not used as a dumping ground for one's private trash, not used for sleeping; and, the overarching rule, that public areas be places where people are required to behave in a civil manner—not necessarily polite or friendly, but, at a minimum, respectful of the other person's right to be left alone. The threshold of safety is met when a failure of public civility is so unusual that it is noteworthy.

REPRISE:
"ENOUGH SAFETY" AS A NATURAL CONDITION
THAT IS OCCASIONALLY UNNATURALLY LACKING

Construing Progress: The Usual Understanding. What I am treating as "safety," an enabling condition for the pursuit of happiness, is usually treated as "the crime problem." The problem is measured by FBI figures on crime rates and by public opinion surveys in which people are asked about their level of fear of crime. The measure of success in government policy has been straightforward: Calculate the crime rate, determine whether it is going up or down, and make policy decisions accordingly. The policy decisions are based on the prevailing wisdom about the causes of crime. If it is thought that crime is the result of poverty and deprivation, as in the 1960s, then programs designed to provide constructive alternatives to crime instead of punishment will be in vogue. If it is decided that crime results when the benefits of crime outweigh the costs, then programs to toughen law enforcement will be in vogue, as in the 1980s.

Recasting the Relationship of Crime and Safety. I have argued that "enough safety" to pursue happiness cannot be defined relative to a specific level of threat. Indeed, there is an intriguing analogy between the unending search for more safety from risk by contemporary policy advocates (some elements of the environmental and consumer rights movement, for example) and the unending search for more material resources. Both searches are ultimately unsatisfying bases for assessing progress in public policy for much the same reasons: No amount of progress is ever good enough, even though common sense and experience tell us that at some point we must pass (or have already passed) the optimum and are doing more harm than good. When one further considers that, as a practical matter, the great majority of readers of this discussion enjoy lives of extraordinary safety anyway, far safer than those of even their parents and orders of magnitude safer than those of their grandparents, just as they enjoy lives of extraordinary affluence, it becomes apparent that the "crime problem" as it is ordinarily conceived is one that seriously impedes the lives of only a small proportion of the population.

If then our topic is the measurement of success and progress in public policy, why bother with this lengthy discussion of safety? Again, there is an analogy with solutions to poverty ("Just give everyone a decent income and be done with it"). In the case of crime, why not simply say, "Extend to those in the 25th Precinct the same level of safety that the rest of us enjoy," and be done with it?

But we cannot do that. The relationship of safety to the pursuit of happiness is not simply a matter of being sufficiently protected against threats (who would choose to live in a sterile bubble?). If we make the people of the 25th Precinct safe by converting their neighborhood to a tightly surveilled armed camp, we have only exchanged one form of threat for another. It may be that the situation is so bad there that the residents would prefer the police-dominated armed camp over an outlaw-dominated armed camp, but we would still be very far from the best of all possible worlds. The discussion of safety as an enabling condition for the pursuit of happiness has attempted first and most importantly to distinguish between *being faced with threats* and *having a satisfying framework for coping with threats*. What has really happened to the people of the 25th Precinct (I have been arguing) is not that insufficient police are assigned to their district, but that the people of the 25th Precinct do not have a satisfying framework for coping with threats.

Using the specific case of crime, I have argued that the framework consists of two aspects. First, for coping with actual physical threats from crime, *the system must above all else satisfy the citizen's need for lawfulness*. The essence of lawfulness is captured by this formulation:

In a lawful community, someone who does something that is both illegal and harmful is sought by the police. If he is caught, he is prosecuted. If he is convicted, he suffers a penalty.

Nothing in the formulation needs imply Draconian punishments, truncated rights, vigilantism, or massive police forces. All it says is that the primal function of the criminal justice system is to hold accountable those who commit crimes. Performing that function comes first. If a residual "crime problem" sufficiently severe to warrant further measures continues to trouble the system, then other things may be added to the criminal justice system *but not substituted for it*.

The reason I include the phrase "both illegal and harmful" in the basic formulation of "lawfulness" is that all illegal things are not equally disquieting to safety. The more directly harmful the act to the immediate well-being of people in the neighborhood the more important (for a sense of lawfulness and of safety) that the criminal be apprehended and stopped. This practical distinction among illegal acts is a reasonable ordering of priorities. It tends to be observed wherever the people who are at risk also control the law enforcement resources.

A major threat to lawfulness is complexity. In the criminal law as in civil law, tax law, and tort law, I have argued that *law sufficiently complex is indistinguishable from no law at all*, from the point of view of the ordinary citizen. Lawlessness exists when the citizen must rely on go-betweens, be they corrupt officials or be they lawyers, to work a system whose workings the citizen cannot comprehend. The point is not that everyone should therefore have a good lawyer, but that an essential element of lawfulness is law which is simple, objective, and consistently applied.

The second half of the framework for coping with threats consists of *the power to enforce community standards of public civility*. Partly, this power directly affects quality of life—when a person cannot walk to the bus stop through a neighborhood park without being verbally assaulted by the gang of teenagers that uses the park as a hangout, that person's daily life is importantly changed for the worse. But apart from that, public civility is intertwined with safety. The reason for keeping drunks from sleeping in the street or for rousting the gang of abusive teenagers is not just to placate people who are offended by such sights, but to preserve a fabric of public order that, once it frays in small ways, begins to rip in large ones.

These two aspects of the threshold condition of safety raise difficult problems of implementation and potential abuse of police power. However, there is merit in separating issues. The assertion here is that, to provide people with the good called safety, the minimal but indispensable requirements are that it consistently and predictably hold criminals accountable for their crimes and that a community be able to enforce its standards of public civility. To say that these functions can be distorted or carried too far is not the same as saying that they are not minimal and indispensable.

Finally, the discussion of safety has raised for the first time a question that will recur frequently in part 3 when we consider the design of policies. I have used the 25th Precinct in East Harlem as an example of one of the comparatively rare places in the United States where physical safety really is a major, life-affecting problem. And yet it is also obviously aberrational. Very few people who live in the 25th Precinct *want* to live in fear of assault and robbery, *want* to submit to the public incivility that surrounds them. If it is aberrational for communities to permit the predators to dominate, the question for designing a safer 25th Precinct is not "How may we engineer better ways of preventing crimes and catching criminals?" but rather "What are we doing to cause this aberration?"

6

Dignity, Self-Esteem, and Self-Respect

WE TURN NOW to a concept that has shaped much of contemporary thinking about social policy but that remains oddly obscure and unexplicated. In editorials and speeches, the concept commonly goes under the label of dignity. Thus it is said that some policies "give dignity" to people, while others "let people keep their dignity" and still others "deny dignity" to people.

Welfare is often at issue. Should people be required to submit to detailed eligibility investigations? No, it is argued, because such investigations are demeaning: They strip the recipients of dignity. Food stamps are argued to be a better way of providing help than doling out food at soup kitchens, because the stamps let people retain more of their dignity. To live in impoverished circumstances is in itself said to be destructive of one's dignity.

It is not just matters of welfare that have been shaped by considerations of dignity. Drug rehabilitation programs, job training programs, services for unwed mothers, prison reform, educational reform—virtually all services designated for poor people—have been designed and evaluated, examined and criticized, according to the effects they are purported to have on the participants' dignity. Employment policy has been decisively affected by attitudes toward dignity. On the one hand, having a job is often argued to be essential to dignity; on the other, being asked to take a menial job (a "dead-end" job in the current phrase) is often argued to be destructive of dignity.

"Dignity" used in this context is a generic label. One might substitute "self-esteem" or "self-respect" in any of the examples I gave and it would carry the same message. And whatever one thinks of the argument regarding any particular policy, the underlying concept is unquestionably important. Indeed, that is why Maslow made self-esteem one of his five essential needs and why it is being included in this short list of enabling conditions for the pursuit of happiness. From the perspective of a different theoretical system, Gordon Allport has written, "If we are to hold to the theory of multiple drives at all, we must at least admit that the ego drive (or pride or desire for approval—call it what you will) takes precedence over all other drives."[1] The classic defense mechanisms of psychoanalytic theory—rationalization, projection, displacement, reaction formation, and repression—"have as their most important single objective the protection of self-esteem."[2] Theorists of all kinds have recognized that the need for self-approval lies at the heart of human behavior.

Thus it is not surprising to find a large empirical literature demonstrating that people who feel low self-esteem suffer thereby. Low self-esteem is one of the distinguishing features of clinical depression.[3] Low self-esteem has been found to be associated with impulse aggression, negative affect states, and somatic symptoms;[4] with submissiveness, autonomic anxiety, and general maladjustment.[5] People with low self-esteem tend to be unimaginative,[6] dependent upon others,[7] less creative and flexible,[8] more authoritarian,[9] and disposed to deviance and criminality.[10] High self-esteem, on the other hand, is associated with "positive mental health,"[11] expressed satisfaction with life,[12] and avowed happiness.[13] But in a sense these data are superfluous. Morris Rosenberg, one of the most prominent contemporary analysts of self-esteem, put it this way:

Few activities engage our lives so profoundly as the defense and enhancement of the self. The self-esteem motive intrudes on many of our daily activities, influencing what we say, how we act, what we attend to, how we direct our efforts, how we respond to stimuli. The individual is constantly on the alert, dodging, protecting, feinting, distorting, denying, forestalling, and coping with potential threats to his self-esteem.[14]

The thing that psychologists call self-esteem is not something that we need to be told is important. All of us prove it to ourselves every day.

But there is more to the pursuit of self-esteem than scratching a psychological itch. There is at issue some construct closely related to "self-esteem" but encompassing more. For the process whereby one feels this whatever-it-is is in part a process of self-evaluation. To think oneself *deserving* of self-approbation is as important as self-approbation itself. And as the word "deserving" implies, this other construct has a rational, objective aspect that cannot be faked.* But what is it that we are talking about? What is the other thing usually denoted by these words "dignity," "self-esteem," "self-respect"? The following discussion falls into two parts. The initial sections try to

---

* It is this substantive, unfakeable aspect that Arthur O. Lovejoy had in mind when he wrote that "some modest measure" of self-esteem is "indispensable to endurable existence for creatures constituted as we are."[15] John Rawls, probably the most influential philosopher of social democracy, had a similarly rational, substantive component of whatever-it-is in mind when he asserted in *A Theory of Justice* that self-respect (or self-esteem—Rawls did not distinguish between the two) is "perhaps the most important primary good," ranked even above the other goods of liberty and opportunity, income and wealth.[16] Rawls writes further: "We may define self-respect (or self-esteem) as having two aspects. First of all, . . . it includes a person's sense of his own value, his secure conviction that his conception of his good, his plan of life, is worth carrying out. And second, self-respect implies a confidence in one's ability, so far as it is within one's power, to fulfill one's intentions." Rawls sees the first aspect of self-respect as being contingent on two conditions: "(1) having a rational plan of life, and in particular one that satisfies the Aristotelian Principle [see chap. 7 of this book]; and (2) finding our person and deeds appreciated and confirmed by others who are likewise esteemed and their association enjoyed."[17]

tease out the crucial features of the underlying concept, using self-esteem and self-respect as separable aspects of it. The latter sections shift to empirical findings and their implications for good policy.

SOME PROBLEMS WITH SELF-ESTEEM AS A BASIS FOR ASSESSING POLICIES AND SOME MERITS OF SELF-RESPECT

In trying to determine what the threshold condition is for this construct that goes beyond self-esteem alone, we are faced with a problem different from those posed by material resources and safety. In the case of material resources, the concept of "enough" has an objective physiological meaning (subsistence-level food, shelter, and clothing). The problem is to determine how much more than subsistence (if anything) is required to reach a threshold condition for the pursuit of happiness. In the case of safety, the nature of the condition of safety can be stated, but the definition of "enough" is elusive—there is no easy analogue to subsistence. In the case of this new requisite for the pursuit of happiness, we begin without even a commonly accepted referent condition, let alone a sense of what "enough" means.

THE DEFINITION OF SELF-ESTEEM

Quantitative students of self-esteem have taken a hands-off stance, morally speaking, in much the same way that they have taken a hands-off stance toward the definition of happiness. "Self-esteem" has been defined in a way that strips it of normative implications.

William James was among the first to state a value-neutral definition of self-esteem, as the "ratio of our actualities to our supposed potentialities," represented in his equation[18]

$$\text{Self-esteem} = \frac{\text{Successes}}{\text{Pretensions}}$$

Subsequent versions have stripped even this much specificity from the meaning of self-esteem. Morris Rosenberg defines self-esteem as "the evaluation which the individual makes and customarily maintains with regard to himself; it expresses an attitude of approval or disapproval."[19] Stanley Coopersmith, another leading investigator of self-esteem, defines self-esteem as a "personal judgment of worthiness that is expressed in the attitude the individual holds toward himself."[20]

In other words, the question asked in the research has been whether people *say* they have high self-esteem (just as they are asked whether they are happy in the avowed-happiness research); the researchers work back from that to the conditions that produce or fail to produce the end result of avowed self-esteem.[21] As social science, this approach has much to commend it; for purposes of policy analysis, it tends to leave us adrift.

THE AMBIGUOUS VIRTUE OF SELF-ESTEEM

The problem with a value-neutral definition of self-esteem is that people can have high self-esteem when they shouldn't. In 1985, for example, a star basketball player in a Chicago high school was walking along the street with his girlfriend and brushed against a youth standing in his path, whereupon the basketball star was shot to death for reasons essentially the same as those that led Porthos to challenge d'Artagnan to a duel in the opening pages of *The Three Musketeers*. The brushed-against youth's sense of dignity had been offended. Where would the young man who did the shooting show up on a sociological measure of self-esteem? Judging from subsequent newspaper accounts, very high. Consider, for example, one of the most commonly used scales for measuring self-esteem. It consists of ten items with which the respondent is asked to strongly agree, agree, disagree, or strongly disagree.[22] The ten items are:

> On the whole, I am satisfied with myself.
> At times I think I am no good at all.
> I feel that I have a number of good qualities.
> I am able to do things as well as most other people.
> I feel I do not have much to be proud of.
> I certainly feel useless at times.
> I feel that I'm a person of worth, at least on an equal plane
>   with others.

I wish I could have more respect for myself.
All in all, I am inclined to think I am a failure.
I take a positive attitude toward myself.

Judging from news accounts, the offended young man probably would have answered most of those questions with the
"high self-esteem" answer. He was a leader. A success in his
neighborhood. True, he was leader of a gang of violent young
hoodlums. But, quite likely, he had very high, if perhaps fragile,
self-esteem.

For the social scientist, this state of affairs may pose no problems. For the policy analyst, however, it should. If we consider
that self-esteem is an enabling condition for the pursuit of happiness, and if by "self-esteem" we mean the sociologist's definition, then we are led to conclude that the young man is doing
fine on this particular enabling condition. *But he isn't*—that
much seems intuitively apparent. The sociologist's definition of
self-esteem is inadequate for describing whatever it is that we
want people to acquire so that they may pursue satisfying lives.
A correct definition should at least give us more leverage in
specifying what is wrong with the young man's status with regard to this elusive quality.

Or I may put it another way. As long as we restrict ourselves
to the sociologists' concept of self-esteem, we are condemning
ourselves to one of two barren courses. Either we are to perpetuate the excesses of earlier years in which everything was
considered to be ethically indiscriminable and the young hood-
lum's self-esteem was to be considered as "valid" as anyone
else's. Or else we must continue to exclude the effects on self-
esteem from our assessments of policy. Neither course is satisfactory, and I therefore want to pursue the notion that a threshold condition of a related but larger quality exists. By the same
token, however, I do not want to rush too quickly into a highly
limited definition of this quality. A good place to begin is by
drawing a distinction between "self-esteem" and "self-respect,"
and seeing where this leads us.

THE DIFFERENCE BETWEEN
SELF-ESTEEM AND SELF-RESPECT

Philosopher David Sachs offers a quick and easy way to confirm that "self-esteem" and "self-respect" are fundamentally

different notions, by asking yourself whether it is possible to have too much of either. "Often it is thought of individuals that they have too much self-esteem," he writes, "and there is no difficulty in understanding the thought. But it is not often thought—indeed it seems a hard saying—that a person has too much self-respect."[23] We know what a person with too much self-esteem is like—puffed up, narcissistic, vainglorious. But what might a person with "too much self-respect" be like? He might be too stuffy, maybe lack a sense of humor, maybe be too unbending—but would he really have *too much* self-respect? Would we want him to correct his defects by diminishing his degree of self-respect, or by coming to understand that self-respect does not require, for example, stuffiness? The latter, surely. As Sachs goes on to point out, such uses of the notion of "too much self-respect" are sarcasms.

One implication of this line of thought is that self-respect is always a good while self-esteem is not. But what is the nature of this good? How are we to distinguish the substance of self-respect from the substance of self-esteem? For that, let us turn to another contemporary social philosopher, Michael Walzer.

Walzer distinguishes between self-esteem and self-respect by employing the concept of "measuring up":

> In order to enjoy self-esteem, we probably have to convince ourselves . . . that we deserve it, and we can't do that without a little help from our friends. But we are judges in our own case; we pack the jury as best we can, and we fake the verdict whenever we can. About this sort of thing, no one feels guilty; such trials are all-too-human. But self-respect brings us closer to the real thing. . . . Now conscience is the court, and conscience is a shared knowledge, an internalized acceptance of communal standards. The standards are not all that high; we are required to be brethren and citizens, not saints and heroes. But we can't ignore the standards, and we can't juggle the verdict. We do measure up, or we don't. Measuring up is not a matter of success in this or that enterprise, certainly not of relative success or the reputation of success. It is rather a way of being in the community, holding one's head high.[24]

It is a convincing description. For our purposes, Walzer's formulation has the special merit of excluding the mindless code duello visions of self-respect without drawing the net very tightly around any particular alternative set of standards. Walzer then goes on to specify that the key feature of self-respect is acceptance of responsibility for the acts that constitute measuring up or not measuring up. "What is dishonorable, above all," he writes, "is the claim of irresponsibility, the denial of self-possession." Sometimes the self-respecting citizen will fail to fulfill the obligations of citizenship, but he "acknowledges his failures, knows himself capable of fulfilling his obligations, and *remains committed to do so*."[25] (Emphasis added.)

I add the italics to that last phrase to emphasize a direct implication that Walzer does not stress but I will: Self-respect must ultimately be grounded in behavior. A person may fail to measure up now and again, but if he truly "remains committed to do so," that commitment will be observable in behavior—if not in success, then in the act of trying.* To stop trying is to lose self-respect. With that lone caveat, I will proceed using Walzer's pair of assumptions that (1) self-respect is a psychological imperative and (2) it has to be grounded in a real (internalized) acceptance of responsibility for measuring up to the basic standards of being a member of a community.

Social Policy and Self-Respect

Boiled down to the essentials, there are two ways to look at the role of the government vis à vis self-respect. One is that self-respect is something like religious conviction. Personal definitions of self-respect can vary widely and, as long as the internalized standards do not demand such things as shooting

---

* The necessity of stating this caveat is more apparent with regard to Rawls than to Walzer. Walzer implies without being explicit that the ultimate test of measuring up lies in behavior. Rawls seems to permit self-respect independent of behavior. It is easy to imagine a person who meets Rawls's conditions for self-respect (having a rational plan of life and confidence in his *ability* to carry it out) who nonetheless fails to carry out that plan for reasons that are his own fault. Does he possess self-respect? If he does (I would argue) it is because he is engaged in some other activity that enables him to see himself as measuring up.

people who brush against you, the government has no right to say that one person's internalized standards are better than anyone else's. All that government can do is avoid degrading people. The alternative approach to social policy is to say that, while internalized standards may vary, there is an underlying set of standards that are inescapable—not because the government says so, but because they are inherent in the nature of being a member of a human community. Public policy should validate the underlying standards.

In recent practice, these two views have had topsy-turvy applications to public policy. The first view sounds noninterventionist and libertarian, but in fact was the justification for many of the liberal reforms in welfare, education, and law enforcement during the 1960s and early 1970s. The second view sounds authoritarian or perhaps theocratic, but in fact tends to lead toward policies that let events take their natural course, which generally means keeping government out of the picture.

THE PUZZLE

This contradictory state of affairs arises from the nature of self-respect. It *has* to be internalized (which means it has to be genuine), and it *has* to be earned—the individual has to do the "measuring up," no one else can do it for him. To accept this and also to assign a high priority to self-respect (which seems equally necessary) creates a disquieting moral puzzle that, generally speaking, policy analysts have dealt with by pretending it doesn't exist.

The nature of the puzzle is illustrated by the recent work of some British sociologists who set out to examine whether being unemployed caused "psychological distress" in young people. They began by placing their work in the context of previous research, noting that unemployment had already been proven to cause psychological distress in many people. They cited the work of Norman Bradburn, who was among the first to establish an empirical relationship between work and happiness, and the work of Angus Campbell and his colleagues, who demonstrated that "life satisfaction" is also related to work.[26] They cited the literature showing that unemployment is related as well to depression, negative self-esteem, and anxiety.[27] So far, no surprises: Most people need no convincing that being unemployed would be very distressing.

But to what extent, the authors asked, did this distress apply to everyone? Might it not be that the only people who felt much distress were those who had "high commitment to the labor market" (meaning that they *wanted* to work)? The answer turned out to be yes. They examined some new data and found that young Britons who had "low commitment to the labor market" (who didn't particularly want to work) didn't mind being unemployed. They felt fine, thank you.[28]

Whence the moral puzzle. In such a situation, what are the implications for good policy? What, if anything, should be done for these young Britons who feel no distress at being unemployed? They are not "measuring up" in the sense of providing their own keep. It seems they must have little self-respect. On the other hand, if they don't seem to know this, what's the problem?

TRYING TO IGNORE THE PUZZLE

Policy analysts in general have sidestepped the puzzle through a line of argument that goes something like this:

For a variety of practical economic reasons, it is a good thing if people have a commitment to the labor market. Therefore we may want to try to encourage the unemployed-but-untroubled young Britons to acquire more commitment to the labor market—perhaps through training and job programs that ease them into the labor market. But this is a practical matter involving macroeconomic objectives, not part of a crusade to make them want to work "for their own good." If they prove to be unresponsive to efforts to get them into the labor market, that does not mean that we should then tell them that they are inferior to people who have jobs.

To assert that having self-respect (measuring up) *must* mean being productive is dogmatic, the argument continues. Many people live happy lives without being productive. Some people live off their parents' money. Others pull strings to get a city hall sinecure where all they have to do is collect their paycheck. Others find a niche in the economy that provides them with a handsome income in return for very little effort.

These people are not really "productive members of the community" in any meaningful sense of the term, but don't they feel self-respect? Why make people who are unemployed measure up to a standard that so many other people evade?

The argument may be embellished by the observation that we do not in practice reserve our affection for only the sternly self-sufficient. Literature is full of lovable ne'er-do-wells (does Bertie Wooster feel self-respect?). In real life, many of us count scamps as friends, often some of our most entertaining ones. The kaleidoscopic variety of people in the world and their variegated sources of self-pride is what makes life interesting. How dull if everyone were a Puritan, even though doubtless everyone would feel self-respect.

And isn't the dogmatic response atavistic? In a subsistence economy, people who fail to contribute to the community in basic ways—getting food, raising children, protecting turf—threaten the very survival of the community. The world no longer works like that. It is no longer essential for the survival of the community that everyone pull his own weight. We can afford free riders. Is there any real reason other than memories of bygone scarcities to believe that work is intrinsic to self-respect?

I will not try to spin out all the variants on such arguments; readers will doubtless be able to think of variants and improvements on them for themselves. My proposition is that all are ultimately unpersuasive. The thesis of the following discussion is that *the threshold condition for self-respect is accepting responsibility for one's own life, for which the inescapable behavioral manifestation is earning one's own way in the world.* I am stating this not as an ethical precept but as a fact about human beings that ought to influence policy choices in important ways. No matter how ready some of us may be to absolve others from this responsibility, it is not within our power to do so. It is impossible to run public policy in a way that both frees people from the necessity to earn their own way and is also the best of all possible worlds in terms of enabling people to acquire self-respect. I will try to make this case in two ways, first invoking shared experience and then offering some relevant empirical evidence.

FREE LUNCHES DON'T NOURISH

"Earning one's own way" may seem equivalent to "having a job," and in that sense is too narrow a construction. "Earning one's life" is perhaps more accurate. People don't necessarily have to get a paycheck for it. There are many ways to earn one's life without drawing a salary as conscientious mothers, studious students, and unpaid contributors to society of all kinds prove every day. But one way or another, we cannot be drawing more out of the world than we are putting back and still retain our self-respect.

We may return to the examples I just cited as exceptions to the rule and reexamine them. For example, what about the person who lives off an inheritance? There is no need for a double standard. A young person who does not feel a strong commitment to be a productive adult is in trouble, and this applies as much to rich people as poor people. (Some possible personal experiences to consider in this regard are young people who have come into independent wealth at an early age.) People with large inheritances and no meaningful vocation search furiously for ways to create a surrogate. Sometimes it takes the form of expensive and often arduous hobbies, sometimes drugs and alcohol. Theirs is not really so different from the behavior of poor young people without work; they just have more exotic pastimes and more expensive anesthetics.

What about people who hold soft jobs, who are employed without being productive? Most readers know such people; they bear contemplating for a moment. Do you really envy them? Would you exchange jobs with them if you could? (The money may be envied, I am suggesting, but not the notion of sitting all day doing no useful work.) One may contemplate the state of mind of people who get kicked upstairs, keeping all their perks, perhaps even getting new ones, but deprived of real job functions. I know of no studies, but judging from accounts in *Fortune* and the *Wall Street Journal*, many resign; many are miserable. Few seem to think that they've finally got it made, with lots of money and status but no work.

I pose this challenge: Try to think of anyone who does *not* have an authentic basis for self-respect as I am using the word and who seems to be happy. My proposition, which I am asking you to test in your own experience, is that self-respect is intimately, inextricably bound up with earning one's own way—measuring up. The unemployed Britons who show no distress at being idle are kidding themselves. Free lunches don't nourish. But rather than try to clarify these points with further hypotheticals and anecdotal data, let me turn to a body of empirical work bearing on such issues.

AN OPERATIONAL MEASURE OF SELF-RESPECT

In the extensive technical literature on self-esteem, one finds very little that talks of "self-respect." It is not thought to be a useful concept for research. But psychologists have over the last thirty years been engaged in several pertinent lines of research. Some of the findings from this work are more salient yet to the discussion of "enjoyment" in the next chapter. But one strand of the work has developed—de facto, not intentionally—a measure of the core concept underlying self-respect, the belief in one's personal responsibility, and has described its role in human functioning. The measure is known as "locus of control."

THE MEASURE

Locus of control, also known as "internal-external control" or simply "I-E," was first developed as a personality measure by psychologists working at Ohio State in the 1950s. I-E did not come into wide currency until 1966 when psychologist J. B. Rotter published an article entitled "Generalized Expectancies for Internal Versus External Control of Reinforcement" which included a twenty-three-item, easily administered test.[29] From nowhere, I-E quickly became an important research interest among psychologists. By 1975, the author of that year's chapter on personality in the *Annual Review of Psychology* could write that locus of control was "Undoubtedly . . . the single most popular topic in current personality research."[30] Through the mid-1980s, the technical literature has grown at the rate of about a hundred titles per year.

The locus-of-control construct is founded on a simple and plausible proposition: People vary in the degree to which they see themselves as being responsible for what happens to them. This variation is represented by a continuum ranging from highly "internal" (at the extreme, belief that one controls almost everything that happens in one's life) to highly "external" (at the extreme, belief that one's life is controlled entirely by luck or outside forces). Very few people are exclusively internal or external. The place where any particular person sits on the continuum between the extremes is determined by asking how much the subject agrees or disagrees with a list of statements such as

Whether or not I get into a car accident depends mostly on how good a driver I am,

or

Whether or not I get to be a leader depends on whether I'm lucky enough to be in the right place at the right time.[31]

To put it in terms of self-respect, an internal has a highly developed sense of personal responsibility for what he does and the consequences of those acts. The external, applying Walzer's language, denies self-possession.

A PAUSE FOR PREDICTIONS

I have superimposed a new meaning on locus of control. Explicitly: To be an internal is to assume self-possession, the key psychological attribute of self-respect. To say this, however, is to anticipate the findings of the research. Perhaps it is useful to pause for a moment and ask: If the I-E scale were being presented to you for the first time, before any research had been done, what would your expectations be?

Absent any theoretical preconceptions, it is not at all clear that externals should be less happy (or productive or cheerful or whatever) than internals. The situation is very different from the one we encountered in the measurement of self-esteem. In that case, it is obvious that people who respond to items such as

I feel I do not have much to be proud of

with "Strongly agree" have real problems. But when the question is

> Although I might have good ability, I will not be given leadership responsibility without appealing to those in positions of power,

to respond with the answer "Strongly agree" is not necessarily a sign of dysfunction. It can be an accurate statement about the reality that confronts a person.

Furthermore, there are a priori reasons to expect that externals are more at ease with the world—better-adjusted if you will—than internals. Where did the phrase "happy-go-lucky" come from, after all? The popular image of people who "take it easy" and who "take life as it comes" is an image of well-adjusted, happy people, *"Que sera, sera"* is usually not taken to be a negative way of looking at life. Nor has a need for personal control gotten a good press in recent decades—descriptors such as "compulsive" and "anal retentive" have been commonly associated with characteristics that often go along with a highly internal I-E score, and they have not commonly been thought of as desirable personality traits.

I mention these points in preface to the results that follow for two reasons. One is to emphasize that the findings are not ones of which we can say, "Of course, everyone knew that." Everyone didn't know that. The other reason is that there has to be a coherent explanation of the results. The intrinsic importance of self-respect—not just "self-esteem" but self-respect, grounded in the acceptance of personal responsibility for one's life—is a persuasive one.

THE FINDINGS

So one-sided have the findings about I-E been that one researcher felt compelled to voice dismay at the way in which her colleagues had been presenting the internals as the "good guys."[32] But there's no way around it. Again and again, the literature documents the ways in which internals do better, in all sorts of important ways.

We may begin with avowed happiness. Two researchers conducted a large-scale study of white males assessing their avowed happiness using Cantril's self-anchoring scale and including among their independent variables a measure of locus of control.[33] Many of the factors usually thought to be related to happiness—age, sex, social contacts, career, marital status, intelligence—had little or no relationship to happiness. Instead three other variables were especially important: self-reported health, "organizational activity" (in effect, links to a social network), and belief in internal control. As it happened, belief in internal control was also closely related to the degree of orgaizational activity. Another study of 437 males in Army basic training found that internals tended to claim greater life contentment while externals self-reported higher levels of depression and anxiety.[34] Experiments with samples of the elderly have shown similar results, as have surveys of the victims of serious accidents.[35] People who believe and act as if they are in control are happier.

These statistical links between internal beliefs and various types of satisfaction and happiness are not the main point, however. It's not so much that internals *are* happier, but that they have such superior tools for pursuing happiness. They function better in a variety of ways that link up directly with enjoying life and making life enjoyable for others.

Internals are healthier, apparently because they take responsibility for taking care of their health and following up on doctor's orders.[36] Internals are less susceptible to pressure from others, less likely to conform for the sake of being part of the group, and more likely to assess material on its merits, not its reputation.[37]

The literature demonstrates overwhelmingly that, even after controlling for socioeconomic and intelligence factors, internals do much better on a wide range of activities that *do* lead to control over their own lives. Internals acquire and retain information better than externals.[38] They take more time to deliberate when facing tough decisions.[39] They outperform externals in school—again, even after controlling for factors such as intelligence and socioeconomic class.[40]

Internals seem to find it easier than do externals to deal with strangers, and are likely to be more comfortable and less prejudiced with people who are "different" from themselves.[41] In dealing with problems, internals rely less than externals on coercion and threats, preferring persuasion instead.[42] Internals even tend to be more attractive than externals on an interpersonal basis. Researchers who conducted a study of interpersonal attractiveness reported with open surprise that people actually *like* people who are internals more than they like externals. Even the externals find internals more attractive.[43]

Finally, internals tend to be happier in their work, with greater job involvement and more job satisfaction. Give an internal and an external the same job, and the internal will tend to do it better and take more away from it.[44]

OF CHICKENS AND EGGS

Any discussion of the merits of being an internal must lead to a question of causation: Is being an internal the cause of these desirable outcomes? Or does being an effective person cause one to be an internal?

The answer makes a big difference in deciding whether to encourage people to adopt internal beliefs. Suppose, for example, that a person truly is ineffectual at accomplishing outcome X. It would then seem to be both inappropriate and cruel to try to convince that person that he is responsible for outcome X— he will only feel unwarranted guilt when he fails. It is the disentanglement of such issues that makes the I-E literature so provocative and important.

The two main points about these attempts are that (1) not surprisingly, I-E beliefs are in part a result of past experience, but (2) the beliefs themselves become a cause of subsequent experience. In the laboratory, this can be demonstrated by assigning tasks that are known to be within the ability of the subject to achieve. Moreover, a great deal of the research has explicitly controlled for intelligence, socioeconomic status, and other variables that presumably affect real (as opposed to perceived) control over events.* The answer to the initial chicken-and-egg

---

* Blacks constitute a special case that deserves mention. Early in the research on I-E, it was noted that blacks tended to be much more external than whites. This was understandable. A black who grew up in an age of systematic segregation and discrimination would be foolish not to answer many of the items on an I-E test

question is not that reality has no bearing on how people answer I-E items when they are tested, but that *independently* of those differences people with internal beliefs do better. To put it another way: If you take two people, identical in intelligence, socioeconomic status, and whatever else you wish to control for, and then give them both the same task, one that is within their capabilities to achieve, you had better bet on the one who brings to that task the belief that he, not luck, is responsible for his life. To believe that one is master of one's own fate is to some degree a self-fulfilling prophecy.

Reprise: Self-Respect as the Indispensable Good That Cannot Be Given

The discussion began on common ground. Some elusive quality that in the policy rhetoric is usually called "dignity" is a fundamental good that people must have if they are to lead satisfying lives. Everyone from editorial writers to psychologists to social philosophers, from political left to political right, seems to agree. But precisely what is this seldom-defined good? In the course of exploring that question, the divergence between the common understanding and the pursuit-of-happiness perspective became very wide.

Construing Progress: The Usual Understanding. "Dignity" as it figures in discussions of social policy is usually used interchangeably with "feeling good about yourself." It is treated as an antonym, roughly, of "feeling humiliated" or "feeling worthless." The key aspect of contemporary political usage is that

---

with "external" answers, because, realistically, much of a black person's world was controlled from outside. In 1969, a group of researchers dealt with this problem by distinguishing between personal control (one's own competence to determine outcomes) and ideological control (the general role of the social system in determining outcomes).[45] Since then, it has also been demonstrated that middle-class blacks show far less racial discrepancy in I-E scores than do lower-class blacks.[46]

dignity can exist or fail to exist *independently of any quality within the person.* Thus we may imagine two women standing in a line to receive some sort of welfare assistance, one a woman who has lost her job and cannot find another, the other a woman who has lived off welfare for years and never tried to work or to be in any other way a useful member of the community. The welfare worker is rude to both of them. Both women find this experience humiliating. The key assumption of the usual understanding of dignity is that if the welfare worker is respectful to both women—better yet, if the check is mailed to the women, so that they don't have to confront a welfare worker at all—then this constitutes progress in promoting the thing called dignity. *Both women* can thereby find it easier to feel dignity.

Recasting the Role of Self-Respect. In the preceding discussion, I have argued that the concept of self-respect is the core of the human need in question, with self-respect defined as measuring up to internalized standards of what it means to be a full-fledged member of the community—of being able to hold one's head high. Applying the argument to the example of the women in the welfare line, a respectful welfare worker might promote *self-esteem* in both women, but can preserve the *self-respect* only of the woman who has a basis for self-respect. The woman who lost her job has that basis. The long-term welfare recipient whom I have described does not—she *cannot* feel self-respect, no matter what is done on behalf of her dignity. Or more ominously, she cannot feel self-respect unless society has been so arranged that "measuring up" no longer has any meaning to her—in which case, self-respect will itself have become a concept without meaning.

I have used divergent routes to the same destination. One may use the language of social philosophy, and say that self-respect is an essential human need and self-possession is essential to self-respect. Or one may turn to the work of the psychologists and conclude that it is tangibly good that people have a highly internal "locus of control"—that they take a high degree of responsibility for their lives and act on that responsibility. I lump such conclusions into this formulation: It is essential to the pursuit of happiness that one earn one's life. The threshold condition of self-respect is that one feel, not in one's public protestations but in one's heart, that he is a net contributor to the world.

It is the kind of homily to which almost everyone pays lip service. The reason why I have nonetheless approached it as if it were controversial is that, if taken seriously, the implications for what constitutes good social policy are nearly revolutionary. To take just one example: No concept has been more unfashionable in social policy for the last twenty-five years than "stigma," and no criticism has been treated as more damning than to say that such and such a policy "stigmatizes" people. If the discussion above is accepted, under what circumstances might "stigma" be an appropriate feature of social policy? If self-respect is not within the gift of any government or any policy, if the only thing that government can do is provide an environment within which people can earn their self-respect, then the implication of the argument in this chapter is that government's duty is to provide an environment in which people accept responsibility for their actions. An acceptable social policy is one that validates the individual's responsibility for the consequences of his behavior. Or to put it another way, a social policy that induces people to believe that they are not responsible for their lives is one that inhibits the pursuit of happiness and is to that extent immoral. Can then a policy that *fails* to stigmatize be a moral one?

I put the question mark because I think that trying to engineer stigma into a policy is as wrongheaded as thinking it can be engineered out. But we will take up that issue in later chapters. For now, the example serves to illustrate how much appears on the table for reconsideration after you take the initial, gigantic step of accepting that for anyone to have a satisfying life he *must* have self-respect, and that his self-respect *must* be earned.

7

Enjoyment,
Self-Actualization,
and Intrinsic Rewards

WHEN JOHN STUART MILL was a precocious youth of fifteen, he set out to reform the world by propagating Bentham's "greatest happiness principle." He found happiness in devoting himself to making the world happy. Then, at twenty, he asked himself what would happen to his personal happiness if he succeeded in his aims for the rest of the world, and he came to the awful realization that the act of achieving his goal would destroy its pleasure. "At this," he writes in his autobiography, "my heart sank within me: the whole foundation on which my life was constructed fell down. All my happiness was to have been found in the continual pursuit of this end. The end had ceased to charm, and how could there ever again be any interest in the means? I seemed to have nothing left to live for."[1]

In the deep and prolonged personal crisis that followed, Mill pondered the internal contradiction of "pursuing happiness," the intimate antagonism between the seeking and the thing-sought. He summarized his conclusion in this eloquent passage:

> I [had] never, indeed, wavered in the conviction that happiness is the test of all rules of conduct, and the end of life. But I now thought that this end was only to be attained by not making it the direct end. Those only are happy (I thought) who have their minds fixed on some object other

than their own happiness; on the happiness of others, on the improvement of mankind, even on some art or pursuit, followed not as a means, but as itself an ideal end. Aiming thus at something else, they find happiness by the way. The enjoyments of life (such was now my theory) are sufficient to make it a pleasant thing, when they are taken *en passant*, without being made a principal object. Once make them so, and they are immediately felt to be insufficient. They will not bear a scrutinizing examination. Ask yourself whether you are happy, and you cease to be so. The only chance is to treat, not happiness, but some end external to it, as the purpose of life. Let your self-consciousness, your scrutiny, your self-interrogation, exhaust themselves on that; and if otherwise fortunately circumstanced you will inhale happiness with the air you breathe, without dwelling on it or thinking about it, without either forestalling it in imagination, or putting it to flight by fatal questioning. This theory now became the basis of my philosophy of life.[2]

The passage also serves to describe the point that our discussion has reached. If you have acquired enough material resources (enough to know that more are not going to make you happier), live in safety, and are secure in your self-respect, you nonetheless may not be happy. But the task at that point is not to search for happiness, but for "things to do" that provide you with continuing enjoyment (or fulfillment or self-actualization or intrinsic rewards—choose the label you prefer). Every once in a while you may observe your life and realize that, by and large, you are happy, but the best way to preserve that happiness is to become immediately reabsorbed in the things that are providing the enjoyment.

But to do so depends on finding "external ends" on which to focus one's attention and energies. And not just that. Popular and scholarly accounts alike indicate that finding them is becoming more and more problematic. This situation has been best documented with regard to a central aspect of life, work.

Work is at the center of life partly as a practical matter, in that work constitutes the core waking hours of most days of the year. "You can't eat for eight hours a day nor drink for eight hours a day nor make love for eight hours a day—all you can do for eight hours a day is work,"[3] as William Faulkner complained. At a more abstract level, work is at the center of life because it is also at the center of our satisfactions. Carlyle is the most florid defender of the proposition ("Produce! Produce! Were it but the pitifullest infinitesimal fraction of a Product, produce it, in God's name! 'Tis the utmost thou hast in thee: out with it, then. Up! Up!"[4]). But such views are hardly restricted to nineteenth-century Britishers, nor to Weber's "Protestant ethic." The belief that a person's work is his chief source of worldly satisfaction is age-old and broadly held. Karl Marx said it as well as anyone: "Only in being productively active can man make sense of his life." Work, Marx asserts, is the "act of man's self-creation," "not only a means to an end—the product—but an end in itself, the meaningful expression of human energy."[5]

Correspondingly, the relationship of economic and social institutions to work has been at the center of debates over public policy for more than a century. Whether it is as sweeping as "control of the means of production" or as specific as legislation requiring employers to offer maternity leave, much of the social policy debate turns on the relationship of people to work, because the nature of that relationship is so crucial to their happiness.

When we turn to the last of the enabling conditions for the pursuit of happiness, what Maslow called "self-actualization," and think about it in terms of social policy, we must therefore confront primarily the world of work and an abundance of evidence that a great many people are unhappy with that world. Most of the hard evidence is to be found in social science journals under the headings of job dissatisfaction, alienation, and anomie. But a more vivid sense of the problem can be found in everyday life, observing in daily encounters the large number of people who seem to be (and often openly state that they are) unhappy in their work, with devastating consequences for their lives as a whole. The malaise is such that Studs Turkel, who got many ordinary people to talk to him about their work, introduced his book, *Working*, by writing that "This book, being about work, is, by its very nature, about violence—to the spirit as well as to the body. . . . It is above all (or beneath all), about daily humiliations. To survive the day is triumph enough for the walking wounded among the great many of us."[6] It is an astounding opening to a book in which most of the respondents were making good money at jobs where they didn't have to work very hard—certainly not "work very hard" in comparison to the norm throughout human history, and the norm everywhere except the developed West.

Turkel was not talking just about migrant workers and day laborers. He interviewed all sorts—white-collar workers, blue-collar workers, technicians, professionals, the miserably paid and the lavishly paid. Few were self-actualized. Few found enjoyment in their work. Moreover, we know from more systematic surveys that the dissatisfaction he found has been increasing rapidly in the last few decades. As recently as 1955, for example, a survey of workers found that 52 percent enjoyed their work so much that they "had a hard time putting it aside." By 1980, the proportion who so enjoyed their work had dropped to only a third of the respondents (33.5 percent).[7] The drop was about the same for everyone, from professional persons to farmers, but it was the largest of all for manual workers. In 1955, 50 percent of manual workers had enjoyed their work so much that they had a hard time putting it aside; by 1980, that figure had dropped by almost half, to 27 percent.[8]

The explanation for such findings is widely suspected to lie in the very process of modernization. Boredom and the loss of a sense of purpose are often seen as a by-product of "progress" as we have experienced it in the twentieth century. Indeed, the very idea of progress (in its former positive meaning) has fallen by the wayside in the twentieth century in large part because of the observation that people who are living longer and better than their grandparents by any quantitative measure seem nonetheless to be enjoying it less.

We are moving into problems of modernity where public policy is not obviously relevant. The decline in religious faith and of "belief in something greater than the life immediately around us" is, as Robert Nisbet has argued, intimately related to phenomena that Turkel observed as alienation and boredom and to an impoverishment of the "eternal ends" that have given meaning to lives throughout history.[9] The "exhaustion of Modernism" that Daniel Bell has described, and the search for a re-energizing, redemptive understanding of how the world works, is a historical phenomenon on a grand scale for which Congress presumably has no quick fixes.[10] There remains, however, a modest corner of the problem for us to examine.

The three preceding chapters tried to give a new perspective on old measures. Poverty, crime, and dignity have always been considered when social policy is assessed; I have argued that they have been misconceived and that they acquire valuable new dimensions when considered in light of enabling conditions for the pursuit of happiness. When it comes to "enjoyment," "self-actualization," or "intrinsic rewards," the task is somewhat different: not to suggest a different way of looking at them, but to suggest that they *can* be looked at. They are not will-o'-the-wisp concepts about which everyone will have different opinions. We know more about them than most people realize, and what we know can usefully be brought to bear on policy issues. Social policy is involved in the same way it is involved in self-respect. The question raised by the discussion in the last chapter was not "How can social policy give people self-respect?" (it inherently cannot), but "How can social policy encourage an environment in which people acquire self-respect?" Similarly, the question to be raised in this chapter is not how policy can make people enjoy themselves or find life fulfilling, but how it can encourage an environment in which enjoyment and self-fulfillment flourish.

We will in the rest of this chapter be considering this proposition: While it is true that the ways in which people enjoy themselves are infinitely various, the underlying reasons *why* things are enjoyable are limited and definable. The discussion proceeds in three parts. First, I present the basis of enjoyment and self-fulfillment as stated by Aristotle, a conception now in the process of being rediscovered by modern psychology. The second part is an account of the nature of enjoyment as revealed by contemporary research. The third part takes up contemporary findings about the conditions under which enjoyment flourishes.

ENJOYMENT AND THE ARISTOTELIAN PRINCIPLE

As with happiness, Aristotle broke ground we still till. As he discussed happiness and its relationship with intelligence and action, he picked his way around a complex thought that he never quite articulated in one place but which emerges unmistakably from his discussion as a whole.[11] John Rawls assembled these related thoughts into the "Aristotelian Principle," which he stated as follows: "[O]ther things equal, human beings enjoy the exercise of their realized capacities (their innate or trained abilities), and this enjoyment increases the more the capacity is realized, or the greater its complexity." Rawls continues:

> The intuitive idea here is that human beings take more pleasure in doing something as they become more proficient at it, and of two activities they do equally well, they prefer the one calling on a larger repertoire of more intricate and subtle discriminations. For example, chess is a more complicated and subtle game than checkers, and algebra is more intricate than elementary arithmetic. Thus the principle says that someone who can do both generally prefers playing chess to playing checkers, and that he would rather study algebra than arithmetic.[12]

The more we learn about human motivation in the laboratory, the more it seems that Aristotle was saying something true and important about how human beings enjoy themselves.*

The accumulation of evidence has been cautious, working slowly away from a consensus among psychologists early in this century that human behavior could be fully explained without

---

* Lest the Aristotelian Principle be taken out of context, it is important to emphasize that Aristotle saw enjoyment as part of, but by no means the same as, a well-lived life. Alasdair MacIntyre said it concisely: "Just because enjoyment of a highly specific kind . . . supervenes upon each different type of successfully achieved activity, the enjoyment of itself provides us with no good reason for embarking upon one type of activity rather than another."[13] Those crucial decisions rest on man's unique capacity for intelligence informed by virtue.

recourse to anything resembling an innate urge to exercise "realized capacities." For several decades following the advent of psychology as a scientific discipline, human behavior was conceptualized as a straightforward stimulus-response pattern. Pavlov's dog learns that a bell means that food is on the way; once that is learned, the dog responds to the stimulus of a bell by salivating. The *motivation* for behavior (why, after all, does the dog respond to the prospect of food?) was seen as ultimately the product of a small number of physiological drives. Freud originally saw two drives—sex and aggression.[14] The empiricists, led by C. L. Hull, saw four—hunger, thirst, sex, and the avoidance of pain.[15]

These determinants of behavior left very little to the discretion of the human being as a volitional, thoughtful creature. Other psychologists, notably E. L. Thorndike and B. F. Skinner, dispensed with the question of motivation and volition altogether.[16] Like Hull, they saw behavior as a product of past reinforcements, but their orientation, labeled operant psychology, treated motivation as a black box. The experimenter introduced stimuli and measured behavioral responses. The rest of what might be going on (if anything) was of no concern to operant theory and its predictive power.

Operant conditioning obviously worked in certain kinds of circumstances. The underlying drives postulated by the drive theorists seemed to be important for explaining certain kinds of behavior. But as time went on and the experimental record accumulated, researchers found that other behaviors stubbornly resisted being pigeonholed. Behavior in both animals and humans seemed to be more complicated and interesting than the existing theories could accommodate.

The first new probings emerged in tests to validate empirically what is sometimes known as the "Wundt Curve," in honor of the psychologist who first hypothesized it in 1874[17] (see fig. 5).

"Stimulus intensity" can refer to degree (saltiness, for example); also to the newness, surprisingness, or complexity of a stimulus. As the stimulus increases in intensity, it becomes increasingly pleasant until one finds oneself in possession of too much of a good thing, whereupon the stimulus shifts from pleasant to unpleasant.[18]

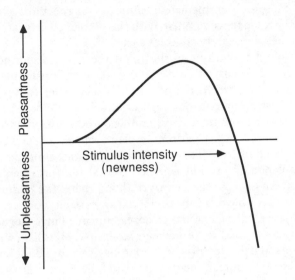

FIGURE 5
THE WUNDT CURVE

When "degree" is at issue, it is not surprising that the reactions of animals of all sorts, including humans, should follow the Wundt curve: Saltiness in food is increasingly pleasant up to a point when the food abruptly becomes "too salty" and then inedible. But the relationships of newness, surprisingness, and complexity to pleasantness were more intriguing. Why, for example, should rats offered equal rewards at the end of a T-shaped or Y-shaped maze tend, in successive runs, to choose the arm they had not chosen in the previous run? The only explanation that fit the data was that the rats sought (in a nonrational sense) to expose themselves to novel stimuli.[19]

Among human subjects, such phenomena have been documented in a variety of experimental situations. Infants given choices among groups of toys consistently tend to choose groups that contain a mixture of unfamiliar and familiar toys, for example, avoiding groups that contain either wholly familiar or wholly unfamiliar toys. Adults asked to judge the pleasantness of shapes that have been gradated by complexity initially regard those of intermediate complexity as the most pleasant; as they become more familiar with the shapes, their preferences shift to the increasingly complex shapes.[20]

Psychologists working in the 1940s and 1950s began producing evidence that this taste for complexity, surprisingness, and newness was related to enjoyment. Among other things, these psychologists began to notice how much of human behavior consisted of exploration, play, and other activities that seemed to be self-sustaining. Children at play were a conspicuous example, but adults too "played." These activities continued even in the absence of any identifiable external reinforcement. People did them because they *enjoyed* doing them, for reasons that had no perceptible relationship to sex, aggression, hunger, thirst, or avoidance of pain. Furthermore, human beings developed. Long after they had acquired their basic survival skills (whether they consisted of learning to hunt or learning double-entry bookkeeping), human beings persisted in maturing, altering themselves in patterned ways that were common across human beings but did not easily fit within drive theory.

By the late 1950s, a psychologist named Robert White was prompted by these anomalies to suggest a new motivational concept. He published an article in *Psychological Review* postulating that human beings took satisfaction from dealing effectively with the environment around them. The reward was a feeling of "effectance," and this reward was sufficient to motivate the behavior—hence his label, "effectance motivation." It was an awkward phrase, and in fact there was a perfectly good everyday word for what he had found. He used it in the title of the article: "Motivation Reconsidered: The Concept of Competence."[21]

By "competence," White was not referring to a specifically human characteristic. In his view, elaborated in a series of articles appearing from 1959 to 1971, effectance motivation characterizes organisms in general. But clearly the notion of "competence" and of satisfactions to be gained from coping with one's environment had immediate implications for studying human behavior. An urge to "competence" had a different weight and feel to it than an urge to satisfy hunger, slake thirst, reproduce, or avoid pain. Amidst the bleak plains of behaviorism, the possibility that man might be human in the Aristotelian sense was putting up shoots.

THE ANATOMY OF ENJOYMENT

In his 1943 article introducing his decidedly non-Freudian theory of human motivation, Abraham Maslow labeled the fifth and last of the needs in his hierarchy "the need for self-actualization." This ultimate need, stated by a twentieth-century psychologist, sounds almost like a paraphrase from book I of Aristotle's *Ethics:*

> Even if all these [lower-level] needs are satisfied, we may still often (if not always) expect that a new discontent and restlessness will soon develop, unless the individual is doing what he is fitted for. A musician must make music, an artist must paint, a poet must write, if he is to be ultimately happy. What a man *can* be, he *must* be. This need we may call self-actualization. . . . It refers to the desire for self-fulfillment, namely, to the tendency for him to become actualized in what he is potentially. This tendency might be phrased as the desire to become more and more what one is, to become everything one is capable of becoming.[22]

The need for self-actualization subsequently led Maslow to formulate the notion of "peak experiences"—self-actualization reified—and to interview people about their peak experiences. He found that they exhibited characteristics that sounded very much as if peak experiences were not just exalting, but intensely *enjoyable.* Indeed, if Maslow's respondents are to be taken at face value, "self-actualization" should be thought of not as some rarefied experience reserved to a few, but as a supreme form of "fun" that everyone ought to be enjoying as often as possible.

A scholar at the University of Chicago, Mihaly Csikszentmihalyi, proposed a frontal attack on the problem. He set out to determine what "enjoyment" means, beginning with the most direct example of enjoyment, man at play. "The simple goal of this study," he wrote, "is to understand enjoyment, here and now—not as compensation for past desires, not as preparation for future needs, but as an ongoing process which provides rewarding experiences in the present."[23] He and his colleagues chose a set of people who "had one thing in common: they consisted of people who devote much energy to some activity which yields minimal rewards of a conventional sort"—30 rock climbers, 22 professional composers of modern music, 53 chess players (30 males of all skill levels and 23 of the nation's top female players), 40 basketball players from high-school teams, and 28 female modern dancers, ranging from beginners to professionals. Csikszentmihalyi and his colleagues called the disparate activities to which these people devoted so much time and energy "autotelic" (from the Greek *auto* = self and *telos* = goal, purpose), and began gathering data about what made them do so. From this exercise came a remarkable description of a process that many had assumed to be indescribable, the process of enjoyment.

"FLOW"

As they analyzed the results, they decided that autotelic was the wrong name. "Autotelic" implied to them that external goals or extrinsic rewards do not exist. Such goals and rewards might in fact exist, the researchers found; they just weren't important. When professional poker players (and many entrepreneurs) claim that "money is just a way of keeping score," they are being literal; the process of winning is the thing, not the winnings themselves. Or as Csikszentmihalyi observed, "We still have to hear of an artist who packed up his brushes after completing a painting, or even paid much attention to a canvas after it was finished. . . ."[24]

Recognizing this, "the autotelic experience" was given a new label, "flow." The authors borrowed it from this description by a young poet comparing the sense of "flowing" that he got from writing poetry with the same sense he got while rock climbing. "The purpose of the flow is to keep on flowing," he said, "not looking for a peak or utopia but staying in the flow. It is not a moving up but a continuous flowing; you move up only to keep the flow going."[25]

The label "flow" has an uncomfortably trendy ring to it, but the phenomenon itself is not mystical nor even rare. Consider the last time that you looked up in surprise after being absorbed in something and said "Where did the time go?" The self-forgetfulness—the complete absorption in the task that John Stuart Mill saw as essential to happiness—is one of several characteristics of what Csikszentmihalyi calls flow.

Another common aspect of flow is that action is joined with awareness.[26] You know exactly what you're doing, but you are not thinking about the fact that you know. Along with this awareness goes a sense of control. The dancer experiencing flow does not worry about tripping; the rock climber does not think about falling. "What is lost in flow," Csikszentmihalyi writes, "[is] the self *construct*, the intermediary which one learns to interpose between stimulus and response."[27] Still another characteristic of flow is that it occurs when attention is centered on a limited stimulus field. A basketball player describes the world as narrowing down to the court; the chess player describes it as narrowing even further, to the squares of the chess board.

One of the most intriguing characteristics of flow is the clarity of "right" and "wrong," "good" and "bad" that seems to be built into the experience. Or as Csikszentmihalyi put it, a flow experience characteristically "contains coherent, noncontradictory demands for action and provides clear, unambiguous feedback to a person's actions."[28] Further, the feedback is built into the process. Thus one young basketball player noted that he could tell how well he was doing when he was playing poorly or playing reasonably well, "but if I'm having a super game I can't tell until after the game."[29] He even loses track of the score. There is a "rightness" to what he is doing that bypasses the ordinary assessment process. An interesting sidelight of this aspect of flow is that *one cannot experience flow while cheating*—not because cheating is morally reprehensible, but because it gets in the way of the essential unambiguity.

The quality of "challenge" that was so essential to flow could occur in almost any kind of activity. Basketball is not cerebral in the same sense that chess is, yet the commonality of the flow experience was evident. The anecdotal evidence available to Csikszentmihalyi for other activities suggested similarly that "people who enjoy bowling or gambling enjoy it for the same reasons that a composer enjoys writing music or a chess player enjoys a tournament."[30]

I have focused on Csikszentmihalyi's findings because they represent the best systematic work that has been done. But a large journalistic literature about people who *do* enjoy their work provides additional evidence. The descriptions of the underlying enjoyment to be had in performing surgery, customizing cars, wrestling with iron beams, or putting out fires are far more similar than the contents of these different jobs would suggest.[31] I will not try to review that evidence here except to illustrate the extremely important point that enjoyment is not restricted to the glamorous or prestigious jobs. One example is especially apt, because the job in question is one that to most people probably seems unusually tedious—the job of a directory assistance telephone operator.

In a recent magazine article about the long-distance telephone system, the writer encountered one such operator and opened the conversation with a question that seems self-evident: "Isn't your job incredibly boring?" But the directory assistance operator said that, no, it needn't be. He quickly acknowledged that it *could* be incredibly boring, if he relied on the computer. But good directory assistance operators don't rely on the computer, he said, and that's what makes the job fun:

> A good directory assistance operator, he continued, works out of personal memory as much as possible, and the job is satisfying to the degree that it can be done out of personal memory. Sometimes when the calls are flowing in, four a minute, and personal memory is knocking them out of the box, one after another, a rhythm emerges and begins to build. The calls lay down the beat, the bass line; the melody floats out of another department in personal memory, picks up the bass and begins to carry it . . . Sometimes he finds himself beating time on the floor, on the sides of his terminal. What makes this possible, he says, is knowing. Not thinking; when a call comes in that takes thought . . . you lose the rhythm. The music stops. What starts it again is knowing. And it is the repetition that makes the knowing possible. And that, he said, leaning back, is why the job isn't boring.[32]

Such testimony suggests that perhaps "flow" is not such a bad word after all for describing the nature of such enjoyment.

The most striking aspect of the directory assistance operator's description is the way in which he *makes* the work more complicated so that he may enjoy it. Many of Studs Turkel's respondents who enjoyed their jobs were doing the same thing, and it made no difference whether the job was one ordinarily thought to be "creative" or one ordinarily thought to be "menial." "I want my hands to be right when I serve," a waitress told Turkel.

> I pick up a glass, I want it to be just right. I get to be almost Oriental in the serving. I like it to look nice all the way. To be a waitress, it's an art. I feel like a ballerina, too. I have to go between those tables, between those chairs . . . Maybe that's the reason I always stayed slim. It is a certain way I can go through a chair no one else can do. I do it with an air. If I drop a fork, there is a certain way I pick it up.[33]

Similarly, people engaged in activities in which they are not expert can find enjoyment in them if the correct balance is found. Thus, for example, the executive who does fix-up chores around the house on the weekend can find himself taking pleasure in patching a leaky roof. The point is not the content of what one is doing as much as it is the content relative to one's own skills. Trying to build a house would be simply dispiriting for the amateur. Patching it, for a person who is pleased if a nail goes in straight, can be absorbing and satisfying.

CHALLENGE AND ENJOYMENT

In *creating* challenges for themselves when the job did not do it for them, the waitress and the directory assistance operator both intuitively recognized the core dynamic of enjoyment that Csikszentmihalyi identified from his analysis of the data. To wit: Enjoyment and challenge are inseparable. Specifically, Csikszentmihalyi identified three elements that seem to play consistent roles in the feeling of enjoyment: a feeling of creative discovery, a challenge overcome, a difficulty resolved.[34] Csikszentmihalyi graphically summarized his conclusions this way:[35]

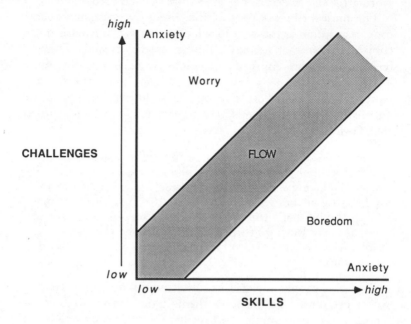

FIGURE 6
THE ARISTOTELIAN PRINCIPLE RECAST

The figure is a graphic representation of the way that enjoyment occurs when challenges are in the correct relationship to skills. When an average chess player is competing with someone at his skill level or slightly higher (that is, someone he can beat only if he tries hard), he can be completely absorbed in the game. As the challenge begins to exceed the skills for coping with it, then worry begins ("I'm in over my head"). When the imbalance is great (the chess player finds himself sitting across from Bobby Fischer), worry about the possibility of failure is transformed into anxiety—about the imminence of failure, the overload on one's capabilities, the prospect of making a fool of himself. If, on the other hand, the skills are greater than the challenge, boredom results. If the skills are *much* greater than the challenge (the same game seen from Bobby Fischer's point of view), then another kind of anxiety occurs, in the form of intense frustration at being prevented from exercising one's skills.

The fit of Csikszentmihalyi's summary with Aristotle's anciently discovered Principle ("Other things equal, human beings enjoy the exercise of their realized capacities . . . and this enjoyment increases the more the capacity is realized, or the greater its complexity") is remarkably close. What brings this from the realm of interesting social science to something that policy analysts ought to ponder is the aspect of challenge. Challenge is a resource for meeting the human need called enjoyment, just as food is a resource for meeting the human need called nourishment. If one measure of a good society is its production and distribution of food, another measure of a good society is its production and distribution of challenges.

But we are not finished with the problem of understanding enjoyment. For while the work of Csikszentmihalyi illuminates the anatomy of enjoyment, it does not address the question of how it is that people become engaged in such activities in the first place. For that, we turn to another body of work.

SELF-ACTUALIZATION AND INTRINSIC REWARDS

Everyone spends most of his life doing things that are not from moment to moment "self-actualizing" and not, from moment to moment, especially "fun." When even the glamorous occupations are examined closely, their glamorous parts are a fraction of the whole. The peak moments of the heart surgeon's professional life, when everything hangs on his knowledge and small motor skills, are few in comparison to the hours he spends doing things as mundane for him as stitching a hem is to a tailor. The moments that an actor spends in front of an audience, that a trial lawyer spends in front of a jury, or that a wide receiver spends catching passes are flashes in their life's work compared to the hours, days, or months spent on preparation for those moments.

Yet some people enjoy themselves at their work nonetheless, not just for a few peak moments but more or less continually.

The trial lawyer may enjoy the lawyer's work-life and the actor the actor's work-life, just as people in less glamorous professions "like what they do"—that is, *take satisfaction* in it as it happens (not just in retrospect), for no reason obvious to the rest of us. They are engaging in a less intense form of flow. Obviously, this gives them an advantage over the rest of the world in the successful pursuit of happiness. The question is therefore especially pertinent: What are the conditions that enable this gratifying state of affairs to exist? What encourages it? What impedes it?

"INTRINSIC" AND "EXTRINSIC" MOTIVATION

During the same years when Csikszentmihalyi was pursuing the nature of enjoyment, other scholars began trying to unravel another aspect of these self-sustaining behaviors. What Csikszentmihalyi treated as "autotelic activities," they treated as the product of "intrinsic motivation," defined as "the innate, natural propensity to engage one's interests and exercise one's capacities, and in so doing, to seek and conquer optimal challenges."[36]

These scholars have not been particularly interested in why things are enjoyable. They are satisfied to take as given that certain activities are self-sustaining, done "for the fun of it," and have tried to determine how this type of intrinsic motivation interacts with "extrinsic" motivation. The first thing they found, to their acknowledged surprise, was something that Mark Twain had pointed out a century earlier.

In *The Adventures of Tom Sawyer* and the famous story of the whitewashed fence, Mark Twain observed that "there are wealthy men in England who drive four-horse passenger-coaches twenty or thirty miles on a daily line, in the summer, because the privilege costs them considerable money; but if they were offered wages for the service, that would turn it into work and then they would resign." Twain was identifying a stubborn and important tension between intrinsic and extrinsic rewards. Paying people changes the terms of an activity. Among other things, it can lead people to treat an activity as something they have to do instead of something they want to do.

That is more or less what the first systematic experiments investigating intrinsic motivation revealed in the late 1960s. Edward Deci, who went on to become the leading scholar in the field, gave block-building puzzles to two sets of college students. One set of subjects was paid for completing the puzzles, the other set was not. When the time was up, the person administering the experiment left the room on a pretext, leaving the students alone. Then the researchers surreptitiously observed the subjects during free time after the experiment. The subjects who had *not* been paid tended to continue working on the puzzles whereas the subjects who had been paid tended to read the magazines that the researchers had left in the room. Like Twain's coach drivers, the puzzle solving had been turned into work for those who had been paid and remained play for those who had not.

As other psychologists tried to replicate his results, the effect Deci had discovered soon proved to be ubiquitous and robust. Calder and Staw asked their subjects to rate how much they enjoyed their task (assembling a jigsaw puzzle), and found that those who had been paid found it less enjoyable than those who had not.[37] Pritchard, Campbell, and Campbell found the same effect among subjects asked to solve chess problems.[38] Other researchers demonstrated the effect for high-school students.[39] Elementary-school students.[40] Preschoolers.[41] The mentally retarded.[42] Yoshimura demonstrated the effect among Japanese and Eden demonstrated it among Israelis.[43] By the end of the 1970s, there was no longer any question whether extrinsic rewards tended to undermine intrinsic motivation.

Why should people like something less *because* they were paid for doing it? As the research accumulated, the psychologists began to converge on an explanation. People tend to categorize the things they do either as ends in themselves or as means to other ends, and the choice has very little to do with the content of the thing-to-be-done. People can be bored doing the most glamorous of jobs; they can take satisfaction from the most menial of jobs.

The act of paying for the performance of the task is important in three respects. First, the payment can tend to establish a criterion of success that interferes with enjoying the thing-for-itself—put roughly, one has to think about two things, what one is doing and the money one is getting for doing it. Or, as Csikszentmihalyi might say, the fact that money is involved distracts from the absorption necessary to achieving flow.

A related but slightly different effect of the act of paying is that the payment signals that the thing-to-be-done is a chore, and something one would not do unless one were paid. If one accepts the notion that things-to-be-done either are or are not enjoyable according to some objective status that cannot be altered by the person doing them, then a chain of reasoning is set up: Since I would not do this unless I were paid, it must be something that is not enjoyable-in-itself. Because it is not enjoyable-in-itself, there is no way that I can make it so. Therefore I cannot be enjoying myself while I do it.

The third and perhaps most important effect of payment on intrinsic rewards is one that relates directly to the Aristotelian Principle: Payment tends to give people an incentive to strip their jobs of the complexity and challenge that create enjoyment in the first place. If I am doing something because I have to in order to obtain some other desired end, then, obviously, I prefer that the job be made as undemanding as possible, and that I finish it as quickly as possible with as little effort as possible. Given such an orientation, the account given by the directory assistance operator is incomprehensible: Why is he making his job so complicated when he could use the computer? The notion of working overtime without pay to finish a job is truly irrational: Finishing the job is not what one is getting paid to do. Thus it is not surprising that three researchers who examined the relationship of task complexity to extrinsic rewards reported just such an effect. People who were paid for doing something made the job as simple as possible.

But they also uncovered a less predictable and more insidious result. Once a person had gotten used to the idea that the job should be done as quickly and with as little effort as possible, that attitude carried over even when the extrinsic reward was removed. For example, children who had learned a game with a reward attached to it subsequently played the game less often, and preferred a simpler version of the game, than the children who learned the same game in a no-reward situation.[44] Or to return to the language of the Aristotelian Principle, the existence of the reward directly obstructed their ability to "enjoy the exercise of their realized capacities." Comparable effects were found by Shapira, who showed that college students given free choice selected challenging puzzles unless there were contingent rewards, in which case they chose easy ones.[45]

Such findings raised a troubling problem. Extrinsic rewards make the world go round. West or East, in capitalist or socialist countries, people are paid for working. If extrinsic rewards always undermine intrinsic motivation, the implication would seem to be that no one can be paid for doing something he enjoys without losing some of that enjoyment. And yet that result does not accord with common sense. Some people who love their work also make lots of money without having their satisfaction impeded. What are the conditions under which extrinsic rewards do *not* reduce intrinsic motivation?

AUTONOMY AND SELF-DETERMINATION

The experiments proliferated, trying different rewards structures—rewards given for participating without regard to performance (equivalent in the real world to most blue-collar industrial jobs), rewards given for the amount of work done (similar to piece-rate systems of pay or commissions for sales), rewards contingent on performance according to some normative standard (equivalent to salaries adjusted according to quality of work), and rewards obtained by direct competition (as in poker). By 1983, these studies had led to a crucial distinction among three types of events that may bring rewards.

The first type is "informational." An informational event provides useful facts for a person to use without imposing guidance about how those facts are to be used. The lack of direction does not mean a lack of structure, however. An "informational environment" is not synonymous with a "permissive environment."

The second type of event is "controlling." Controlling events pressure the person to think, feel, or behave in specified ways.[46] This can occur in a number of ways, from the controlling influences exerted by the status of another party (a parent or boss, for example) to the controlling influences exerted by contingent rewards.

The third type of event is labeled "amotivational," prompted by the studies of what is called "learned helplessness." Learned helplessness has involved some of the more brutal experiments (at least to the layman's eyes) in motivation, wherein subjects are "taught" by experience that their behavior has no influence on events—for example, by giving the subject an electric shock independently of whether the subject performs his assigned task correctly.

To simplify the results, these "events" may be thought of as feedback. Informational feedback gives the subject unadorned, correct information about how the subject is doing; controlling feedback adds pressure to the information (e.g., "Do better next time!"); amotivational feedback keeps the subject from having any reason to think he is "doing" anything in the way of effective action.

The effects of these types of feedback were systematically related to the effects of rewards on behavior. Amotivational events tended to extinguish behavior altogether, as subjects who learned that their behavior didn't matter stopped trying.[47] Controlling events could produce results, but they also undermined intrinsic rewards.[48] Informational events were the best: They tended to permit intrinsic rewards to continue even when extrinsic rewards were present.[49] To date, the only combination of rewards and feedback that seems to improve intrinsic motivation over the baseline condition of no reward at all and no feedback at all is performance-based extrinsic rewards (rewards that depend not only upon doing the task, but upon how well it is done) plus informational feedback.[50]

So we know it is possible to sustain or even to increase intrinsic motivation in the presence of extrinsic rewards. But to do so, it seems essential to work with that exotic notion that Robert White advanced so tentatively in the 1950s: "competence." Intrinsic motivation is intimately bound up with people functioning as autonomous, self-determining, competent human beings. Such is the conclusion, at any rate, of the most recent and comprehensive synthesis of the data by Edward Deci and another leading authority in the area, Richard M. Ryan. In their 1985 book, *Intrinsic Motivation and Self-Determination in Human Behavior*, they drew three propositions from the literature. I summarize them below, taking two kinds of liberties. One is stylistic (see their text in the notes) for purposes of communication.[51] The other is substantive. Deci and Ryan refer to perceived causality, perceived competence, perceived self-determination, and perceived autonomy. I recast their wording to assume real causality, real competence, real self-determination, and real autonomy, for reasons I will expand upon later.

Their first proposition ties personal control to intrinsic motivation: *When people are in control of an activity, they enjoy it more*. When people are passive, not in control, they enjoy it less.[52] In part, Deci and Ryan justify this proposition through the evidence that money payments diminish intrinsic motivation by changing the locus of causality from internal to external ("I am no longer doing this because I want to; I am doing it because someone is enticing me to do it with money").[53] But they are also able to draw on a variety of other evidence that events which undermine self-determination (internal causality) also undermine intrinsic motivation, whether the events be the threat of punishment, the promise of nonmonetary rewards, or constraints such as surveillance and evaluation.[54]

The second proposition borrows from Csikszentmihalyi's (and ultimately Aristotle's) notion of optimal challenges. *People have a deep need for the sense of competence that comes from mastering something that is difficult*. When external events promote this competency, intrinsic motivation is enhanced. When external events prevent such demonstration of competence, intrinsic motivation is diminished.[55]

The evidence for the notion of "optimal challenge" draws from the study by Shapira (see above) and another study by McMullin and Steffen, who found that students who worked on puzzles that got more difficult with each trial displayed greater intrinsic motivation than students who worked on puzzles at a constant difficulty level,[56] plus additional studies dealing with small children.*[57] The experimental evidence on behalf of the proposition is based on a number of studies in which subjects received both positive and negative feedback

---

* Specialists in child development will recognize in "optimal challenges" similarities to Piaget's teachings on moderately assimilable stimuli and Montessori's on the need to organize stimulation relative to the child's internal organization.

(which were assumed to bolster and undermine perceived competence respectively). As might be expected, intrinsic motivation followed suit. In studies with positive feedback, the undermining effects of the tangible rewards on intrinsic motivation seemed to be counterbalanced by the positive effects of the enhanced perceived competence.[58] In studies with negative feedback which did *not* help the subject attain competence (note the important caveat), intrinsic motivation decreased. Detailed analyses of the data indicate that the mediating factor was a drop in perceived competence.[59]

The third proposition summarizes the findings regarding the effects of "informational," "controlling," and "amotivational" events on intrinsic rewards. Informational events are good, heightening perceived competence. Controlling events are bad, because either way of controlling—giving people orders or taking them under one's wing—causes people to feel less in control and undermines their enjoyment. Amotivational events are bad—telling people that the situation is beyond their control makes them feel helpless and discourages any sort of behavior.[60]

Deci and Ryan have systematized a body of scientific literature by scholars of many perspectives that is increasingly leading others to similar ways of looking at the role of competence and self-determination.[61] And, as with Csikszentmihalyi's elaboration of autotelic behaviors and flow, the underlying concepts are familiar and even commonsensical to the lay reader. The novelty of Deci and Ryan's outlook lies not in what they say about the sources of human enjoyment, but in the fact that they can once again, after nearly a century's lapse, make such statements with the imprimatur of science behind them.

REPRISE:
SELF-ACTUALIZATION AS ENJOYMENT AND ENJOYMENT AS THE EXERCISE OF COMPETENCE IN THE FACE OF CHALLENGE

"Self-actualization," like the word "happiness," tends to be used so glibly that the problem in analyzing it is first of all to bring it down to earth. The best place to begin is with the observation that sometimes human beings do, in point of fact, enjoy themselves, do become absorbed in and are gratified by certain kinds of activities, and that they can enjoy these repeatedly, over long periods of time, without becoming bored. Since we all recognize that such enjoyment occurs, why not (I have suggested) forget about "self-actualization" for the moment and think instead about how it is that human beings come to enjoy themselves, assuming that a person who enjoys himself for great stretches of his life is likely to be self-actualized as well. The reason for inquiring into this topic is the hope that understanding the nature of human enjoyment might be useful when we begin to think about designing good social policy.

Construing Progress: The Usual Understanding. The debate over social policy has impinged on this topic only indirectly. Policymakers and analysts think in terms of "progress" regarding material resources, crime, and even dignity, but I cannot think of an example of policymakers or analysts asking the question, "What constitutes human enjoyment, and how does this relate to what we're doing?"

Still, there are a few themes in contemporary assessments of social policy that relate indirectly to the topics we have been reviewing. For example, leisure is commonly assumed to be a good—people with more leisure are tacitly assumed to have more enjoyable lives than people with less leisure—and therefore a shorter work week (for the same pay) is evidence of progress. Another example is the curious way in which the enjoyment to be gained from a particular job has been confused with (or submerged by) considerations of money and prestige. Thus, being a doctor is assumed to be undifferentiatedly "better" and "more challenging" than being a nurse, and one seldom hears in public dialogue that some people will enjoy being a nurse more than being a doctor. It is as if the only reason one would be a nurse instead of a doctor is because one was denied the opportunity to be a doctor. Similarly, one does not often hear it argued that, for some people, being a waitress will be more enjoyable than being a nurse, being a mechanic will be more enjoyable than being a lawyer, or (unspeakable thought) being a secretary will be more enjoyable than being an executive. In the best of all possible worlds, according to the usual understanding, people will work short hours and everyone will have a job that is "meaningful," with "meaningful" tending to exclude low-skill physical labor and tending to include any of the professions and any supervisory position.

The usual understandings on these issues also tend to disregard the satisfaction of overcoming difficulties. This is not surprising, since the purpose of most social policies is to reduce a difficulty, lower a barrier, or insure against a risk. Therefore people who design policy have never started from the assumption that overcoming obstacles can be a source of pleasure, as well as of self-respect, in itself. Many of the difficulties and barriers that social policy is meant to address are perceived as being unfair; it is an easy jump to assume that all are unfair, or at the least, undesirable. These are understandable reactions, but they also mean that the contemporary dialogue about policy is almost completely silent on the question raised by the discussion in this chapter.

Recasting the Role of Enjoyment. How can social policy facilitate human enjoyment if that enjoyment is intimately linked to the exercise of competence in the face of challenge?

The immediately obvious and the unthreatening answer is that social policy must facilitate the acquisition of competence by all its citizens—an answer that, among other things, can be translated into a call for better educational programs so that people will become more competent.

But such answers are sufficient only insofar as we assume that competence and autonomy are qualities that are pumped into people, not things evoked from people. Once we entertain the kinds of questions raised by the psychologists' probings of the sources of human enjoyment, the answers become more provocative, not to say radical.

As in the case of the findings about self-respect, the implications for social policy are far reaching only if one takes the findings about competence and autonomy literally. One may instead treat them in terms of *perceptions* of causality, competence, self-determination, and autonomy, as Deci and Ryan did in the three propositions that I recast (see the endnotes).

By recasting their propositions to assume real causality, real competence, real self-determination, and real autonomy, I meant to emphasize the same reality test that underlay the discussion of self-respect in the preceding chapter. In that case, I argued it was not enough that people say that they are "committed to measuring up" and urged that authentic commitment must be reflected in behavior. In this case, I conclude that we must avoid thinking in terms of how people can be made to "feel as if" they are in control of events; rather, they must *be* in control of events. It does no good to try to persuade people they are competent if they are not acting competently. It misses the point to tell people they are self-determining human beings if they really are not. The question is not how government can organize a good PR campaign, but how society can be organized so that people are authentically in control of their own lives and possess authentic competencies in which they can take pleasure.

We are left at the end of the discussion of enabling conditions with this contrast: The enabling condition that has dominated American social policy since the 1960s (and European social policy since long before that) has been the distribution of material resources. But if one asks, "What do we know about the importance of material resources to human happiness?" the answer is that the relationship—after subsistence is reached—is complex and ultimately determined by a number of other factors. At the other extreme, the enabling condition that has been virtually ignored by social policy has been enjoyment and the processes that produce human enjoyment—which turn out to be closely linked to challenge, competency, and autonomy. If one asks, "What do we know about the importance to happiness of being a self-determining, competent human being?" the answer is that these qualities are consistently and decisively important.

What happens when we try to make the priorities for assessing policies fit the priorities for pursuing happiness?

PART THREE

TOWARD THE
BEST OF ALL
POSSIBLE
WORLDS

The science of constructing a commonwealth, or renovating it, or reforming it, is . . . not to be taught *a priori*. . . . That which in the first instance is prejudicial may be excellent in its remoter operation, and its excellence may arise even from the ill effects it produces in the beginning. The reverse also happens; and very plausible schemes, with very pleasing commencements, have often shameful and lamentable conclusions.

—EDMUND BURKE

Governing a large state is like boiling a small fish.

—LAO-TZU

8

Policy and
an Idea of Man

NOTHING THAT has gone before lines up neatly with practical politics. The discussion of material resources can be used to defend a miserly floor on income assistance to the poor ("If wealth doesn't buy happiness, why give people more than subsistence?"), which would be conservative. It can also be used to defend a low ceiling on permissible wealth ("If wealth doesn't buy happiness, why let people accumulate huge fortunes?"), which would be liberal. The discussion of safety argued for just deserts and public civility, which sounds like code for "lock 'em up," the conservative prescription; but the concern was to protect poor people, not suburbanites, which sounds liberal.

The discussion of self-respect argued for the importance of making one's own way, an argument usually identified as conservative. But the definition of self-respect was lifted verbatim from the middle of a passage arguing that such self-respect is best fostered by a welfare state. The discussion of enjoyment celebrated individual achievement and autonomy, a theme of the right. But the thinker who stated the Aristotelian Principle and assigned it a central role in human happiness was John Rawls, the philosopher of social democracy, writing in *A Theory of Justice.*

What follows, then, is not a "therefore . . ." but something less dogmatic. The findings and argumentation of the last several chapters may be used to develop an internally consistent case on behalf of socialist states or capitalist ones, communitarian states or libertarian ones, or (to state the dichotomy more accurately) powerful states or limited ones.

The continental divide that forces the flow of the logic one way or the other is defined by one's idea of man. Solutions to social problems that call for a central government to intervene are not attractive or workable without one set of assumptions about man, a limited government is not attractive or workable without another, and the elements of the two sets are not interchangeable. Indeed, they are antagonistic.

WHAT DOES AN IDEA OF MAN HAVE TO DO WITH POLICY?

By "idea of man" I am speaking of issues that reach beyond anything that can be fully resolved by the psychologists' experimental data, for the topic is not only what man is, but what man might be. Martin Diamond, writing the lead article for a collection subtitled *An Inquiry into Fundamental Concepts of Man Underlying Various U.S. Institutions*, explained why.

Politics, he acknowledged, begins with practical questions about how to get the garbage collected or how to get along with the Russians. But "whenever we ask what to do about any particular problem, large or small, we are, of course, asking what it is *best for us* to do in the circumstances."[1] To answer "What is best for us?" requires us to have "some notion of who we are and want enduringly to be."[2] The question of what kind of people we want to be must then be grounded in some still broader notion of what is good for human beings in general. And if voters or policymakers are to decide what is good or bad for human beings in general, they must have a view on what it means to be human: "that is, on an idea of what are the human needs and their order of dignity, on what are the human capacities, possibilities, and limits—in short, on an idea of man."[3]

These ideas are a mix of our ideas about man-as-he-happens-to-be (which can be informed by data of the sort presented in part 2), but also about man-as-he-would-be-if-he-realized-his-essential-nature, which is much more elusive.[4] This is why two people may accept exactly the same data-based statements about man in part 2 and reach polar disagreement about the policy implications. A specific illustration comes to mind:

In George Gilder's account of life in the Albany ghetto, *Visible Man*, the main character, pseudonymously called Sam, is a person of intelligence and natural talents who has grown up in a classically deprived environment.[5] As an adult, he cannot hold onto a job, wastes good opportunities when they are proffered, lives off welfare at second hand by living with women who are on welfare, fathers children he fails to support, and is generally irresponsible (from one point of view) or unable to cope (from another). Then he is arrested and jailed. During the period in jail, Sam is a different man. Outside, he has been oblivious to the rules. In jail, he knows the rules inside out and wrenches from them every possible fractional inch of latitude. Outside, he had been indolent. In jail, he is constantly busy with entrepreneurial schemes for making the best of his situation. Outside, he had been incompetent. In jail, he is highly competent. If only Sam would behave outside as he behaves inside, Gilder concluded, he would be making a middle-class income within a few years.

What are the implications of such a story for public policy, assuming agreement on the facts as presented? I am suggesting they cannot possibly be defined by data. Even if we could agree (which is problematic in itself) that man-as-he-is does tend to respond to challenge as Sam did, our notions of "what it means to be human" would lead us to radically different prescriptions, liberal and conservative, and more data would not change our minds. Too much of what goes into our prescriptions is based on what man could be and should be, not just what he is.

Thomas Sowell traces such disputes to conflicts of "visions" of man. "Visions" as Sowell uses the word are pretheoretical, "what we sense or feel *before* we have constructed any systematic reasoning that could be called a theory, much less deduced any specific consequences as hypotheses to be tested against the evidence. A vision is our sense of how the world works."[6] In the chapters that follow, the logic will be underwritten, inevitably, by the vision that I hold, my understanding of the amalgam of man-as-he-happens-to-be and man-as-he-would-be-if-he-realized-his-essential-nature, just as your reaction to it will be shaped by your vision of the nature of man.

There is no point in trying to "prove" one set of views about this Brobdingnagian topic, but neither need we ignore it. Just being explicit about who believes what will help. First, I will associate myself with a particular set of views. Reduced to their essentials, these views are that man acting in his private capacity—*if restrained from the use of force*—is resourceful and benign, fulfilling his proper destiny; while man acting as a public and political creature is resourceful and dangerous, inherently destructive of the rights and freedoms of his fellowmen. I will explain these views using the language and logic of the American Founding Fathers. Next, I will suggest that if one accepts that set of views of man, the way we assess social policy is pushed in certain directions. Then in subsequent chapters we will get down to cases.

A Brief Note on This Particular Use of the Founders as Authorities

In 1987, the celebration of the bicentennial of the American Constitution prompted lavish invocations of what the Founding Fathers would and wouldn't think of contemporary American problems. Much of this use and misuse of the Founders centered on debates about interpretation of the Constitution by the contemporary Supreme Court, just as much of recent political philosophy has been concerned with whether the Constitution should be interpreted literally according to its text, according to "original intent," or as a "living document" that must be reinterpreted for each generation. To avoid possible confusion, let me emphasize that the center of attention in the discussion that follows is quite different. The Constitution itself is not the topic, nor any specific provision of the Constitution. Rather, it is argued that the Founders (taking their thought as

a whole, encompassing the thinking behind the Declaration and
the Constitution) drew from common eighteenth-century understandings of man's potential and of man's limitations, and that
these understandings (not any particular point in the Constitution) provide an important and persuasive perspective on how
to approach contemporary policy issues.

A second potential point of confusion is the way in which I
am treating the Founders as "authorities." The chain of reasoning in many of the recent invocations of the Founders seems
to be either

The Founders were brilliant men.
The Founders thought X.
Therefore we in contemporary America should think X.

Or, just as bad,

The Founders were slaveholders [or males or members of
an economic elite, etc.].
The Founders' views on X were thereby affected.
Therefore, the Founders' views on X are not germane to
contemporary America.

In the following pages, the use of the Founders is something
closer to this:

In the eighteenth century, a coherent and impressively argued set of views about man was set forth, in somewhat
different but related ways by different thinkers. I am persuaded of the continuing truth of those views, and of their
continuing applicability to the way governments function.
The people who most directly applied these views to the
government of an actual nation were the Americans
known as the Founding Fathers.

As I expatiate on civics-class standbys that you have been
hearing about since you were a sophomore in high school, the
underlying question will be: What if these fellows were right?

The Potential of Private Man

The founding of the nation was an affirmation of the potential
of individual human beings and in that sense was profoundly

optimistic. Two features of man especially captured the imagination of Americans of the Revolutionary era: his capacity to act as an autonomous being, and his equality as an actor.

AUTONOMY

The Founders' ringing defense of man's *right* to act independently is different from their analysis of man's *capacity* to act independently. The Declaration hailed the inalienable right, in the words that were once part of the secular catechism of every school child.[7] The theory that undergirded it drew from John Locke's theory of natural rights as expressed in his *Second Treatise of Government*.[8] But along with the right of man to be free and independent (no matter whether he used that freedom wisely), there was a strong sense that man was at his best operating as an individual. The Founders came to this conclusion from two different lines of reasoning, the second of which I find more persuasive than the first.

The Moral Sense. In the mid-eighteenth century, one of the liveliest issues of political philosophy had to do with the question of whether men were Hobbesian brutes or had within them a "moral sense," in the language of the Scottish philosophers. Jefferson was one of the most optimistic Founders on this score, although his remained a guarded optimism. Men did have a moral sense, he argued; more importantly, the moral sense was part of the heritage of all men—not learned, but instinctive. It was as much a part of man "as his leg or arm."[9] Acting from this moral sense, men left to their own devices tend to act virtuously toward their neighbors, observing when they are distressed and responding to those distresses with assistance.[10] Jefferson was aware that human nature (the other half of the compound) was such that men could behave badly, but believed they were seduced into behaving badly by bad government. Good government left men alone to behave as they had it in them to behave. As Diggins put it, "Classical political thought aspired to make man dependent upon the state, to whose civil ideals private interests would be subordinate; Jeffersonian liberalism aspired to free man from the state to pursue his own interests. . . ."[11]

•

Approbativeness. Many of the Founders were more skeptical than Jefferson. Perhaps, they thought, man did not have an instinctive moral sense after all. Or perhaps, even if he did, the moral sense was so tenuous that it could not be relied upon. Nonetheless, man still functioned best (they argued) as an autonomous being, not because he had a moral sense but because of his instinctive desire for approbation—what Arthur O. Lovejoy later labeled "approbativeness."

Approbativeness refers to the ineradicable desire of men to receive approval and to avoid disapproval.[12] Adam Smith, in *The Theory of Moral Sentiments,* gives one of the most complete analyses of this instinct, arguing that it is an unavoidable result of society.[13] A man raised alone on some desert island, without any communication with another human being, could not possibly think of his own "character," Smith pointed out, any more than he could think of his face as being "beautiful." He would lack any frame of reference. But put him together with other human beings and he *cannot avoid* having a frame of reference for considering his own character, just as he cannot avoid having a frame of reference for assessing the beauty or deformity of his face.[14] Smith's subsequent argument is far more subtle (and persuasive) than can be conveyed here, but for our purposes it comes down to the straightforward proposition that man comes to society with an "original desire to please, and an original aversion to offend," feeling pleasure from approbation *for its own sake,* and pain from disapprobation.[15] These reinforcements may be in the form of fame and fortune, in the good opinion of coworkers or neighbors, in the praise of one's boss or in the admiration of one's children. Seen from a contemporary perspective, Smith is in some respects discussing the need for self-esteem and self-respect that was documented in chapter 6.

Approbativeness serves as a replacement for the "moral sense" (should it be lacking after all) by leading people to behave in ways that are functional for the society in which they wish to reside. Approbativeness will tend to produce behaviors quite similar to those that we hope will be prompted by the moral sense: Communities function better when people exhibit a certain degree of cooperativeness, mutual regard, and generosity; that being the case, behaviors that are cooperative, mutually respectful, and generous tend to receive approbation; therefore, people who want the approbation of their fellows have a strong incentive to behave in these positive ways. Reason and virtue might fail to govern human behavior, but "the substitutes—approbativeness or self-esteem or emulation or all three together—are, by the beneficent dispensation of Providence, capable of producing the same effects in outward conduct as reason and virtue themselves."[16] John Adams nearly paraphrased Smith, writing in 1790 that "as Nature intended men for society, she has endowed them with passions, appetites and propensities calculated . . . to render them useful to each other in their social connections. There is none more essential and remarkable" than this desire of every man "to be observed, considered, esteemed, praised, beloved, and admired by his fellows."[17] To a twentieth-century reader, there is nothing strange in the thought, even if the wording is sometimes archaic. It seems to be an empirical fact that everyone wants to be well-thought-of, and a reasonable conclusion that the desire to be well-thought-of is a force for maintaining a civilized society.

EQUALITY

The other revolutionary aspect of the Founders' optimism regarding the nature of man had to do with that word which has in the twentieth century been used to mean so many things, "equality."

The Founders were not egalitarians nor even very good democrats. Men *are* unequal, they observed, and these inequalities should affect the way a government is structured. This is a far different thing from saying that the inequalities are unjust and should be reduced (the twentieth-century issue), for the inequalities that concerned them were inequalities of virtue, accomplishment, and judgment, not inequalities of material condition.[18] When it came to government and what was meant by "the consent of the governed," the Founding Fathers were generally persuaded that one could easily go too far. Thus Jefferson could write easily of a "natural aristocracy" of virtue and talents that "I consider as the most precious gift of nature, for the instruction, the trusts, and government of society."[19] Madison took as the limit of his "great republican principle" that the common people would have the good sense to recognize the rarer men of virtue and wisdom who were fit to serve as their representatives.[20] Such features of the Constitution as the electoral college and provision for the selection of senators by the state legislatures were a few of the concrete expressions of the Founders' doubts about the masses.[21]

In the twentieth century, the Founders' unflattering vision of the common man has come under sustained attack. One history widely used as a university text, *The American Political Tradition* by Richard Hofstadter, is a good example, pointing out that an essential purpose of the Constitution was "cribbing and confining the popular spirit."[22] The Founders "did not believe in man," the author wrote, and had "a distrust of man [which] was first and foremost a distrust of the common man and democratic rule."[23]

Hofstadter was right. The Founders *were* distrustful of democratic rule. But the Founders believed that men *were* equal in another and crucial sense, and the affirmation of that equality was perhaps the most revolutionary and optimistic aspect of the Founders' conception of man.

Their view was revolutionary first in that it broke with the assumption that inequalities were governed by class. The few who were fit to govern were not necessarily to be drawn from an economic or social aristocracy. Alexander Hamilton, in many ways the most elitist of the Founders, wrote matter-of-factly that "experience has by no means justified us in the supposition that there is more virtue in one class of men than in another." On the contrary, he continued, the only difference among the social classes is the type of vice that predominates, not its quantity.[24] But beyond this pragmatic recognition that virtue and intelligence can reside in anyone was a broader affirmation of equality. The nobility of the American experiment lay in its allegiance to the proposition that everyone may equally aspire to happiness.

This seems hardly a radical position to modern eyes, but radical it was. From the most ancient times until the Founding Fathers broke ranks, governments had been based on the opposite premise, that only a few men have the potential for (in modern terms) self-actualization. All men may exhibit rudimentary good qualities or experience primitive feelings of pleasure, it was believed, but attributes such as virtue and meaningful happiness might be achieved by only an exceptional few. A primary function of government was to nurture these few. "The classical idea of human nature is, as it were, aristocratic," as Diamond put it. "All men are human but some are more so, and that is the crucial political fact." The Founding Fathers began a new tradition that is now as unquestioned as the old one: "The modern idea of human nature is democratic: No difference among us can reach so far as to alter our naturally equal humanness, and *that* is the crucial fact."[25] That also is the underlying assumption of equality and democracy that makes it reasonable to seek the best of all possible worlds in one that makes the enabling conditions for pursuing happiness available to everyone.

In terms of practical politics, the Founders' prescription was simple. Equality meant that all men shared as their birthright the same natural rights of liberty. All were equally immune by right from the arbitrary coercion of the state. This did not have anything to do with equality of outcome. Edmund Burke expressed the prevailing view when he wrote that "All men have equal rights, but not to equal things."[26] The essence of this constrained vision of equality, as Thomas Sowell has pointed out, is process—providing a level playing-field, to employ a modern analogy.[27] Even this formulation permits semantic games, but the underlying meaning is reasonably clear. If your competitor comes to the playing field after months of practice, with professional coaching and superior ability, it is no doubt true that you will not derive much advantage from a level playing field. But there is a qualitative difference between your disadvantage under those circumstances and the disadvantage if *the rules* specify that the referee give you three strikes and your competitor four, or (worse) that no matter what, your competitor *must* win. For if you have superior abilities or even just superior determination, what you need most of all is a level playing field. What is deadening to the soul is not to lose, but to be forbidden to win. Until relatively recently in American history, such logic was taken for granted.

A COMMON PERSPECTIVE

In this short review I necessarily ignore the rich variation in the views of the Revolutionary period, but the variation is less striking than the degree of consensus. In later years, John Adams, referring to the Declaration of Independence, wrote that "There was not an idea in it but what had been hackneyed in Congress for two years before."[28] It was a sentiment that Jefferson himself endorsed, writing in a letter to Richard Lee in 1825 that the Declaration of Independence "was intended to be an expression of the American mind." Originality of thought was not the object; the essential thing was to "place before mankind the common sense of the subject," drawing upon "the harmonizing sentiments of the day, whether expressed in conversation, in letters, printed essays, or the elementary books of public right, as Aristotle, Cicero, Locke, Sidney, etc."[29] In trying to capture this consensus, one can do no better than did Bernard Bailyn as he concluded *The Ideological Origins of the American Revolution:*

> The details of this new world were not as yet clearly depicted; but faith ran high that a better world than any that had ever been known could be built where authority was distrusted and held in constant scrutiny; where the status of men flowed from their achievements and from their personal qualities, not from distinctions ascribed to them at birth; and where the use of power over the lives of men was jealously guarded and severely restricted. It was only where there was this defiance, this refusal to truckle, this distrust of all authority, political or social, that institutions could express human aspirations, not crush them.[30]

Such was the vaulting optimism about what free men might accomplish, what free men might be.

THE DANGERS OF PUBLIC MAN

The nation was founded as an affirmation of the private man but was to survive because of profound pessimism about the public man. The construction of the American polity was grounded in the understanding that men acting as political animals are dangerous, and that what men might do innocuously as individuals is far different from what men might do innocuously as groups. Man's potentialities are grand; his human nature constantly threatens to prevent him from realizing those potentialities.

This understanding was expressed in the Constitutional Convention, in the minutes of the state ratifying conventions, in the public and private correspondence of the leading figures, and (in a losing but influential cause) by the Anti-Federalists. But to a remarkable degree the theory has been handed down to us in a single text, *The Federalist,* the collection of eighty-five letters written to newspapers in New York State in an effort to persuade the voters of New York to ratify the Constitution. The byline on the letters was "Publius," the nom de plume of Alexander Hamilton, who instigated the project, John Jay, who soon had to drop out because of bad health (he was injured in a street riot), and James Madison, a Virginian who chanced to be in New York that winter of 1787–88 for the sitting of the Continental Congress. It was a haphazardly conceived and hastily conducted effort that gave birth to the most enduringly influential document in American political history save only the Constitution itself. Jefferson (who had no part in either the convention or the writing of *The Federalist*) expressed the general opinion of the Founders when offering bibliographical advice to Thomas Randolph in a letter written just two years later. Adam Smith's *Wealth of Nations* was the best book in political economy, he wrote, and John Locke's "little book on government" (meaning the *Second Treatise*) was "perfect as far as it goes." But when it comes to arranging a practical government, "there is no better book than the Federalist."[31]

All of this contrives to make *The Federalist* almost inaccessible to us today. It is a classic as Mark Twain defined one, a book that people praise and don't read. Nor is it an easy read, written as it is in the cadences and with the vocabulary of the eighteenth century. But it remains a critically important document for contemporary policymaking. *The Federalist* is not about the eighteenth century. It is about how humans function when given access to public power.*

---

* Both the scholarship and the disputes about what Publius thought of human nature are extensive. I have skirted issues that are not directly germane and tried to make my summary statements no

FACTION, AND ITS ORIGIN IN HUMAN NATURE

Republics don't last. Democracies don't last. This was the stark empirical truth that faced the Founders. It is a fine thing to say that government derives its just powers from the consent of the governed, but it is exceedingly difficult to translate this aspiration into policy.

The reason why it is so difficult, Publius concludes, is that men, given a chance, will destroy their freedoms under a representative government. The bludgeon with which they do so is called faction, defined by Madison in No. 10 as "a number of citizens, whether amounting to a majority or minority of the whole, who are united and actuated by some common impulse of passion, or of interest, adverse to the rights of other citizens, or to the permanent and aggregate interests of the community."[32] Faction is something with which the political system must live, because eliminating the phenomenon is out of the question. To endure, the system would either have to suppress faction—which requires a totalitarian state—or else convince everyone to share the same opinions and interests, which is impossible even in a totalitarian state.

It is impossible to avoid the coalescence of factions because "the latent causes of faction are . . . sown in the nature of man."[33] Publius saw the proof everywhere—in the histories of the classical period as in the struggles that had attended the Confederation. "Has it not . . . invariably been found," Hamilton asked in Federalist No. 6, "that momentary passions and immediate interests have a more active and imperious control over human conduct than general or remote considerations of policy, utility, or justice?"[34] The modern reader may pause at

---

more argumentative than necessary—for example, there is considerable controversy about the degree to which Madison had a pessimistic view of human nature; there is much less disagreement that he was suspicious of man acting as a public person. I have limited myself to the latter and less contentious line of argument. Readers looking for a thorough analysis are referred to White's *Philosophy, The Federalist, and the Constitution,* which devotes three chapters to Publius's view of human nature and includes an excellent review of other scholarship through the mid-1980s.

the phrase "momentary passions"—a modern rendering might be "one's current personal priorities"—and the optimist will balk at the word "invariably," which is possibly too strong. But with these qualifications, subsequent history seems to bear Hamilton out.

Readers who find this too cynical are invited to try to think of a single social measure, including in your consideration the ones passed with the highest-minded of intentions, that was supported by a majority consisting of people whose *own* priority interests were being seriously impeded. Perhaps the archetypal contemporary example is school busing to achieve racial balance. White politicians and journalists living in Washington, D.C., who spoke and wrote in support of busing almost without exception kept their own children in suburban or private schools.[35] Busing was a good thing for other people's children and a step toward social justice—but it was a measure whose consequences could be evaded for their own children. The assertion here is not that people are without idealism (many who supported busing did so at political cost to themselves) but that the laws people support very rarely violate Hamilton's generalization. In the busing case, some were willing to suffer some consequences for themselves; few were willing to budge when it came to the interests of their children.

It is important to emphasize, however, that factions were an inevitable result of man acting in a *public* setting, not a reflection of an intrinsically deficient human nature. Hume, from whom Madison drew his own views on this matter, put it succinctly: In forming a system of government, "every man ought to be supposed a knave" even though "at the same time, it appears somewhat strange, that a maxim should be true in *politics* which is false in *fact*"—for, Hume observes, "men are generally more honest in their private than in their public capacity."[36] To concur with Publius, one need not believe that men are depraved, only that, by and large, they are self-interested and prone to calculate their self-interest in fairly simple, immediate terms.

GIVEN FACTIONS, WHAT IS TO BE DONE?

Factions will form, inevitably, and they will seek to obtain advantages over other factions, to obtain special favors, to accumulate power, to work their will on the polity. We cannot rely on enlightened statesmen to adjust these differences for the common good, partly because, as Publius noted, "enlightened men will not always be at the helm" and partly because in many cases there is no way to determine the public good "without taking into view indirect and remote considerations, which will rarely prevail."[37] The conclusion? "The inference to which we are brought is that the *causes* of faction cannot be removed, and that relief is only to be sought in the means of controlling its *effects*."[38]

To some of the influential Americans of the period, there was no way at all to provide such relief in the context of a strong federal government. These men, known as the Anti-Federalists, read the same accounts of past republics that Madison and Hamilton read and came to the conclusion that men acting in a public capacity were so intrinsically bound to form factions and expand their power that the only relief lay in decentralization.

The Anti-Federalists lost the argument and have therefore been largely lost to history. Read today, some of their writings seem almost prescient. Here, for example, is Brutus (the Anti-Federalist's closest counterpart to Publius, generally thought to have been a prominent Albany lawyer named Robert Yates[39]), regarding congressional authority versus the state legislatures. "It is a truth confirmed by the unerring experience of ages," he begins, "that every man, and every body of men, invested with power, are ever disposed to increase it." Therefore, Brutus did not need to know exactly what the rationalization for expanded federal authority would be—he didn't need to know about modern communications or complex economies or any of the other ex post facto justifications. He knew that, one way or another, it would happen: The disposition to expand power "is implanted in human nature" and will inevitably "operate in the federal legislature to lessen and ultimately to subvert the state authority."[40] Having made that prediction about the federal legislature, Brutus made this confident forecast about the Supreme Court:

[T]he judges under this constitution will control the legislature, for the supreme court are authorized in the last re-

sort to determine what is the extent of the powers of the
Congress; they are to give the constitution an explanation,
and there is no power above them to set aside their judge-
ment. . . . There is no authority that can remove them,
and they cannot be controlled by the laws of the legislature. In short, they are independent of the people, of the
legislature, and of every power under heaven. Men placed
in this situation will generally soon feel themselves independent of heaven itself.[41]

As I associate myself with the thinking of the Federalists, I cannot suppress the seditious thought that just because the Anti-
Federalists lost doesn't mean they were in the wrong of it.

They did lose, however. Madison, Hamilton, and the rest of
the Federalists calculated that the importance of an effective
central authority outweighed the risks it entailed and they were
able to make their view prevail. But though they won, the Federalists were no less absorbed than the Anti-Federalists by fears
for the survival of democracy over the long run.

If the faction consists of less than a majority, Publius wrote,
then an easy remedy presents itself. "Relief is supplied by the
republican principle, which enables the majority to defeat its
sinister views by regular vote." The minority may "clog the
administration, it may convulse the society," but it cannot
win.[42] For Publius, the much greater problem was what happens when the faction consists of a majority. A time arises
when, for whatever reason, a majority of the people is in favor
of a bad policy. It has the votes; it can pass its "sinister views."
What then?

And thus the "great object" facing Publius, facing the Founding Fathers, and facing the United States of America throughout its history up to the present day: How to "secure the public
good, and private rights, against the danger of such a faction."
From that aim flows the Federalist's discussion of representative
government vs. democracy, checks and balances, the role of a
strong executive, and the other features that were to protect
against the destruction of the country by faction. Madison put
his case in Nos. 10 and 51, Hamilton his in Nos. 9, 70, 71, 76,
and 78. The central message is that people with a passion to do
things their way and impose their will on others are a danger so

great and so unending that all the structures of the government must be arrayed against them. Madison stated the theme most powerfully in the famous passage from Federalist No. 51:

> It may be a reflection on human nature, that such devices [as the separation of powers] should be necessary to control the abuses of government. But what is government itself but the greatest of all reflections on human nature? If men were angels, no government would be necessary. If angels were to govern men, neither external nor internal controls on government would be necessary. In framing a government which is to be administered by men over men, the great difficulty lies in this: You must first enable the government to control the governed; and in the next place, oblige it to control itself. A dependence on the people is no doubt the primary control on the government; but experience has taught mankind the necessity of auxiliary precautions.
>
> This policy of supplying, by opposite and rival interests, the defect of better motives, might be traced through the whole system of human affairs, private as well as public. We see it particularly displayed in all the subordinate distributions of power; where the constant aim is to divide and arrange the several offices in such a manner as that each may be a check on the other; that the private interest of every individual may be a sentinel over the public rights. These inventions of prudence cannot be less requisite in the distribution of the supreme power of the state.[43]

There is no better statement of the pessimism with which one must view man acting as a political creature.

THE CONTINENTAL DIVIDE, AGAIN

I began the chapter by observing that the discussions of the enabling conditions—material resources, safety, self-respect, enjoyment—lent themselves to internally consistent social policies that were poles apart. Which way one goes depends on how one perceives human nature. Having presented an overview of one perspective, I should add that there are many able proponents of the proposition that the Founding Fathers were wrong.

Indeed, in the twentieth century it has been intellectually fashionable to believe that they were, joining in Hofstadter's opinion that "No man who is as well abreast of modern science as the
Fathers were of eighteenth-century science believes any longer
in unchanging human nature. . . . Modern humanistic thinkers who seek for a means by which society may transcend eternal conflict and rigid adherence to property rights as its inte-
grating principles can expect no answer in the philosophy of
balanced government as it was set down by the Constitution-
makers of 1787."[44]

And that is the kernel of the debate over policy choices.
Most of what we know as contemporary social policy is based
on the tacit assumption that the Founders were wrong. It is believed, apparently by a large majority of people, that humans
can act collectively with far more latitude than the Founders
believed they could.

If the Founders were wrong, we may conduct social policy
on the assumption that if humans seek a more even distribution
of resources, for example, they may achieve it. If humans want
an end to racial inequality or sexual inequality, it is within their
grasp to have it; all they have to do is pass the right laws. The
world can be made constantly fairer if human beings use the
instruments of government to reduce unfairness. If the Founders were wrong, we may continue to be optimistic in the face
of failures, and assume that when one attempt at a solution
doesn't produce the desired results, the proper response is to
try again with another and better political solution. Most importantly: If the Founders were wrong, then we may assume
that this expansive use of a centralized government *can continue over the long run,* because men have it in them after all
to act collaboratively in their public capacity.

Suppose, however, that the Founders were right. If one accepts their optimistic view of private man, then centralized
governmental solutions are not attractive. What allows man to
fulfill his own nature in the Founders' vision is the process of
individual response to challenge, risk, and reward. Each of
those words—"individual," "challenge," "risk," "reward"—grates
against the rationale for centralized solutions. Centralized solutions from the left urge that the collective society has a moral

claim on the individual; they seek to dampen risks and increase predictability, and use as primary measures of success the achievement of security and equality. Centralized solutions from the right urge that the state has the right to impose beliefs on individuals; they seek to restrain by law individual variations in social behavior, and use as primary measures of success the degree of conformity to the righteous way. If man has the autonomy and equality that the Founders saw in him, these goals are not "bad" but wrongheaded. They do not liberate humans to fulfill their potential. They do not nourish the human soul.

If the Founders were right about *public* man, then the practical options for seeking solutions to social problems through a centralized government are highly constrained for two reasons.

First, such solutions will be impossible to sustain over time without also sacrificing democracy. If Publius was right, republics collapse when a faction is able to use the state to impose its vision of the good on the rest of society. And a relentless use of the state in just that fashion—to let a majority faction decide what is right for everyone and impose that vision on everyone— is the very essence of legislation that requires either school prayer on behalf of religious values or school busing on behalf of social justice.

Accepting Publius's analysis, one should view the Western democracies as in a process of transition. Sooner or later the genie will get out of the bottle. If one permits the government to do one thing for everybody in the country because it is the "right thing" to do, every once in a while the government will do another thing for everybody in the country that is the wrong thing. And as time goes on, and as the limits on what it is permissible for government to do are loosened, there will be no defense against any number of bad things being done in the name of good.

Second (and less apocalyptically), policies that attempt to use the state to redistribute goods or increase equality will tend to fail. The ubiquitous "unintended outcomes" that have been found by the evaluators of social programs would not have mystified Publius. Constituencies of persons, Publius already knew, would seek to use the reforms for their own ends. They would form factions, bringing pressures to bear on the politicians who design the policies and the bureaucrats who implement them. The politicians and bureaucrats themselves would have ambitions that affect the way that the programs are run, not to mention other human frailties of vanity, ineptitude, and foolishness that would obstruct the implementation of the great schemes. And if all that were not enough, Publius knew, the very definition of what constituted "serving the common good" would be impossible for anyone not omniscient and of Olympian detachment to discern. A central message for modern times to be drawn from *The Federalist* is that one cannot use central governments to do such things—not just "ought not" use them but *cannot*, successfully. To work, to be just, to be stable, centralized social reforms demand every quality of public man that the Founders did not believe in.

I said at the outset of the discussion that one cannot try to prove that one view of human nature is correct; not, at any rate, within the confines of this book. Similarly, proof that these links between the Founders' view of man and the limits of government are true for all time and all circumstances is beyond me. The purpose of the discussion has been to lay bare underlying assumptions. We are about to set the discussion of the enabling conditions side by side with ways that social policy might work. In that discussion, I will be assuming that man is as the Founders saw him, sharing equal dignity with all as an autonomous actor, filled with exciting potential, seeking happiness in the free working-out of his life, perhaps inherently moral but at the least "fitted for society"—and at the same time irredeemably problematic whenever given even a little rein to advance his own interests in the political arena.

9

Asking a New Question, Getting New Answers: Evaluating Results

THE THREE LARGE assertions of this book so far have been that we ought to use the pursuit of happiness as the criterion of success in making social policy, that the design of policy solutions must reflect one's understanding of human nature, and that these things constitute not just a theoretical exercise but something that policy analysts ought actually to do as they go about their work.

It is time to take up the last assertion, that all this has some relevance to the real task of devising better policies. In this and the following chapters I will discuss two specific ways in which the framework I have presented might be employed in assessing policy. This chapter will deal with the problem of evaluation: the art of measuring whether we are making progress, of deciding what (and how much) has been accomplished by a policy. The next chapter will begin to take up the design question: Given the existence of a social problem, how is one to divine a solution? Because the way we design solutions is so dependent on the way we assess results, I begin with the evaluation function.

•

The Inevitability of Evaluating

Despite the frayed reputation of social scientists as interpreters of social policy and its effects, there's no way around it: People are going to make claims about the effects of social programs, and they are going to be based, for better or worse, on specific measures, specifically operationalized, of what has been accomplished. The fundamental question that has always been asked by presidents and congresses alike is "Will policy X produce the intended result Y?" The more precisely one attempts to answer it, the more one is driven toward methods very like the ones that social scientists use.

Policy analysis (as I will refer generically to this type of social science) is predominantly quantitative. The techniques are numerous, each technique has its own idiosyncrasies, and the debates about technical issues are unending. But the esoterica of statistical analysis are not our concern. We will focus on a basic issue that receives too little attention, what I will call "the dependent variable problem."

THE DEPENDENT VARIABLE PROBLEM

Seen through the lens of evaluation statistics, the world is divided into "dependent" variables and "independent" variables. If one thinks in terms of cause-effect relationships, the independent variable is the cause, the dependent variable the effect. (A mnemonic for keeping them straight: An effect "depends upon" its cause, hence is dependent.) If one thinks in terms of social policy goals to be attained by social programs, the program is the independent variable (or "the intervention") and the thing-to-be-attained is the dependent variable. For those who think in terms of conventional statistical notation, independent variables are the Xs and dependent variables are the Ys. In a graph, the independent variable is shown on the horizontal axis, the dependent variable on the vertical axis.

The social scientist's assessment of whether progress is being made depends on the measuring stick he employs for the dependent variable. Almost all of the technical debates about the results of evaluation focus on the difficulties associated with the actual data gathered and analyzed. (Is the measure valid and reliable in the statistical sense of those terms? Are the data accurately recorded? Is the sample correctly chosen? Are the statistical techniques used appropriately?) But long before the sample is drawn or any data are collected, the investigator has, whether he has thought about it or not, made two other decisions that will decisively shape his conclusions. The first has to do with the way that the *construct* that is the "real" dependent variable is translated into *measures*, the second with the unit of aggregation that will be used to describe the effect.

OPERATIONALIZING THE CONSTRUCT

Almost nothing having to do with social policy that we can measure directly is the construct we are really interested in. This has been a leitmotif throughout this book, but it is time to be more explicit. When we measure poverty, we are not really interested in whether the person in question has an income above or below the number of dollars that happens to represent the poverty line that year; we are interested in whether that person is living in a state of poverty. The poverty line is our best effort to operationalize the construct called "living in poverty." When we examine grade-point averages (GPA), we are not really interested in the letters A, B, C, D, or F that teachers have written onto school records, but in a construct called "learning" for which grades are a shadowy representation. In the jargon, GPA is an operational measure of learning; "an income lower than a certain number of dollars" is the operational measure of poverty.

The extent to which the operational measure truly represents the construct is crucially important to the results of an evaluation. Let us continue with the relationship of GPA to learning as the example. Suppose that GPA is a perfect operational measure of learning: It always increases when learning increases and never for any other reason. In that case, if a new education program makes grades go up, we can be absolutely sure that learning has increased as well. Suppose, however, that learning is only loosely related to grades. In this case, a program can produce an increase in grades that fools us into thinking that learning has increased when it has not. We have not only failed to increase the student's learning, we are under the illusion that we have succeeded, and the problem we set out to solve remains unsolved. We have used the wrong operational measure. Or it is equally possible that a poor operational measure will fail to reflect a change in the construct—for example, fail to register an increase in learning, if the increase in learning is not captured by the grading process.

You will find oddly little said about this issue in the press or even in the technical journals. Much more attention is given to whether the measure is calibrated accurately. With regard to the poverty index, for example, elaborate studies have been devoted to the question of how to assign a cash value to noncash benefits such as Medicaid and food stamps. The Labor Department works hard to improve the accuracy of the data it uses to calculate the unemployment rate and consumer price index. Almost never does anyone call into question fundamental issues about how well or poorly the operational measure corresponds to the thing-in-which-we-are-really-interested: "being without the resources to live a modest but decent material existence" in the case of poverty, "wanting a job but unable to find one" in the case of unemployment. It is an important flaw in the public dialogue about policy. Politicians, television anchormen, editorial writers, and social scientists constantly write about (and interpret) rises and falls in the indicators; few ever stop to question whether they measure what they're supposed to measure. This defect in the public dialogue about policy, important all by itself, is magnified by the problems associated with choosing the unit of aggregation.

DEFINING THE UNIT OF AGGREGATION

The "unit of aggregation" as I am using the term here refers to the set of people that we use to evaluate the policy implications of the results.* Suppose, for example, we are evaluating the Job Corps, and the measure of success is "the state of being employed after graduating from Job Corps." We have a choice about the unit of aggregation we use to assess the size of the

---

* "Unit of aggregation" has another technical meaning. I am using the term for the specific purpose described in the text.

outcome. We may express it in terms of the gain in employment for some large number of Job Corps trainees, or we may express it in terms of the improved odds of employment for any particular trainee.

Our choice makes a big difference in how we view the results. If we value the macroeconomic effects of the Job Corps program, we will probably want to examine the overall change in employment status, compare that to the costs of running the program, and produce a cost-benefit analysis. But suppose instead that we are advising a particular youth whether to go into the Job Corps. The same results can produce completely different implications. I elaborate on this example later in the chapter, but, for introductory purposes, suppose that Job Corps graduates are found on the average to make $3.30 more per week than people who don't graduate from the Job Corps.[1] This may well be enough to claim that the Job Corps is cost-effective (depending on collateral assumptions I won't bother with here), but it doesn't give me much incentive to join the Job Corps if I am a youth in the inner city who happens to hear about the results.

When the way we add up results is combined with the difficulties of operationalizing hard-to-reify constructs, the nature of what I call "the dependent variable problem" becomes clear. If the dependent variables in social policy have been properly defined, measured, and aggregated, we will eventually make progress even if we make mistakes with our policies—*because mistakes will be recognized.* If in contrast we have misconstrued the dependent variables, no degree of skill in implementing policies or of precision in calibrating results will prevent us from making disastrous mistakes, because mistakes will not register as mistakes on our measuring devices.

The "dependent variable problem" is that the policy-making process has become boxed into assumptions ensuring that some types of outcomes of social policy—some dependent variables—will be measured and others will not. It is not just that policy analysts are measuring progress inaccurately, yielding results with a larger margin of error than we would prefer. Rather, I propose that domestic policy-making in the United States has gone fundamentally awry. We use yardsticks thinking they are thermometers. We try to measure whether we are doing

better or worse, and we keep coming up with meaningless answers—worse, misleading answers—because the way in which
we measure our progress in the pursuit of happiness unavoid-
ably skews the way in which social policy permits certain kinds
of happiness to occur. The people who analyze policy, make
recommendations about what to do next, who write bills and
regulations, have been shooting at the wrong targets.

THE PURSUIT OF HAPPINESS AND
THE 55-MPH SPEED LIMIT

Let me try to set the nature of the evaluation problem as it relates to the pursuit of happiness by using a homely example:
the national 55-mile-per-hour speed limit enacted in 1974.

The Congress originally enacted the 55-mph speed limit as
a temporary measure in response to the Arab oil embargo. Its
purpose was to save fuel. As it turned out, this objective was
unrealistic. Instead of the 10 to 30 percent reductions that had
been predicted, the actual savings were trivial. And the fuel
shortage quickly dissipated, so even if the law did save fuel, it
wasn't helping solve a national emergency. But by that time it
had been learned (or thought it had been learned) that lives
were being saved, so obviously the law had to be a good thing.
In 1974, Congress made the national speed limit permanent so
that more lives could be saved.* And thus began a sort of national schizophrenia.

A Gallup survey in 1981 (typical of others) illustrates how
zany the situation became. A large majority of the people polled,
75 percent, proclaimed their support for the speed limit. But
only 29 percent said they obeyed it consistently. Even among
those who said they favored the law, 42 percent conceded that
they observed the law "not very often or never."[2] The problem was that the lives-saved argument meant that it was not
nice to be against the 55-mph speed limit. It was not nice even
to *think* that one was against it. If you were against the 55-mph

---

* More precisely, the law said that federal highway funds would be
withheld from states that did not enact the 55-mph limit.

limit, you were in favor of people dying of car accidents that you could have prevented. And so it came to be that a large majority of Americans supported the law, including a large majority of congressmen and senators, and a large majority of Americans disobeyed it, and nowhere more uniformly or flagrantly than on the beltway surrounding Washington, D.C.

In 1987, a bill was finally passed that permitted states to raise the speed limit to 65 mph on rural interstate highways. The debate over the eventual modification of the law recalls Oscar Wilde's remark about the difficulties of reasoning a person out of something he has not reasoned himself into. The Congress extricated itself not so much because its original expectation for the law was false, nor because the data on savings of lives were refuted, but because so many Americans hated the law they said they supported. Those who led the public opposition to the 55-mph limit never proved that the law did *not* save lives, nor did any other rationale for changing the law gain wide acceptance; rather, after years of frustration, they won what must seem to an impartial observer to be an irrational victory.

In reality, I will argue, the debate over the 55-mph limit exemplifies the problem of defining dependent variables. The opponents of the speed limit were not ignoring "the good." They were construing it differently. And in this difference lie lessons that apply to a variety of contemporary issues.

Let us imagine we are examining the 55-mph speed limit afresh, divorced from political pressures. Our objective is to decide systematically, unemotionally, based on data, whether the law is, on balance, beneficial or harmful—whether we have approached the best of all possible speed limits.

THE CONVENTIONAL GOOD

We begin by arraying the dependent variables to be assessed. They are:

1. Human deaths and injuries (expected to go down).
2. Fuel costs (expected to go down).
3. Other economic costs associated with travel (expected to go up).
4. Noneconomic and nonhealth costs associated with travel (expected to go up).

The first three of those outcomes lend themselves to straightforward quantitative measures. The calculations cannot be precise, because it is difficult to get data on all of the potential economic costs. Causal attribution will be imprecise, especially for the estimate of lives-saved. But the procedures for identifying and developing measures and for assessing causality are methodologically straightforward. The unit of aggregation for measuring these costs and benefits will be "the nation."

When we conduct the analysis, we find that the 55-mph speed limit has saved 7,466 lives per year since it was enacted—by the end of 1986, a grand total of almost 90,000 people saved by this one law.* For practical purposes, this finding ends the analysis. We may add the savings in injuries. We may compute dollar savings in hospital bills and the economic benefits of the increased lifetime earnings of those who were saved, and we may subtract from those totals the costs associated with longer travel time. But these conclusions will make little difference.† Surely, it is an open-and-shut case. Thousands upon thousands of people, perhaps including some of the readers of this book, are alive because of this law.

Meanwhile, we have reached our decision without even getting to that fourth dependent variable, the "noneconomic

---

* For verisimilitude, I am using the figure from a specific published estimate.[3] I have no faith in this particular number, nor in the numbers produced by any other analysis with which I am familiar. I am not even endorsing the thesis that the 55-mph speed limit has saved a lot of lives. This discussion simply says, "Suppose it has," and uses a specific number for convenience.

† To elaborate: The same analysis (Forester et al.) calculated that for 1978 the 55-mph limit caused the nation's citizens to spend a total of 456,279 extra person-years on the nation's roads, and concluded that the reduction of 7,466 fatalities per year attributable to the speed limit is outweighed by economic costs when a variety of standard procedures for valuing lives are used.[4] The analysis also concluded that the main mechanism by which the speed limit saves lives is not by lowering speed, but by concentrating speeds within a narrower range. These conclusions, no matter how justified they may be from a technical standpoint, are bound to get lost in the public dialogue—as indeed they have been. How many readers have ever heard of them?

and nonhealth costs associated with travel." What might these costs be?

It depends on where I live. If I live in the mountain and desert states of the American West, a strictly enforced 55-mph speed limit can mean several dozen extra hours per year spent on the highways. But in most cases these would show up under the calculation of "economic costs." More commonly, the non-economic costs are not especially dramatic or urgent. If I am driving from Washington to New York to see friends and drive 55 instead of 70, it takes me an extra hour to get there. Or: I get bored sitting in the car, and so want to complete my journey faster. Or: I enjoy driving fast.

Economists have ways of dealing with these reasons for wanting to drive faster than 55 mph, but they come down to one form or another of "opportunity costs" that are assigned a dollar value, usually based on wage rates.[5] To assign a dollar value in this instance sidesteps the problem. To illustrate, consider the case of a man whose decrepit old car is not capable of going any faster than 55 mph. He drove down to Washington for the weekend and wants to get back home to New York in time for dinner, but to do so he will have to skip a visit to the National Gallery of Art. Whichever choice he makes, he will incur an opportunity cost. The way I have set up the example, the man is facing a standard problem of deciding what he wants, how much he wants it, and what he's able or willing to pay for it. Time is a scarce commodity. If he wants to expand his "disposable time," he will have to incur a cost by procuring a faster means of transportation. Somehow he will have to come up with the price for that benefit. It would be nice if such benefits were free, but they aren't.

Suppose, however, that his car will go 70 mph but the law says he must not exceed 55 mph. The nature of the opportunity cost changes subtly but very importantly. He has acquired the necessary resources to permit him to visit the National Gallery of Art and still get back to New York for dinner. He has paid all the prices necessary to do so. There is no necessary opportunity cost. The only reason he has to choose between the options is because of the law. The government has said, "There is a safety interest that justifies removing from you this degree of freedom." The point is not yet whether the law is good or bad. The only point I am making now is that the ordinary calculus of choice has been taken out of the chooser's hands and the ordinary ways of construing opportunity costs are changed. The government has created the cost.

To return to our analysis of the costs and benefits of the 55-mph speed limit: Whether we use ordinary or extraordinary methods of calculating dependent variable #4, "the noneconomic and nonhealth costs of travel," makes no difference. Given the terms of reference we applied to the analysis—what are the aggregate costs and benefits for the nation?—aggregate noneconomic costs will look trivial in importance next to the 7,466 lives per year being saved.

So our fresh look has decided that the 55-mph speed limit is a good thing. We do not want to repeal it. But this leads to a fascinating question: *Why not lower the speed limit to 50?* We can demonstrate (using the same methods that yielded the figure of 7,466) that doing so may be expected to save a certain number of additional lives. Economics do not prevent us from taking such a step. Let's lower the speed limit to 50 and save even more lives!

Why hasn't this happened? Why is it that no one in public life ever suggested that we lower the speed limit even further? It is unlikely that in 1974 Congress stumbled onto precisely the right speed limit. Surely there is some number lower than 55 that would provide the optimum. And yet no one is seeking it.

As we in our imaginary deliberations take up this question, it becomes clear why it has not been discussed in the real world. The debate as we confront the problem of determining the optimum speed limit becomes increasingly divided between a rational and an irrational component. For if it is true that a 50-mph limit will save lives, how many more will be saved by a limit of 49 mph? 48 mph? And so on.

Our choice of dependent variables is such that we cannot find a place on the slippery slope to stop short. There is no point at which economic savings clearly become more important than savings in lives. Our objective is to be rational, to decide on a speed limit that maximizes "good," and we have two sets of measures for maximizing "good"—human lives and economic efficiency—and when changes are at the margin, it is impossible to rationalize any stopping point. By the same token, we know—irrationally, it would seem—that even at 50 mph and certainly at 45 mph, the costs are too high. People won't stand for such a limit, no matter how rational it may be. Those ephemeral "other outcomes" that we couldn't value have become so important that we know (without being able to specify the algorithm by which we know) that such speed limits are too low. Don't ask us to defend this conclusion, because we cannot (the lives-saved case for lowering the limit just one more mile per hour will always be irresistible). But that foggy, unarticulated set of "other factors" out there will finally be too strong to ignore.

The only reason that this commonsense assessment of the situation appears to be irrational is because we have construed the safety variable in ways that ensure it. We have artificially constrained and distorted the policy assessment so that it is impossible for people to defend doing what seems to them to be reasonable and desirable. There must be another way to look at the costs and benefits that accords with common sense.

AN ALTERNATIVE GOOD

We turn the analysis on its head. We are no longer holding in our head a concept of the aggregate public good, nor in our cost-benefit calculations are we trying to estimate savings for the nation as a whole. Rather, the concept of the good is individual happiness. Policy is to be assessed according to whether it increases or decreases the conditions for pursuing happiness. We consider the question of the 55-mph speed limit—for the time being, the only option on the table.

Safety is by no means irrelevant. It is difficult to pursue happiness if you are dead, so safety remains a dependent variable. So do dollar costs and benefits, and so do nondollar costs. This is the array of dependent variables:

1. Human deaths and injuries (expected to go down).
2. Fuel costs (expected to go down).
3. Other economic costs associated with travel (expected to go up).
4. Noneconomic and nonhealth costs associated with travel (expected to go up).

The dependent variables are not changed in their content but in their unit of aggregation. Now, we are trying to calculate the cost-benefit ratio *for the individual driver.*

Costs and Benefits for the Individual. We begin by assuming a 250-mile trip from New York to Washington as the example. Let us assume that our individual has no moneymaking use for the time he will save—variable #3 (economic costs other than fuel) is set to zero. Let us assume that the driver who observes the 55-mph limit gets 25 miles per gallon, that gasoline costs $1.00 per gallon ($10.00 for the trip), and that the driver who drives at 70 mph pays a penalty of 10 percent in gas mileage, getting 22.5 miles per gallon. Variable #2 is thus set to $1.11.

Now for the safety variable. In 1983, drivers or their passengers incurred 19,613 fatalities in the course of 819 billion vehicle miles on highways posted with a 55-mph limit.[6] Or in other words, there were .000006 fatalities per trip of 250 vehicle miles (approximately the distance from New York to Washington).* If we assume that, without the 55-mph law, 7,466 more lives would have been lost that year on those highways, then there would have been .000008 fatalities per trip of 250 vehicle miles.

Both figures represent an exceedingly small risk, and I could use them in the analysis that follows without changing the results. But in fact they represent an inaccurate starting point, and in the imprecision lies a highly salient point about measuring the safety effect of a speed limit, a point so tightly packed with implications that it provides an excellent test case for deciding what you think about many issues. Here it is for the 55-mph speed limit.

For any driver, the safety value of a 55-mph speed limit lies in what it adds to the level of safety that he could unilaterally achieve for himself by choosing to drive at 55 miles per hour.

---

* The odds are based on the probability of surviving all 250 miles. The algorithm is $(1-p)^k$, where p is the probability of a fatality in one mile and k is the number of miles.

Do you agree or not? Technically, the statement is (I think) indisputable. If you choose to drive at 55 mph you immediately obtain for yourself all the safety advantages associated with your own control of your car. You can stop more quickly, the car is easier to maneuver, you have more time to react, and so on. The only thing that a (strictly enforced) law requiring *others* to go no more than 55 mph does for you is reduce the likelihood that because of *their* mistakes at higher speeds they will ram into you or otherwise cause you to have an accident.

If you do not agree, I think it has to be because of one of two other rationales.* The first possibility is that you want to save the lives of others even if your own is not at risk—the value of the 55-mph speed limit is *not* just the good it does for you, but also the good it does for others. The label that many would rush to put on this motivation is altruism. But altruism has the meaning of "devotion to the welfare of others." These "others" too have the option of driving at 55 mph if they so desire, but some of them will not exercise that option. You want to force them to exercise that option for their own good—which, of course, raises the age-old question: By what right do you presume to impose your judgment of the other person's welfare over his own? The answer ultimately comes down to the presumption that those "others" are exercising poor judgment, that you know better, and it is okay for you to tell them what to do.

I believe that such reasoning is inherently dangerous. But without trying to make that case here, let me suggest simply that the quality of debate on social policy will be considerably improved if the terms are clearer. There is an important distinction between arguments on behalf of a public good, which

---

* A common rationale for supporting the 55-mph speed limit (and compulsory seat belt laws, motorcycle helmet laws, etc.) is that people who are injured in accidents cost other citizens money in the form of medical services and disability payments. This is irrelevant to the issue of safety being discussed, falling instead under "other economic costs." I have not included it in the discussion, though my general response should be obvious: If that's the logic, is it then okay for me to go without a helmet if I guarantee to pay for the ambulance and all subsequent costs?

the 55-mph speed limit is usually conceived of being, and arguments on behalf of making people do things for their own good, which is a large element of what the 55-mph speed limit actually tries to do.

The other rationale for rejecting my statement of the value of a 55-mph speed limit might be that the existence of the law makes one behave in ways that one ought to behave.[7] Such a person knows he should drive no faster than 55, but if there weren't a law he would go faster, and the government is substituting for the self-discipline he lacks. This argument is quite different from the "doing it for other people's good" rationale, which assumes that others are ignorant of their own best interest. To justify a speed limit via this reasoning, people who hold this view must in effect round up all the people who think they would benefit from the law by being saved from themselves and demonstrate that they constitute a large enough number of people to warrant getting their way. But what an extraordinarily self-absorbed message they are sending: "We favor a restrictive law that affects the lives of 250 million people, whether or not they need it, for no better reason than that we, ourselves, need the law to provide us with the discipline we lack." The customary "doing it for their own good" argument at least has the virtue of good intentions toward others. As far as I can tell, this second rationale must rest ultimately on the egoism of small children: "You have to do it because we want you to."

In any event, it remains true, and consistent with the unit of aggregation (the individual) we are employing, that if all the fatalities saved by the 55-mph speed limit would have been incurred by the occupants of vehicles that were exceeding 55 mph, there would be no added safety at all for the driver who chooses to drive at 55. The value of the 55-mph speed limit lies in its control over the behavior of other people who are endangering one's life by speeding. To calculate the added safety value of a 55-mph speed limit, the question we want to answer is: How many of the 7,466 saved-lives consist of people who could save their own lives if they choose *unilaterally* to drive at 55 mph?

A technically complete estimate of the answer to this question is unnecessary here. A rough method of calculating the estimate is shown in the endnotes, and working through it is useful for thinking about the nature of the safety value of a speed limit.[8] (But if you don't like my numbers, feel free to change any of the values of the parameters to ones that seem more reasonable to you. Within all plausible ranges, the estimates are identical for the first six decimal places.)

The results I get are: If you choose to drive at 55 mph from New York to Washington, the odds of being killed in an accident caused by someone exceeding 55 mph are 0.0000004 with the 55-mph limit and 0.0000006 without it. In other words: For any individual, the effective safety value of the 55-mph speed limit on a 250-mile trip is zero. There is no aspect of your life or your decision making that you calibrate to the seventh decimal place.*

If you doubt this—if you think the reduction in the probability of being killed by a speeding driver from 0.0000006 to 0.0000004 while driving from New York to Washington is meaningful—consider all the other things you do before getting in your car and on the road that are having (by comparison) huge effects on the odds of an accident—from such comparatively suicidal behaviors as having even a single drink or driving while sleepy to such nearly universal behaviors as daydreaming behind the wheel. It is likely (I know of no data on the subject) that having an animated conversation with another passenger while you drive has several times the effect of the 55-mph speed limit on your chances of getting in an accident. If I could prove that, would you consider requiring everyone in your car to keep silent while you drive? Or passing a law requiring silence? Every waking moment of the day, you are knowingly making choices (knowingly, in the sense that you would realize if you stopped to think about it) that increase your danger of death by many orders of magnitude larger than

* For those readers who reject my argument about "added-safety to unilaterally driving 55 mph," and who want to include *all* the fatalities in *all* kinds of accidents, the sentences should be amended to read: "There is no aspect of your life or of your decision making that you calibrate to the sixth decimal place." The basic conclusion is unaffected.

those associated with repealing the 55-mph speed limit, even though the benefits of those choices are far less concrete and important than the benefits of saving an hour of time.

To reemphasize the main point: *I am not arguing that the extra hour of time is "worth more" than the increase in safety, but that there is no balance to be struck.* The effective value of the safety variable is zero and the "noneconomic costs" variable is significantly greater than zero. For you, as an individual, there is no meaningful increase in safety at all from the 55-mph speed limit during the course of that 250-mile journey. Or to summarize our analysis, the costs are: zero in safety, $1.11 in gas. The benefits are an hour of your time spent doing something you enjoy more than driving a car.

The Terms of Debate. What if the changes in safety were to be calculated over a much longer period approximating the rest of your life—say, for example, 200,000 miles of highway driving? It is not a notably realistic way of looking at the problem (if you took 5,000 times getting into a bathtub as the frame of reference for calculating the risk of hurting yourself while taking a bath, you might never take another one), but it nonetheless offers another useful perspective for illustrating the problem of the dependent variable.

Applying the data we used for the one-trip example, 200,000 miles of highway driving under a 55-mph speed limit would reduce your chances of being killed (beyond the safety you would achieve by unilaterally driving 55 miles per hour) from 0.0005 to 0.0004. It is still an extremely small effect, and once again there is a long list of behaviors that have decisively greater influence on your safety than the 55-mph speed limit. But at least the meaning of one-in-ten-thousand can be grasped, whereas a change of two-in-ten-million cannot. Cautious people could (I suppose) argue that improving their lifetime odds by one part in ten thousand is worth it to them.

The merit of having switched the dependent variable is that so doing offers an alternative frame of reference. For public consumption, the 55-mph speed limit has been touted as a safety measure for the individual. That's why the advertising campaigns have been based on slogans like "A law you can live with." But that doesn't explain why so many legislators and editorial writers and members of the public at large supported the law so valiantly even though many of these same people were themselves disobeying the law. I suggest that such persons drew from another kind of argument: Even if you don't obey the law, it is uncivic to oppose it. You ask yourself, in effect,

> Should I support a law that saves 7,466 lives every year, even if I personally disobey it?

The way of stating the question forces the answer. You are thoughtless and selfish if you answer no. It then becomes easy and natural to answer the next question:

> Is it justified to require other citizens to join me in my support of this law?

You know that the 55-mph speed limit coerces some of your fellow citizens into doing something they do not want to do, but right is obviously on your side. They are being thoughtless and selfish, whereas you are trying to rise above that.

When we ask the question this way:

> "Do I support a law which, over the course of a lifetime, diminishes the probability that an individual will die in a car accident caused by someone else from .0005 to .0004?

you may or may not answer yes. But it becomes much harder to give a reflexive answer to the next question:

> Is it justified to require other citizens to join me in my support of this law?

It becomes too obvious to ignore that answering yes imposes your own rather idiosyncratic, extremely cautious view of life on other people "for their own good." It becomes too obvious that you have many other unilateral steps you could take (but aren't) that would accomplish the same increase in safety. Reasonable people will say that they do not want the added protection of the law. It becomes obvious why, even if a majority of people in one part of the country think one way, people in another part of the country should not have to conform.

The discussion has led in the direction of a libertarian conclusion ("the risks I choose to take are none of the state's business"), as will some of the conclusions in the chapters that follow. Without rejecting that interpretation, let me point out that it is irrelevant to the present issue. The question is not whether the state has the *right* to pass a 55-mph speed limit. The question is whether it *makes sense,* and the point of the example has been that it stops making sense when we reconsider what we are trying to accomplish.

I have deliberately chosen to assume for this example that the "social program" in question had a major, positive effect. Seven thousand four hundred and sixty-six lives is a lot of lives. And one may cling to that aggregate numbers of lives-saved to convince oneself that it's a good thing to cut the speed limit. *But it is not the appropriate measure of success in deciding what laws to pass and what laws not to pass.* It is a pernicious measure precisely because it makes it easy to evade the question, "What constitutes progress?" We can always save more lives. Cut the speed limit to 40. Ban the sale of cigarettes. Compel everyone over 50 to get an annual physical examination.

Perhaps this *real* safety goal of the 55-mph limit—promoting an environment in which a driver is not endangered by the actions of others—can be achieved by more patrol cars and stricter enforcement of laws against dangerous driving; perhaps it cannot. The ways of producing the desired environment is an empirical question, and it does not necessarily rule out speed limits as solutions. The point is simply that the objective is protection of the individual from risk from other drivers, and this way of putting the objective suggests many other more directly useful things to do than an across-the-board speed limit.

Let me try to generalize from this specific example to some larger principles about evaluating results.

Recasting the Criteria of Success

It cannot be that the criteria we commonly use to assess social programs are to be taken literally. It cannot be, for example, that the objective of a program is to save lives. It may be the *operational* measure of success, but it cannot be the *construct*, to return to the distinction I introduced at the opening of the chapter, because it has no discriminatory power. If "saving lives" is all there is to the objective that falls under the heading of "highway safety," then the measure that saves the most lives is the best measure. But that cannot be, for one can too easily think of measures that will save lives efficiently but are also totalitarian. Similar remarks apply to objectives such as "get people jobs," "clean up the environment," "give people a decent education," and "provide people a decent living." All are statements of desirable end states that in themselves give very little guidance to policy.

My first general point thus has nothing to do with the pursuit-of-happiness theme per se. Rather: *The abbreviations with which we express operational goals have over the years displaced the constructs that should be motivating them.* In conducting the evaluations of social programs, assessing the results, and deciding how these should be translated into policy, policy analysts have gotten lazy. They have stopped specifying *at any point* in the process the construct that lies behind the operational measure. I have further been proposing that this laziness has tangible results: It truncates the analysis. If analysts go to the trouble of spelling out what it is that we are really trying to accomplish with a given program, that process will of itself improve policy. In some cases it will clarify what needs to be done to make good on the real objectives; in other cases it will reveal how foolish the underlying rationale for a program has been, giving people a better chance to say "Wait a minute, that's not what we're really after."

Turning to the pursuit-of-happiness framework, my point is as simple as can be: The evaluation of policy should use the individual as the unit of aggregation. The question that evaluations must first address is, How does the impact of program X look from the point of view of the individual who is directly affected by it? I am not saying that the application of such a criterion of success will lead to any particular set of programs or laws; rather, I am saying that applying it will lead to better debate, more reasoned decisions, and ultimately lead us closer to the state of affairs that we are really trying to accomplish.

In the case of the 55-mph speed limit, the good was highway safety and the people-directly-affected consisted of all people who use the highways—the population as a whole, in effect. But the principle applies as well to the kind of goods that social programs have tried to foster for specific target populations.

Return to the case of the Job Corps that I raised earlier. You are contemplating whether you support the Job Corps, or what kind of Job Corps you might be prepared to support. I am arguing that the evaluations of the Job Corps that you will find in the archives are largely based on cost-effectiveness analyses and aggregate results that tell you very little worth knowing. Instead, suppose that you envision a youth in the inner city with a poor education, no job, living in a neighborhood with a high unemployment rate. The question is, what should he do next? Take a bus downtown and see what the job market is like there? Move to another place where the unemployment rate is lower? Go into the Job Corps? Spend an hour a day more-than-he-has-been looking for jobs? Go to night school? Hang out at the street corner? Deal drugs? Snatch purses? There are dozens of options, some he knows about, some he doesn't. We, with knowledge about the options, have as one of our responsibilities steering him in the direction that will be most beneficial to him. *In the interests of better policy for unemployed youth, it is very useful for us to know whether going into the Job Corps makes sense for that individual youth.* If it does not—if the odds that going into the Job Corps will provide him with a job he wouldn't have gotten otherwise are, say, about 1 in 25—then a much different set of questions arises about what to do next than if we have been told that "Job Corps trainees have a post-program unemployment rate of 36% compared to an unemployment rate of 40% in the control group" (which is where the 25-to-1 statement came from).[9] The downside of such programs becomes apparent (How many unmet promises does it take to produce learned helplessness?). And from a highly pragmatic, atheoretical perspective, there is this simple question: Would you really advise a youth you knew and cared about to invest his hopes and efforts and time in a Job Corps that produces such results? Or would you push him toward one of the other options open to him?

Suppose we are determined to make training programs work better. In that case, looking at the results from the point of view of the individual trainees raises an obvious and important follow-up question. For example, *How can it be* that if a youth goes into a training program for twelve months or longer and works hard, the likelihood of reward is so low? Which then in turn raises important questions about how the program is functioning, how the youth is functioning, and how the results might be improved. For example, suppose that the answer is that it doesn't make any difference how hard the youth works in the program, because the training is geared to the level of the slowest ship in the convoy. That finding suggests important changes in the way the program operates. Suppose the answer is that the trainees who do work hard in the program have a much better than 1-in-25 chance of benefiting—which might suggest changes in the way the program operates and in the way that trainees are recruited and screened.

I will not try to spin out the example further. All of these questions are diagnostic ones that should be asked of every social program that tries to change the behavior or the life chances or the life circumstances of individuals. But if you pick up a stack of evaluations of social programs and try to find the answers to such questions, you find very few, and then usually as a secondary job, divorced from the presentation of the aggregated results that have driven the policy debate.

My general statement is that the usual method of presenting aggregated results tends to obscure these useful questions and useful findings, tends instead to pose policy choices in ways that perpetuate bad programs and retard the improvement of those that can be improved. Worse yet: Relying on aggregated results has tended to encourage self-delusion among the people who want the programs to work. To begin asking of social programs how they affect the pursuit of happiness of individuals, with emphasis on "individual," is in this sense to begin to think about the welfare of others as you think about the welfare of yourself and of those you care for.

10

Asking a New Question,
Getting New Answers:
Designing Solutions

THE LAST CHAPTER was about the evaluation of policy when the pursuit of happiness is the criterion. This chapter is about the design of solutions. The theme is that the conventional paradigm for designing social programs doesn't work very well, and that using the pursuit of happiness as a backdrop for seeking solutions is more productive.

To make this point, I am going to slow the pace, using an extended example involving a single social issue (education) that stretches through this chapter and the next. I devote so much time to a single issue for an important reason.

I favor a way of approaching social problems—involving education, but also crime, racism, poverty, welfare dependence, drugs, and the rest—that is radically different from the approach that currently dominates. Such advocacy must deal with a curious asymmetry: In designing conventional social programs, the reasons why the program should work are obvious ("If people have no job skills, of course a job-training program will help") and the reasons why it won't are subtle. Approaches that assume a limited role for government are in precisely the opposite fix: The reasons why the solution *won't* work seem obvious ("There's no plan; you're just assuming people will do the right thing on their own") and the reasons why it might work are subtle. Thinking about them requires a leisurely spinning-out. And that is the purpose of this extended example: not to persuade you to support any particular reforms in education, but to provide an elaborated example of a different way of thinking about a familiar problem. It introduces motifs that I hope you will find to be broadly applicable.

For the illustration, I have tried to pick a problem in the middle range: critical, but not catastrophic; a live political issue, but not rabidly partisan; difficult, but not so difficult that no one has any ideas for solutions. I have also sought a problem that will be relevant to the personal concerns of many readers. My choice has been the general problem of deficiencies in public education—specifically, an aspect of it that has been much in the news, the need for better teachers.

THE TEACHER PROBLEM

In recent years, a considerable portion of the controversy about public education has centered on teachers. There has been anger and unhappiness on both sides. We read in the newspapers that not only do teachers feel they are underpaid, the best ones are voting with their feet and leaving the profession. We also read (and sometimes observe in our own children's classrooms) that too many teachers joining the profession aren't very good. Sometimes they don't know the subject matter. Sometimes they don't know how to deal with children. Sometimes they are unmotivated. Sometimes they just aren't smart enough.

Social scientists have tools for determining whether such public perceptions are well-founded and have discovered that, indeed, the public is right. Overall, teachers are drawn not just from the average college graduates, which would itself be cause for concern, but from the below average. To take just one indicator (the evidence is extensive, but proving the existence of the problem is not our purpose here), the high-school senior who is planning an education major in college has an SAT-Verbal score that puts him at the 39th percentile of college-bound seniors.[1] Then it gets worse: Among college graduates who took the Graduate Record Examination (GRE) intending to major in education during graduate school—in other words, those who will be running the school systems of the future—the GRE-Verbal score put them in the bottom third of new graduate students.[2] There are other indicators as well. The turnover statistics reveal that large numbers of well-qualified teachers are leaving the profession. Opinion surveys show widespread teacher dissatisfaction with their profession. A documentable problem exists.

So we have the kind of problem that requires a good, hard-headed policy analysis. How are we to put fine teachers into the nation's classrooms?

A CONVENTIONAL APPROACH

In 1985, the Carnegie Corporation, an entity with a long and distinguished history of involvement in American education, established a task force headed by a panel of distinguished educators to design solutions for the teacher problem. In May of 1986, the task force released its report, entitled *A Nation Prepared: Teachers for the 21st Century*.[3] I use it as the paradigmatic example of contemporary policy analysis not because it is bad, but because it is good—knowledgeable, thoughtful, and in many respects courageous.

The task force's central thesis was that the teaching job as it now stands is not designed to appeal to first-rate people. It does not give them the working conditions, money, or status that they can get elsewhere. The solution it proposed is to convert the teaching occupation into a profession: "In a nutshell," the task force reported, "recruiting the most able college graduates to teaching will require the schools to offer pay and conditions of work that are competitive with those to be found in other places where professional work is done. That means fundamental change in both the schools and the profession of teaching."[4] The Carnegie Corporation's own contribution to this goal was to be a National Board for Professional Teaching Standards, which would certify teachers in much the same way that physicians' organizations certify practitioners of medical specialties. More broadly, the task force urged three steps:

much better pay to make teaching competitive with other professions, reforms that would give teachers the same job supports and autonomy that professionals in other fields enjoy, and better certification standards.[5]

Suppose that we as policy analysts are considering whether these measures should be adopted. How are we to decide?

THE LOGIC BEHIND THE PLAN

The first question, put bluntly, is whether we have a reason for thinking that the idea will work even if everything goes according to plan. It may seem like a simple thing ("Of course we're going to get better teachers if we pay them more money"), but we might as well spell out the logic. In this case, it is straightforward. For convenience, I summarize the expected chain of events (sometimes called a "program rationale") in figure 7.

The rationale depicted below is only an overview of the program's logic. A full-scale rationale would be more sophisticated, incorporating more variables expressed in greater specificity than shown above. Furthermore, I assume away many problems, taking as given that the components of the plan that I do not show in the program rationale have been put in place. Even in this simplified form, however, the logic is not unreasonable. It makes sense that higher pay, more professionalization of the working environment, and certification will help attract and keep better teachers.

A JADED EVALUATOR'S PREDICTIONS
ABOUT WHY IT WON'T WORK

But it won't work. It may seem to make good sense. The pieces of the program each seem doable. But even if Congress were to pass a national program mandating the implementation of the plan, the safest prediction is that a few years later the teachers will be no better and may actually be worse.

The failure will not be immediately apparent. In the first months, promising evidence of progress will be reported on the evening news. The program will probably survive, and its funding may even increase, as budgets for unsuccessful programs have been wont to do. But the evaluators will find that

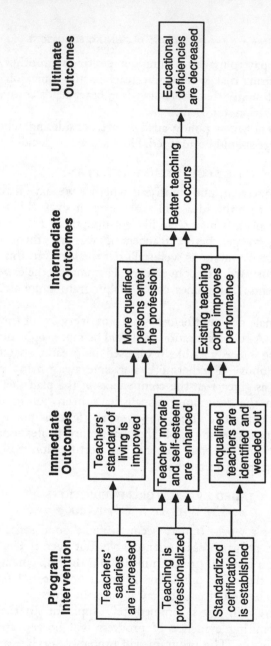

FIGURE 7
A SIMPLIFIED PROGRAM RATIONALE
FOR GETTING BETTER TEACHERS

the apparent successes were misrepresented or short-lived and that the overall quality of teachers has not changed. Worse, as time goes on it will be found that a number of undesirable unintended outcomes have occurred. Sometimes these will be outcomes that adversely affect the thing-to-be-improved (education, in this case); sometimes these will be outcomes that have inadvertently spilled over into another area, in the way that deinstitutionalization of the mentally ill contributed to the problem of homelessness.

Something—several "somethings," in reality—will have prevented the program from accomplishing its goals. The evaluators will identify what the somethings were, and recommend different ways of doing things. But if the recommendations are adopted and the revised program is implemented, it will be found that a new set of "somethings" has popped up that will continue to prevent the program from operating as planned.

The gloominess in these remarks reflects in part the fact that a former evaluator of social programs is writing them. Long exposure to evaluations of large social programs tends to do that. Sociologist Peter Rossi, who led the early evaluation efforts for the War on Poverty and since then has remained a leading scholar and practitioner of program evaluation, has expressed his frustration in what he calls Rossi's Iron Law of Evaluation:

> The expected value of any net impact assessment of any large scale social program is zero,

and the Stainless Steel Law,

> The better designed the impact assessment of a social program, the more likely is the resulting estimate of net impact to be zero.[6]

Taking the evaluation literature as a whole, Rossi's laws seem no more than a statement of fact. Small-scale demonstration programs sometimes succeed, especially if the program has been implemented by its designer. But large-scale programs do not. Or, as Rossi writes:

> It is possible to formulate a number of additional laws of evaluation. . . . [T]hey would all carry the same message:

The laws would claim that a review of the history of the last two decades of efforts to evaluate major social programs in the United States sustains the proposition that over this period the American establishment of policy makers, agency officials, professionals and social scientists did not know how to design and implement social programs that were minimally effective, let alone spectacularly so.[7]

Rossi remains committed to the attempt to do better. Milton Friedman suggests that the attempt is futile. He has a label for the "somethings" that always seem to prevent success: The Invisible Foot, a twist on Adam Smith's "invisible hand" that guides social progress in a laissez-faire economy. It is an especially apt play on words, for the reasons why new "somethings" are guaranteed to pop up are the mirror image of the ways in which Adam Smith described the workings of the invisible hand. A large-scale intervention requires hundreds or thousands of people representing many different agencies—factions, in Publius's terms—and as many different personal agendas as there are individuals in the program. Human transactions in pursuit of these factional and individual ends bring about aggregate results in infinitely complex ways. This is true even of the transactions in which people are consciously trying to help the program work—the things that social programs seek to accomplish are often exceedingly difficult under the best of circumstances. But more importantly, *any social program, no matter how innocuous, requires some actors (whether administrators or clients or bystanders) to do things they would not do on their own, or things they do not particularly want to do, or things that they consciously wish to avoid doing.* No social program, no matter how ingenious, can anticipate and forestall the myriad ways in which people will seek to get their way and thereby frustrate, with or without intent, its aims.

To this extent, I am making a generic prediction. If the program rationale were about building a bridge, and the boxes referred to such things as peak loads per square inch, then one might look for quite specific (and then avoidable) flaws in the steps. When the boxes refer to such things as the weeding out of incompetent teachers, I am in effect saying that we don't even need to look for the particulars. Somehow, the Invisible

Foot will step on this shiny new toy too. But it is useful none-theless to identify a few of the specific ways in which this reasonable strategy for improving the quality of teachers is likely to disappoint us.

STANDARDIZED CERTIFICATION AND

GREATER AUTONOMY

Many professions successfully certify their members. Physicians do it. Lawyers do it. Why not teachers?*

First of all, one must consider the built-in tension that plagues any sort of certification test: The more credible it is, the more often it mistakenly rejects qualified people. This is an inevitable characteristic of testing. A test that may rightly be called "valid and reliable" by the psychometricians has a high degree of accuracy for scores at the top and the bottom. People who score near the top are almost 100 percent certain to be competent; people who score near the bottom are almost 100 percent certain to be incompetent. In between, however, is a gray range in which a person may or may not be competent, depending on qualities that the test does not measure. This holds true for any certification test, even the best ones. One has only a choice between evils: to err on the soft side (passing people who really are incompetent) or the hard side, (refusing to certify many people who would be marginally competent). Toward which direction may one predict that the certification process for teachers will err?

Ordinarily, we can be confident it will err on the side of

---

* The text does not return to the question of why bar exams (which are administered by the state) seem generally to be tough and selective, and why teachers' certification couldn't be so as well. The short answer is that lawyers have no lever on the state to make the exams easier, and those who are already lawyers have an interest in not making it any easier for new competition to join the profession. Imagine the different situation that would prevail with bar exams if all lawyers were paid by the state, were unionized, and the bar exam were being installed for the first time (or it was proposed that the existing bar exam be made tougher), and if lawyers already working on the state payroll would have to pass this exam as well. In such a case, the prospects for the bar exam would be the same as the prospects for demanding teacher certification.

weakness. If it is true that large numbers of teachers are incompetent, the last thing that large numbers of teachers will want is a tough certification test. This seems certain. Now, what happens when we map this fact onto the prevailing environment in which the reforms are to be implemented? For example, what may we expect to happen in environments where there is a strong teachers' organization, as exists in most urban school districts? Because the raison d'être of a teachers' union is to protect the interests of its members, the people who are already teachers, one quite reasonably comes up with the hypothesized sequences of outcomes as shown in figure 8.

The chain of events is not only logical; everything we know about the behavior of teachers' unions leads us to believe that something very like this sequence will actually happen. We have numerous examples from the recent attempts (by Texas, most prominently) to administer tests for minimum qualifications of its teachers: The tests are resisted fiercely, and are finally so watered down that anyone who is barely literate can pass them. In Texas, the teacher test was not only made extremely simple, teachers who failed it the first time were given a chance to take it again.

In Virginia, the Fairfax County school system provides pertinent evidence from its experience with an attempt to install merit pay for teachers. A rating system was established, and the high-rated teachers were supposed to get bonuses. But after the first year, the county's teachers' union announced that major changes were needed. All classroom observations of teachers would have to be followed by a conference between observer and teacher, for example. The teachers who got just a middle rating on the five-step scale ought to be allowed to apply for bonuses as well as those who got the top two ratings. Formal adoption of the plan should be delayed, the head of the teachers' union said, because the union's poll of teachers showed that most were now unsure that the new plan is an improvement over current practice. And one other thing: The union would shortly file suit in federal court to block efforts to deny pay raises to teachers who received low ratings.[8]

Suppose that we anticipate such natural reactions by teachers and think about ways in which we can protect the integrity of

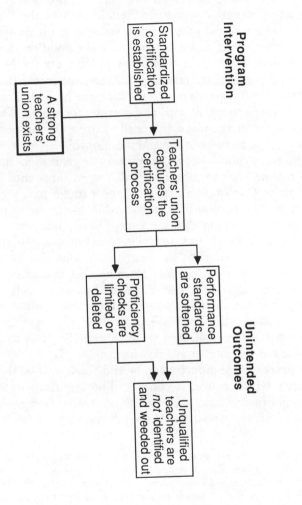

FIGURE 8
AN INVISIBLE FOOT AND ITS LIKELY CONSEQUENCES

the certification process. Is there any way to do so? The Carnegie Corporation, which proposes to develop its own certification process, presents an attractive solution. Carnegie will have no power to force local school boards to accept its certification. The only reason that local school boards will tend to hire Carnegie-certified teachers is because the local school boards have found that it *means* something for an applicant to be Carnegie-certified. Carnegie, to make good on this expectation, *must make the certification process err in the direction of rejecting qualified teachers*—for the same reason that a manufacturer that depends on a reputation for high-quality products must install stringent quality control procedures. The exigencies of the marketplace will tend to drive the Carnegie certification process to be tough and meaningful.

So far, so good. But those teachers' organizations are still out there, and their members are still just as threatened. So if the Carnegie Corporation does produce a tough test, we must expect fierce criticism of it from within the teaching profession. And since teaching ability is exceptionally difficult to measure, and since a tough test *does* falsely reject competent teachers, we may be confident that the critics will be able to make their case that the test is invalid (meaning that it is often in error). It is impossible—not just difficult, but impossible—to create tough teacher certification procedures that are not vulnerable to plausible challenge.* What will the Carnegie Corporation do when those challenges are mounted? Stick to its guns? Or revise the "passing" grade downward?

It makes little difference. The end result will be the same no matter which course it chooses. The argument over the test will not be the good guys (tough on standards) against the bad guys (soft on standards). Many prominent professors of educa-

---

* In the text, I am assuming intellectual neutrality toward the idea of certification. The less optimistic reality as of 1988, however, is that the Carnegie Corporation is trying to create the certification standards in the midst of continuing hostility toward measures of skills based on test scores. Such objective measures inherently *must* be an important part of a tough certification process. One must anticipate not only authentic questions of validity and reliability, but reflexive opposition based on ideological differences.

tion and other experts will be criticizing the test on valid technical grounds and with heartfelt conviction that the certification tests should not be used.*

Either the certification will be made less demanding until it makes very few false rejections of the qualified (in which case it will be certifying large numbers of the unqualified), or it will be so clouded by the controversy that (a) many school boards will believe it is improper to use it, or (b) the local teachers' organization will be able to make the case that the test is invalid. The only public schools that will want to use a tough certification in assessing its teachers will be ones that don't need it, school districts which are already blessed with good (and confident) teachers.

To this point we have merely identified reasons why the certification reform is unlikely to work. Now, let us incorporate with this line of thinking a second reform recommended by the task force, that the teacher's job be made more like that of other professionals. We assume that the support aspects have been installed (better materials, etc.), and focus on a key aspect of professionalism stressed by the task force: autonomy, or the freedom to do the job according to one's professional judgment.

To increase teacher autonomy (which can be a very good thing when the teachers are competent) means, by definition, that the principal has less control over a teacher. The difficulty with this outcome is that the principal of the school is known to be one of the most powerful forces in improving a school. This finding has been confirmed and reconfirmed in a wide

---

* In the rare instances when a test criterion actually *has* been met and there are no credible technical challenges, the hostility to tests can still mean the downfall of standards. The most notable recent example is the attempt by the city of New York to develop a police sergeant's exam that was free of racial bias. The city was successful in that no one has been able to advance a plausible explanation of how the test items retain a racial or cultural bias. But the test *results* have nonetheless been downgraded in promotion decisions simply because they continued to show large racial differentials. Such experiences do not augur well for the Carnegie Corporation, especially since the effects of certification on minority teachers will be so highly sensitive (as the task force's own report notes).

variety of circumstances and seems to apply even in the worst situations. Install the right principal in a bad school, and the school can be turned around.[9] These same studies also reveal, however, that the principal achieves these good results by setting standards and, by fair means or foul (the best principals also often break rules), getting teachers to go along with his way of doing things. But if we are right about the prospects for the certification process, and if both the certification process and the autonomy reforms are implemented, and *if the autonomy reforms are implemented as planned and successfully enforced*, what follows is shown in figure 9.

Nothing remarkable has been imposed on the original logic of the program—no exotic hypotheses, no unforeseeable circumstances—but what was originally a plausible and laudable plan now looks somewhat different. Given the most ordinary considerations about how human beings behave and calling upon some of Publius's observations about the workings of faction, a credible conclusion is that a certification plan in tandem with greater teacher autonomy will make matters worse.

In reality, this is probably too pessimistic. For things actually to get worse, the plans for greater teacher autonomy must work, and as many things can go awry with that element of the intervention as with the certification process. The more likely outcome is that neither the "greater autonomy" *nor* the "standardized certification" elements will work, and nothing will change.

WHY RAISING TEACHERS' PAY WILL BARELY MAKE A DIFFERENCE AND CONCEIVABLY WILL MAKE MATTERS WORSE

Now we come to the reform that surely will make a difference, raising teachers' salaries. The logic seems irresistible: We need talented people to be teachers; these talented people can make more money at other professions; let's raise salaries so that talented people don't have to make as much of a sacrifice. Table 3 shows the average salaries in the Carnegie Forum report.

Teachers are clearly lagging behind the other professions, behind mail carriers and barely ahead of plumbers. Furthermore, raising salaries "enough" to have an effect seems financially

215

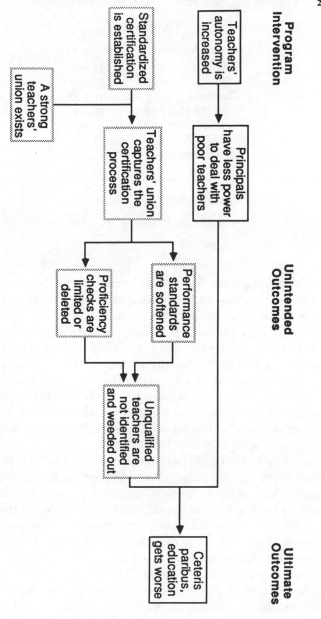

FIGURE 9
THE SYNERGY OF UNINTENDED CONSEQUENCES

TABLE 3

AVERAGE ANNUAL SALARIES IN 1985

Lawyers	$51,400
Engineers	39,500
Chemists	39,200
Systems analysts	36,500
Accountants	31,300
Buyers	26,900
Mail carriers	24,232
Teachers	*23,500*
Plumbers	22,412
Secretaries	19,534

SOURCE: Data from *A Nation Prepared: Teachers for the 21st Century*, 37.

feasible at first glance. In 1980, for example, the distribution of salaries for engineers and for elementary and secondary school teachers looked like figure 10.

All one has to do, it seems, is slide the distribution for teachers over to the right a bit, and the overlap will be so great that teachers' pay will be "competitive enough" to lure some people into teaching instead of into engineering. It would seem that the primary problem is not a design issue at all but the political difficulty of obtaining these obviously useful raises in the face of voter opposition. But let us go more slowly, and ask how much good raising salaries might do.

First, I should concede two obvious points. One is that raises always work, in the sense that a change in salary means a change in one of the important incentives governing behavior. If salaries for teachers are raised faster than salaries in the general economy, one should expect (for example) that applications to schools of education will increase and that the SAT difference between the average college-bound senior and the one planning a career in education will diminish. This will be a *valid* indicator that more talented people are being attracted to the teaching profession, but it will not necessarily be a *meaningful* indicator: What we want in our classrooms are fine teachers, not teachers who are a little less unsatisfactory than they used to be. Suppose,

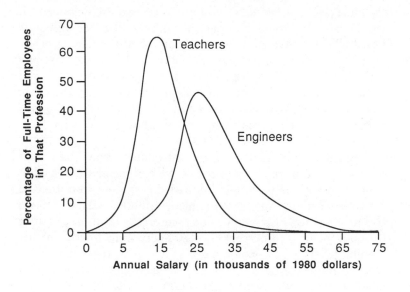

FIGURE 10
MAKING TEACHERS' SALARIES COMPETITIVE

SOURCE: Bureau of the Census, *Money Income of Households, Families, and Persons in the United States: 1980* (Washington, D.C.: Government Printing Office), table 55.

for example, that the SAT math score of prospective teachers shot up by some fifty points and thereby equaled the national average. That would still leave the mean score at only 475 (1985 data). Four hundred and seventy-five is still a pathetic score, considering the questions on the SAT-Math test. One suspects that most readers of this book would be upset to find that their children were being taught math by a person with that level of aptitude. To say that raising teachers' salaries "works" has to mean something more than a statistically significant change.

The second obvious point is that, at the limit, raises will work in a meaningful sense as well. Pay teachers $100,000, and there will be no shortage of first-rate people entering the profession. The key question is, who will be attracted by the level of raise that is within the realm of possibility? If, for example, we were to make the salary structure of elementary and secondary-school teachers equivalent to that of engineers, it would cost in round numbers something like $60 billion a year.[10] That's obviously too ambitious. But even to raise the salary to the level of accountants (one of the lowest paid and least prestigious of the professions) would cost on the order of $25 billion. A still more modest program to raise the mean teacher's salary to $30,000 would cost $14 billion (using the 1985 numbers from the Carnegie report).[11] These are all very large numbers in an era of tight budgets.

Faced with this reality, we are not talking about the effects of raising salaries to be competitive with other professions, but about raises of a few thousand dollars. Let me use an optimistic scenario which assumes that the median teacher salary is raised to $30,000 (the $14 billion option)—meaning, let us also assume for convenience, 28 percent increases across the board, for beginning teachers and senior ones. Whom will this increase attract to the teaching profession? The answer is that *a modest salary increase will attract the marginal teacher, the second-rater, the very person we want to get rid of.*

To see why this is the case, consider first that the big economic difference between a teaching career and other professions is not so much the initial salary or the average salary as it is the cap on maximum salary. The mean salary of someone who goes to work for a corporation as a trainee may be only a few thousand dollars higher than that of the beginning teacher, and it may be possible to match that initial salary. But the corporation's division managers make six figures, and those who reach the top echelons become multimillionaires. Lawyers, physicians, dentists, engineers, and businessmen all have salary trajectories that keep on increasing.

Now, consider the prospects facing the kind of youth we want to attract to teaching—one who is bright, energetic, good with people. When he considers whether to become a teacher or a lawyer, he is not focusing on what he will make the first year. He is thinking of his aspirations, and how likely these aspirations are to be fulfilled. The more confident and able that young person is, the more likely that those aspirations will be high. But even after taking the raise into account, the best that the young teacher can hope for is $40,000 or $45,000 (optimistically) in current dollars, to be achieved after years of accumulating seniority. The change in initial salary doesn't do much to change that fundamental contrast.

We turn to a second youth, not so able. He was a mediocre student in high school and barely got into college. He is not a risk-taker, not especially ambitious. What is he going to do with his life? He is not going to become an engineer or a physician or a lawyer—he doesn't have the intellectual tools. If he drops out of school, he will end up in a skilled blue-collar job that might eventually pay $25,000. If he stays in school he will probably get into a white-collar job paying somewhat more, but not a lot. Or he can be a teacher.

For him, a preraise median salary of $23,500, plus fringes, job security, and a good pension is already attractive. For him, the status of a teacher is not low but high, compared to the blue-collar or low-level white-collar job he might otherwise expect to hold. Raise that median to $30,000, with a starting salary of about $17,000, and the teacher's job becomes not just an attractive option but alluring, dominating the other options. And it is a possible dream. He can pass the courses in teachers' college. He can acquire the credentials. And once he gets his foot in the door, all he has to do is hold on for the first few years until he has seniority, then not do anything to rock the boat for the rest of his career. To summarize: A substantial but not gigantic salary increase creates an asymmetrical incentive. The increase in pay will make it only slightly less sacrificial for the talented to be teachers, but much more attractive for the second-rate to become teachers.

Let us shift focus now from the prospective teachers to the ones who are already in the system. Imagine that the salary increase (28 percent, to a median of $30,000) is being debated in the legislature. The teachers who are already on the payroll are going to be digging in like the French on the Marne. It must be remembered that the salary increase is not intended to reward underpaid teachers, but to get better teachers into the classroom, and the reason it is necessary is because so many teachers in the existing corps of teachers are incompetent. But

they will still be in place on the day after the pay increase, and
while they may not be terrific teachers, they are smart enough
to recognize that the pay increases are highly threatening. Pay
increases will be accompanied by intensification of teachers'
union activities designed to protect their position against what
they will perceive to be the threat of talented youngsters coming in to replace them. This means struggles against attempts
to identify and reward excellence (which inevitably means
identifying and penalizing incompetence—remember the example from Fairfax County). These teachers will be lobbying for
alternative ways of identifying "good" teachers, through by-
the-numbers "qualifications" for pay increases such as summer
school credits that they can meet (without becoming good
teachers).

In response to these maneuvers, the school system will find
it very hard to push through meaningful reforms by offering a
quid pro quo (such as, "If you will accept a stiff certification
and job-performance system, we will give you a big pay hike").
The mediocre teachers prefer the job they have to a better-
paying job that they will be fired from.

I could continue to play out other unintended outcomes. For
example, the harder the second-raters work at protecting their
position, the less attractive the work environment will become
for people who are the best teachers. But I will not try to push
the scenario any further. Let me conclude with the minimal observation that salary increases are risky. If salaries are increased
without any other changes in doing business, the wrong people
are likely to end up more firmly in control. And the experience
of recent years offers far more failures than successes in getting
school systems to change their ways of doing business, for the
persuasive, faction-based reasons we have discussed.

Salary increases have been so popular recently, and so widely
assumed to be necessary to getting good teachers, that perhaps
it is necessary to address the obvious question. All this theoriz-
ing aside, am I really serious in thinking that we could raise
teachers' salaries substantially and still not get better teachers?
Of course we can. *We've raised teachers' salaries for years without getting better teachers.* Figure 11 shows the history (in
constant dollars) from 1930 to 1986.

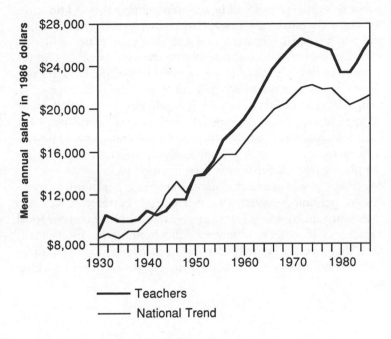

FIGURE 11
REGARDING THE ASSUMPTION THAT
RAISING TEACHERS' SALARIES HELPS . . .

SOURCE: National Center for Education Statistics, *Digest of Education Statistics 1987* (Washington, D.C.: Government Printing Office, 1987), table 53, p. 63. National trend data refer to average annual earnings of full-time employees in all industries.

The graphic gives one pause. The only extended period in which teachers' real incomes rose faster than wages elsewhere in the economy—just a bit more than 28 percent overall, coincidentally—was from 1961 to 1972, a period coinciding with what is generally accepted as a precipitous deterioration in American education. This does not prove that raising teachers' wages makes things worse, but it is very difficult to see in these data an argument that they help.

But this time, things will be different—won't they? This time, we will coordinate the changes—put in place the certification and the professionalization and the salary increases and deal with the teachers' unions and get parents more involved and try innovative new ideas. . . . Never mind *how* these miracles will be performed; never mind that for every pitfall I have mentioned are dozens that have been ignored; never mind that every attempt to circumvent the pitfalls will open up new ways for ingenious interested parties to protect their interests. The history of social engineering is endlessly optimistic that this time the plan will work the way it was supposed to.

Perhaps it will work this time. But if my pessimism is overdrawn, perhaps we can agree that getting better teachers into the classroom by using the plan generated by the conventional paradigm will at the least be very difficult, not to mention expensive. If we really want better teachers, it can do no harm to look for another way of perceiving the problem and seeking solutions.

Good Teachers and the Pursuit of Happiness

The problem remains the same: Teachers are unhappy with their jobs, parents are unhappy with the teachers. But we back away from the conventional policy paradigm, step outside the framework of the education problem, and ask the pursuit-of-happiness question: How does this problem bear on the way that people find long-term, justified satisfaction with their lives?

TEMPLATES INSTEAD OF MAPS

If the analogue of the conventional paradigm is a map, the analogue of the pursuit of happiness alternative is a template. The issues involved in the pursuit of happiness do not constitute a variable to be put in one of the boxes in the rationale, but rather a template against which the policy in question is placed, so that we may examine the "shape," if you will, of the discrepancies between the existing situation and the one in which people are fully enabled to pursue happiness.

The most convenient place to begin is with the people who are most intimately involved in reaching a solution—teachers—and to ask how any solution will impinge on their pursuit of happiness. I will review the situation in terms of the enabling conditions:

Material resources are not directly involved. Low as the teachers' pay may be relative to what others make in American society, the average salary in the average city enables teachers to live at a level that is palatial by any standard of material well-being other than that which prevails in the Western democracies.

To say this in the context of the 1980s seems naive nonsense, of course. The reality is that teachers *want* more money, and want it so badly they are leaving the profession to get it. Another reality is that Americans nowadays, from richest to poorest, seem to use money as a primary measuring stick for assessing one's status. But bear with me for the moment. As always when considering material resources, it is useful to begin with the unadorned question. Granted that low pay creates dissatisfactions because of invidious comparisons, acquisitiveness, and the like, nonetheless: Does the average teacher live at a standard of living such that his ability to pursue happiness is not constrained by sheer physical deprivation? The answer is yes.

Safety is involved for many teachers in urban schools. Some are in physical danger. A much larger number must work in the midst of the kind of incivility that creates fear and apprehension in the school. One clear-cut step in the right direction is to provide the teacher with both the appearance and the reality of safety. But to point out that teachers are not safe raises for the first time what will be a continuing theme in this discussion: How strange that this should be a problem. It is not "natural" that teachers should be in physical danger from their students. On the contrary, for them to be in danger from their students is an historical aberration and extremely odd.

Esteem and self-respect constitute an issue, especially the esteem of others, which teachers feel is lacking. This is odd, too. Why is it that the community does not feel gratitude and a full measure of respect for someone who has taught its children? In historical terms, this is another aberration. The teacher in a younger America had a secure place in the community's status hierarchy. It is also an aberration cross-nationally. In most countries, teaching is a high-status occupation. In Third World countries, it is typically near the top.

Intrinsic rewards are at the very center of the discussion, for this is the oddest thing of all about the teacher problem: Many teachers are not enjoying teaching. And yet the instruction of children yields some of the most vivid, enduring satisfactions of any job in society's offer. Not everyone thinks so; it is in the nature of intrinsic rewards that one person's reward is another person's hard labor. But the world has never lacked for people who take great satisfaction from teaching, for much the same reason that the world has never lacked for people who enjoy raising children.

Thus an initial look at the teaching problem from the point of view of the teachers' pursuit of happiness yields this conclusion: *It's damned odd.* Odd that so many teachers are intimidated or endangered by their students, odd that so many aren't given much respect, odd that so many don't take pleasure in their work.

Since we began by asking the obvious and simple question, let us continue on the line of least resistance and consider this most obvious and simple implication: If it is odd that these problems exist, if it is "unnatural" that human beings behave in such ways, and if we have assumed that human nature is essentially unchanging, shouldn't it also be true that human beings (including human beings who live in a late-twentieth-century affluent society) left to themselves would not behave in ways that create these problems? In other words, I am drawing from this line of reasoning a hypothesis that *the task in solving the teacher problem is not to engineer solutions but to strip away impediments to behaviors that would normally occur.* It's time for another thought experiment.

A HUNDRED PARENTS HIRE TEACHERS

We imagine a group of a hundred parents who for some reason find themselves without a school for their children and no way to get one except to set one up for themselves.* The public school system has disappeared—never mind why or how.

The hundred parents are contemporaries from this society. To simplify this version, we will assume they are neither very rich nor very poor but somewhere in between. Also for purposes of simplification, I will be discussing them as if they live in an isolated town with other people who are not parents. We will later consider the dynamics when these simplifying assumptions are discarded.

Will They Set Up a School at All? In a free country, they will. They always have. Whether they were the earliest English colonials, illiterate European peasants, or freed slaves, American parents have set up schools always and everywhere that they were left free to do so. Alexis de Tocqueville, writing of America before the public school movement began, marveled at the state of American education. People who had not mastered the basics of knowledge were rare, he found, and a man completely without education was "quite an oddity" in the settled areas of New England and only a little less so in the most remote frontier. "I know of no other people who have founded so many schools or such efficient ones,"[13] he wrote.

Without digressing into a historical treatise, I must stress the precondition that the society be free. People do not as naturally set up schools in other environments. As late as the 1830s, when Tocqueville wrote, education among the common people of European societies was exceptional. Even within the United States, the relationship between the expectation of individual liberty and the universality of schools was striking: By

---

* The number one hundred is chosen mostly for convenience, but it also happens that the colony of Massachusetts Bay, in 1647—only twenty-seven years after the Pilgrims landed at Plymouth—required that "where any town shall increase to the number of one hundred families or householders, they shall set up a grammar school, the master thereof being able to instruct youth, so far as they may be fitted for the University; and if any town neglect the performance hereof above one year, then every such town shall pay five pounds per annum to the next such school, till they shall perform this order."[12]

1800, New England had for practical purposes a system of universal free schools, while the South, retaining slavery and a more feudal social and economic system in other ways, had only scattered schools well into the period of the common school movement.[14]

The relationship between the degree of Lockean freedom and the impulse of parents to set up schools is not a matter of chance, then or now. It relies on the primitive motivation of parents that their children do well, conjoined with the factual reality that, in a free society, education means more opportunity for their children to do well. I make this obvious point because it is so overlooked as a force that might be used to design educational policy. In a society where more education means more opportunity, parents of all classes left to their own devices have done whatever was necessary to educate their children. If our hundred parents live in a free society, they will without doubt set up some sort of school.

Who Will Be the Teachers? Some from among the hundred parents or from among the other people in the community must be persuaded to act as teachers. Will anyone be willing?

We return to the observation that the instruction of children is one of the most intrinsically rewarding occupations that society has to offer. Large numbers of talented people quite reasonably find teaching children to be highly rewarding. If any substantial number of people seek independently for ways to spend their working lives that will give them satisfaction, some of them will leap at the opportunity to teach school. This has not changed (I submit) in the late twentieth century. At least, it seems difficult to make the alternative case that modern society has created an array of new, more intrinsically rewarding occupations than teaching. More often, occupations that were once intrinsically rewarding have been stripped by technology of much of their content (being the pilot of a 747 is much safer and physically less taxing than being the pilot of a DC-3, but not as much fun). Teaching remains one of the relatively few occupations that can have the same rich rewards (for people who are drawn to it) that it has always possessed.

The Natural Constraint on Salaries. A school will be set up and people will want to be teachers. At this point, however, a reality intrudes, shaping the tacit contract that is drawn between parents and teacher: *Both teachers and parents want the classroom to be small.* If it is large, both the students and the teacher will suffer—the students because they get too little individual attention, the teachers because teaching is no longer as enjoyable. Everyone's preference will be for a relatively low teacher/pupil ratio. If it is in the neighborhood of one teacher to 25 students, the parents will need four teachers for every 100 school-age children. That being the case, however, the salary for teachers is going to be fairly low—except in a very wealthy community, one hundred parents cannot meet their families' other needs, pay their taxes (i.e., hire the other people, such as policemen, who are necessary), and still come up with large salaries for that many teachers.

What if a person says "Double the salary, and I'll take a classroom of fifty instead"? That's no good either: Any person who would prefer the extra money in exchange for that kind of sacrifice in the enjoyment of teaching has exposed himself as someone who doesn't care much about teaching, and is not the kind of person that the parents want to teach school.

How Are the Prospective Teachers to Be Enticed? Obviously, since the monetary rewards are limited, the nonmonetary rewards must be sweetened. There are three ways to do so.

The first has to do with respect. Our hundred parents trying to set up a school are not in the position of conferring riches on a grateful applicant (unless that applicant is too incompetent to make as much money in any other occupation). Instead, they are trying to lure able people to come forward to teach their children despite the monetary sacrifice. In other words, the teacher is doing the parents a favor—providing the parents with something they deeply value (an education for their children) despite other more lucrative options. Under those conditions, respect from the parents is as natural as their respect for the physician who cures their ailments.

Respect for the teacher from the children follows as naturally. The parents see to that, for the teacher holds a terrible threat over the parents: quitting. If young Tommy is making life miserable for the teacher, the teacher can either do whatever is necessary to bring Tommy into line or, if that fails, tell Tommy's parents to keep him at home. To whom are Tommy's parents to complain? To the other parents? The other parents are going to care far more about their own child's education than Tommy's, and their message to the parent is likely to be, If you want Tommy to stay in school, get him to behave. Odds are, that's exactly what Tommy's parents will do.*

The same dynamics that produce respect also produce a classroom in which the teacher is able to teach. Classrooms will be orderly. The students will do their homework (or be flunked if they don't). The teacher will have a good deal of autonomy in teaching methods (having taken the job with an understanding of the general style that the parents want). All of these good things will happen because they are things that a good teacher can make happen if left alone to do his job. The only reason they don't already happen in every school in the country is because good teachers are impeded from doing so. And the reason that a good teacher will be left alone by the hundred parents is *because* (not in spite of) the low salary. A good person working cheaply is very hard to replace, and accordingly has great bargaining power over job conditions.

If the teacher turns out to be a brute or an incompetent and many of the students are unable to get along with him, then the teacher may be replaced, but there is a built-in validity check—not because parents are making abstract judgments about good pedagogical practice, but because they are making expert judgments about what they want for their children. When enough of them think that they can get a better education for their children by getting another teacher, the teacher will come under pressure to change his ways or get out. If there is a broad difference in views among the hundred parents—if fifty are in favor of a Montessori approach and the other fifty like a traditional approach—they can split up the classes, split up the schools, or otherwise go their own ways. But the homeostatic

---

* I take up the question in chapter 11 of what happens to Tommy if his parents fail to get him to behave.

resting place in this cycle of events will be parental pressure on the students to conform to whatever norms of respect and classroom environment the teacher wants.

The same high demand for "good people who work cheaply" works to the teacher's benefit if the hundred parents turn out to be too obtuse to know what they're getting. Suppose that the hundred parents insist that their children be taught that the earth is flat. This catches the teacher by surprise (for some reason he was unaware that the parents felt this way before he took the job). But the parents do not have much of a club to hold over his head. If he decides it is an issue worth quitting over, there are plenty of other parents elsewhere waiting to hire a good teacher who wants to teach that the earth is round.

Other Enticements. For those who at a young age find they have a true vocation for teaching, this combination of incentives—a good teaching environment and respect from the community—will be enough to make up for the low salary. But people with true vocations can be hard to find, and, while the hundred parents can probably expect a few such persons to come forward, they cannot rely on finding enough to fill out the needed number of teachers. Something else has to happen to bring in the people who would like to teach, who would be good teachers, but who are not committed to teaching as a way of life. Either pressure must be brought to bear (a teacher "draft" of some sort) or some additional inducement must be offered, to ensure a sufficient supply.

In past periods of American history, the answer was often a sort of pressure: Teaching was one of the few acceptable careers for educated women, and the teacher pool was thereby artificially augmented by women with no other choice. We cannot count on that in our community of a hundred parents. On the contrary, we are assuming that the talented people we want to teach our children have all sorts of alternatives. What is the additional inducement?

The additional inducements consist of fringe benefits that are free to the community but can be extremely valuable to the teacher. Such as:

Teaching is one of the best of all "temporary" jobs. Consider (for example) the situation facing a married woman with an advanced degree who pursued a career for a period of time, left her job to raise her children, and now wants to move back into a satisfying job. One option may be to return to her previous career. But some careers are hard to resume, and there is another consideration: Her priorities and interests may well have changed since she chose her initial career path. For example, she may have enjoyed teaching her own children far more intensely than she would have expected when she was twenty and deciding on a major in college. Our hundred parents now say to her: Why not teach third grade for a few years? The pay is terrific (when you think of it as a second income), you'll love the work, you get three months off every summer, and you'll step right into the full "position" immediately—the first day on the job, you will be teaching a classroom of children.

Our hundred parents make the same point to the young man who graduated with honors in math but wants to take a few years off before he goes back for his Ph.D. Teach school while you're making up your mind, they tell him—you're young, single, don't need a lot of money, you'll enjoy the work. They make a pitch to a retired military officer with an engineering degree or years of experience in training young recruits. The shop class is taught by a master welder in his fifties who is good with kids, doesn't need the overtime pay now that his own children are out of the home, and wants to pass on his craft—or, for that matter, the master welder who was displaced when the plant shut down.

Our hundred parents have access to large numbers of people who would be willing and excellent teachers for a few years but not for life. And since the hundred parents have no teachers' union to worry about, they have no constraints on their ability to identify people who are happy with the whole package that the parents can offer. And when the parents hire the wrong person, next year they don't renew his contract.

Is the school public or private? Do the parents establish a school that all the children can attend or only those who can afford to pay? These decisions may go either way, depending on circumstances. The initial, limited point has nothing to do with mandating a national solution. Rather, it is this: The "goods" associated with the teacher's job do not have to be manufactured. No one has to design a program. They come about naturally.

THE HUNDRED PARENTS AND REAL SOLUTIONS

The hundred families example has been a limited scenario. "Limited" is not the same as "unrealistic," I hasten to add. The scenario has been highly realistic with reference to parents who care about their children's education and who have money. The dynamics I have described are very similar (for example) to those that enable private schools to obtain fine teachers at lower salaries than the public schools offer. But it is limited in that I said nothing about how the hundred families would function if half were rich and half were poor, or if the hundred families lived not in an isolated community but in the midst of a city. The scenario does not reveal what will happen to Tommy if his parents cannot make him behave. More generally, it is very unclear how the lessons to be drawn from the analysis are to be applied to the formation of real policy for a real, contemporary society.

On the other hand (and as in the case of the 55-mph example), it is not necessary to have a particular prescription in mind to reach a point at which one may design *better* solutions (even if they are not optimally "best" in my view) by using the pursuit of happiness as a template against which to examine problems. Just thinking about the ways in which the lack of good teachers is unnatural leads the topic away from salaries as a dominating issue and toward letting people enjoy being teachers. This, I suggest, is a significant improvement, just as thinking about the dependent variables for the 55-mph speed limit from the individual's point of view instead of society's is a significant improvement. Better policy will be made because the thinking that goes into the formation of policy has been enriched.

Still, more needs to be said. What about the problem cases that arise when the parents are poor, discriminated against, or ineffectual? And how, if one gets down to specifics, is an ideal case to translate into policy?

11

Searching for
Solutions That Work:
Changing the Metaphor

SINCE LARGE-SCALE social programs began, the metaphor for the process by which the government attempts to solve social problems has been engineering. The words that are used for the policy-formation process—design, evaluation, inputs, outcomes, cost-benefit—and the very notion that a discrete "program" may deal with a discrete "problem" all bespeak an engineering perspective. The logical expectations that drive the solutions lend themselves to the same kinds of schematics that engineers use for wiring diagrams, structural blueprints, and PERT charts. The metaphor has not been lost on the critics of such programs—that's where the label "social engineering" came from.

In arguing on behalf of the pursuit-of-happiness criterion for thinking about social policy, I am in effect arguing on behalf of a metaphor that describes social problems in terms more like the healer's than the engineer's. The parallel is not precise—surgery is not the kind of healing I have in mind—but it captures the notion of social policy as something to be applied to an organic system, not as a process of hammering a selection of raw material into the desired shape.

The view of society as an organic whole was nearly a universal image until the eighteenth century and has continued to be used with great effect by conservatives from Edmund Burke to Robert Nisbet.[1] Having acknowledged this, however, I must separate the discussion that follows from that tradition. Once again, I am adapting a majestic concept for some nuts-and-bolts uses. I am suggesting that if policy planners—diagnosticians?— are to be successful, they must think in terms of solutions that permit a naturally robust organism to return to health. Does the nation suffer from schools that don't teach? The task is not to figure out better teaching techniques; we've known how to teach children for millennia. The task is to figure out what is keeping us from doing what we already know how to do. Does the nation suffer from too many children being born into fatherless families? The task is not to devise a public relations campaign to discourage single teenage girls from having babies, but to neutralize whatever is impeding the age-old impulse of human beings to form families. Does the nation suffer for lack of low-income housing? The task is to understand why an economic system that pours out a profusion of cheap-but-decent shoes, food, clothes, and every other basic of life is prevented from pouring out a profusion of cheap-but-decent apartments for rent. And so on through the list of problems that customarily preoccupy planners of social policy.

In proposing a metaphor of healing, I am proposing as well two quite specific and important characteristics of solutions that work. The first is that such solutions are quite fragile, in this sense: They are not comprised of modules that can be connected or disconnected or grouped in combinations. They don't work because of gimmicks; they don't work by twiddling one bit of a mechanism without affecting anything else. Instead, they work because they tap natural and deeply embedded responses. Such solutions tend to be of a piece, and they tend to be simple.

The second characteristic (which seems at first to be paradoxical) is that the solutions if implemented as a unitary piece will themselves be robust. In sharp contrast to social engineering solutions (which tend to be disrupted by almost anything), solutions that tap dynamics which "will naturally occur if you let them" will tend to work even in the tough situations and to spin off *positive* unintended outcomes—they are serendipitous. In this chapter I take up each of these characteristics in turn, once again using the education problem for illustrative purposes.

A DELICATE BALANCE

The core of the healing metaphor is the concept of interconnectedness—of causes, of effects, and of causes with effects. A great virtue of the pursuit-of-happiness criterion in assessing social policy is that it forces these interconnections to the surface.

Part of the interconnectedness was implicit in the discussion of the enabling conditions. It is not easy to augment material rewards without affecting self-respect, not easy to induce people to enjoy intrinsic rewards unless they already see themselves as self-determining individuals. The constituent elements of the pursuit of happiness are organically linked. The interconnectedness becomes even more apparent when we consider what happens to programs. Milton Friedman's Invisible Foot (the mysterious force that inevitably makes something go wrong with social programs) is the observable consequence of our inability even to identify, let alone control, the interconnections. But in the search for better solutions, it does no good to get a better understanding of the nature of the problem if one then proceeds to try still one more ad hoc solution.

One might conclude from the analysis based on the hundred parents, for example, that more decentralization of educational decisions is desirable. One might decide therefore that some decisions about curriculum and school operation should be returned to parents and to communities, but only some (to protect against mistakes that parents will make if left *entirely* to themselves). The logic is, "Let's keep the virtues of local decision-making, but improve on them." It is not at all clear that this is possible.[2]

Let us suppose it is decided that, yes, education works much better when the parents are directly involved. But if teachers are as valuable to society as has been asserted, then as a matter of fairness they should be paid what they're worth, which is more than most communities will pay if left to their own devices. Therefore, financial support from the federal government to local school districts is required to produce equity. We will still have the benefits of decentralization, the argument goes, but also the inducement of higher salaries—the best of both worlds.

To see how even the most innocuous attempt to give nature a hand may backfire, we return to the thought experiment.

NOW WE CAN RAISE TEACHERS' SALARIES, CAN'T WE?

The school has been established and has been operating for some years. At this point, a generous outside agency (a GOA) decides to give the hundred parents a lump sum of money. The only stipulation is that it be used to increase teachers' salaries. Nothing else has changed—and yet, in the perverse tradition of social programs, we find that within a few years the attractions of the hundred-parent system have fallen apart. For by the simple act of supplementing the teachers' salaries, at least four sets of dynamics were set in motion.

Set 1: The Pool of Applicants Is Augmented by the Wrong People. During the years in which the school has been operating, the parents have by trial and error found the salary level, consisting of X dollars, that attracts able and dedicated career teachers who form the backbone of the school plus other able people who enjoy teaching and are doing it as a precareer or second-career job. In all cases, the teachers could be making more than X dollars if they chose, but the nonmonetary benefits of teaching bring them into that job. Another set of less able people think that X dollars is a wonderful salary, more than they could hope to make otherwise, and want to be hired. But they seldom are, for the same reason that employers seldom choose poorly qualified people when they can obtain well-qualified people for the same wages.

We may visualize this in terms of a Venn diagram (see fig. 12).

The shaded portion of the small circle consists of the people from among whom teachers tend to be hired when X dollars is "just high enough." I am arguing, in line with basic principles of the labor market, that our hundred parents will over time discover how much that amount is.

What happens when the GOA offers the teachers a salary supplement? The total salary is now a new quantity, $X + Y$

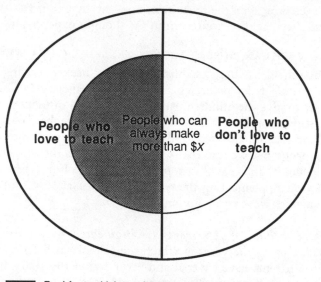

Pool from which teachers are hired

FIGURE 12
THE POOL FROM WHICH TEACHERS ARE
HIRED AT THE NATURAL SALARY OF $X

dollars. The following year, applicants for the new jobs are interviewed. The room is a little more crowded than the year
before. The reason is that the augmented salary is now attractive to a certain number of people who don't particularly like
teaching. Before, they could make more than X dollars in many
other occupations, and so, having no special attachment to
teaching, they went to jobs where they made more money (or
to jobs that they found more intrinsically rewarding). For people who can *always* make more than the augmented salary,
teaching still holds no lure. But for those who could make more
than X dollars working at something else, but cannot otherwise
make more than the $X + Y$ dollars the parents are now offering, the teaching job becomes monetarily more attractive than
any other option.

The problem is that the people interviewing the candidate teachers cannot tell the new class of candidates from the old ones. A vocation for teaching is not emblazoned on foreheads, and the new applicants are otherwise equivalent. Some of those who have been enticed to the teaching profession because of the augmented salary will have degrees from excellent schools. They will be good in front of a classroom (when they feel like it). They will be personable. They are able to teach about as well as the ones hired the year before—they are drawn from the same pool of talent as the current teachers (see fig. 13).

The people who can always make more than the augmented salary $X + Y$ are represented by the new circle set within the one in the previous diagram designating the people who can always make more than X. The newly shaded area indicates

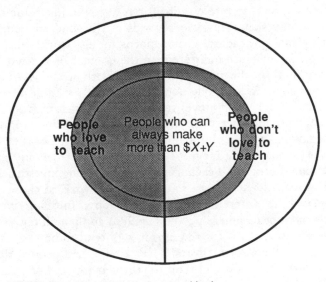

People who love to teach

People who can always make more than $X+Y$

People who don't love to teach

▨▨▨ Pool from which teachers are hired

FIGURE 13
THE POOL FROM WHICH TEACHERS ARE HIRED
WHEN THE NATURAL SALARY OF $X
IS ARTIFICIALLY AUGMENTED BY $Y

the new people who will come to be interviewed and will tend to be hired—because they are just as skilled in every way save one, the "skill" of vocation.

Because the new people may also be good teachers, there need be no immediate educational consequences. The immediate unhappy consequence is a more subtle one that in conventional policy analysis is disregarded altogether: The augmented salary is encouraging a mismatch between people and the jobs that will make them happy. With the augmented salary in place, the ranks of teachers will have more people who do not particularly enjoy teaching. This is bad for them: People should find vocations, and the more advantages a person has, the less excuse for not finding one. And it is bad for the person who *does* have a vocation for teaching, displaced by a person who loves the job less.

It is also bad for the rest of the teachers already hired. One may reread the literature on intrinsic rewards and be reminded of all the ways that intrinsic rewards can be undermined, or one may look instead at what happens in any work situation when people who are indifferent to the content of the work— who are "in it for the money"—are mixed with people who love it. When one is in love, one does things that look foolish to an outsider. A teacher who loves teaching is no different from the computer programmer who is wrapped up in a new program or the lawyer who is obsessed with preparing a case—they all voluntarily contribute far more hours to the job than any employer could demand. Teachers who love teaching invest themselves in the students, in the school, in their work, in the ways that make the difference between a happy, fulfilling work setting and a place where people punch in and punch out. The teachers who are in it for the money will tend to be unenthusiastic about these extra efforts. They are not bad people, they are not lazy, but they will tend to see their job as just that—a job. If just one teacher in the school is like that, he may be socialized (or pretend to be socialized) by the dominant culture. But the dominant culture is very fragile, because ultimately its defenders cannot defend it rationally. The reasons why they are investing so much of themselves in their job has to do with intangibles and values, and often it means doing specific tasks that they do not want to do.

Introducing into such an environment people who are in it for the money is like introducing a virus into a system with no immunity. The unconverted will ask of the teacher who has gone out on a rainy evening to attend a boring school function, "Why are you doing this?" The true answer is "Because doing this, while I don't particularly want to, is inseparable from everything else that makes teaching valuable to me." It is an embarrassing answer when the questioner is not a fellow believer. It is much easier to answer, "Because the headmaster says I have to"—and in the act of saying that, beginning to believe it (as experts on cognitive dissonance will confirm). To reap the intrinsic rewards of teaching, teachers must teach in the company of others who believe as they do. Raising the salary beyond X lowers the dues for membership in the club and lets the wrong sort in.

Set 2: Good Teachers Are Told They Are in It for the Money. All of us seek and gladly accept more money for our work if we can get it. Thus the news that the GOA has decided to augment the teachers' salaries is going to be joyously received in the teachers' lounge. Do the findings reported in the discussion of intrinsic rewards really apply? Are the underpaid teachers really going to lose their intrinsic motivation to teach as the extrinsic rewards are increased? Or were these just experimental effects that don't apply to the teachers hired by the hundred parents? If the teachers have adequate intrinsic motivation at X dollars per year (which is X dollars worth of extrinsic motivation), why should a little more make any difference?

In approaching this question, the first step is to realize that at X dollars, the teachers do *not* have X dollars of extrinsic rewards, but zero. For practical purposes, the teachers in the preraise phase are working for no extrinsic reward at all. On the contrary, *they are paying for the privilege of teaching.* They are working for X dollars despite many options to work for more than X dollars. In this sense, the raise provided by the GOA is directly analogous to the payments given to the people in the experiments reported in the discussion of intrinsic rewards, and there is no reason to think that the effects on them will be any different than the robust effects reported for other populations: They will be more inclined to see teaching not as an end in itself, but something validated to some extent by the money paid for it. Further, one recalls the many experiments demonstrating that underpaid people are especially good at finding and taking pleasure in intrinsic rewards—again, the need to resolve cognitive dissonance leads them to coordinate what they are doing with what they are thinking. When the underpayment ceases, that internal pressure to find and value the intrinsic rewards diminishes as well.

But the effects of the salary increase may be translated into more concrete terms. Suppose, for example, that the GOA is not a government at all, but a rich alumnus who has died and left this onetime salary endowment. In such a case, the raise might not produce any ill effects. The teachers at that particular school would be in the position of having won a lottery. Everybody could congratulate the others on their mutual good fortune and go back to work as before. If instead the GOA is a government, the teachers cannot possibly consider their raise as a windfall. The raise will instead be perceived as the right and fair thing for the government to have done (for the teachers will naturally have considered themselves underpaid all along). The question then inevitably arises: Why not more? What makes the GOA think that this raise brings them to the level that teachers deserve? The GOA has conceded the essential point, that it is proper for it to intercede on behalf of equity. The only question now is how to get it to do the *really* right thing and get the teachers another and bigger raise.

Because of the GOA's intervention, the basis of the teachers' relationship to their job has fundamentally changed. Before, the salary was a given. The hundred parents were not making their decision about salary on the basis of "equity," *and the teachers knew it*. The parents wanted good teachers for their children, wanted to spend as little money as possible to get them— *couldn't* spend a lot of money to get them—and so came up with the package of minimum salary and maximum nonmonetary benefits that would attract the right people. Now, when equity is the principle for determining salaries, the salary is a sign of the teacher's worth to society—the GOA has said so, in quite explicit terms. Consequently, the teachers' self-respect (as well as the natural human desire to have more money if it is obtainable) now is linked with this badge of status in a way it previously was not.

Another result will be the formation of a teachers' organization, eventually linked with those of teachers in other schools, given the mission of lobbying the GOA to intervene again. And that organization will begin to behave as a faction. It will develop its own agenda, and among other things it will constantly remind its members that they are being underpaid by society.

These specifics are perhaps unnecessary. The antagonism between intrinsic and extrinsic rewards is demonstrably real, and there are convincing explanations why it should be so. There is no reason to think that teachers are exempt, and many reasons to think that they are not. But the specifics are in themselves important, and may be expected to have the effect of exacerbating the natural loss of intrinsic motivation.

One other possibility presents itself, however. Extrinsic rewards do not necessarily undermine intrinsic motivation when they are linked to performance and perceived competence. Why not tie the salary increase to a merit system? And that brings us to the third set of dynamics.

Set 3: The Parents Think of the Teachers Differently. The hundred parents find themselves with this extra money from the GOA. It has to be provided for salaries. How do they react?

First, their relationship to the teachers is altered, just as the teachers' relationship to their job was altered. In the pristine case, the parents were as much supplicants as suppliers of jobs. They had to be attentive to the teachers' needs for an environment in which they could enjoy their work.

Upon receiving the money from the GOA, it is conceivable that the hundred parents will breathe a sigh of relief that at last the teachers are getting closer to what they're worth and that nothing else will change. It is far more likely that their expectations will change subtly. Psychologically, the parents' (very useful) solicitude for the teachers' nonmonetary perks will be diminished. After all, the teachers have gotten a big raise, maybe a lot bigger than some of the parents got last year. And there is also the natural reaction: "What are they going to do to earn it?" The teachers are getting more money; it follows that they should be doing something in response. One may expect that in subsequent years conditions will be attached to the raises. But as the conditions are attached, they eat into the non-monetary rewards that made the job attractive. Gradually, the augmented salary tends to shift the terms of debate about job satisfactions and dissatisfactions away from intrinsic rewards and toward extrinsic ones.

Worst of all, the parents might decide to try to give out the money on a merit basis. They have to divide up the salary somehow and they want to reward the best teachers, so they institute some system that tries to identify the best teachers and pay them accordingly.

Why is this bad? In most settings, paying people according to their productivity and excellence is desirable. And since the theme of the discussion has been that a free market in teachers will find the right salary of X dollars, why not trust the market mechanism to work in the case of individual teachers? The best ones will get paid more and still retain all their intrinsic motivation, and other teachers will have an additional incentive to do well. To answer the question, we must ask why it is that the hundred parents didn't set up a merit system on their own.

One reason is that the parents couldn't agree on what test they wanted the teacher to meet. The parents who wanted their children to get into Ivy League schools lobbied for a merit system tied to their children's test scores. But other parents, whose children were not especially smart, argued that they didn't want teachers to be spending all their time drilling the smartest students. What all the parents wanted in different ways was that the teachers "teach well"—which, among other things, means being flexible and imaginative in responding differently to the needs of different children. Developing an objective system for ranking teachers on such dimensions was beyond them.

Another reason the hundred parents didn't set up a merit system on their own is that they discovered that the teachers, *including the best teachers*, didn't want one.* If one assumes

---

* A handful of good teachers in a school filled with incompetent

that teachers must be motivated to try hard, merit pay makes sense. If one assumes that a teacher wouldn't be taking the job unless he were already motivated, then a merit system is not a plus but a minus.

There are a variety of technical reasons why a merit-pay system is a bad idea, having to do with the difficulties of measuring teacher productivity. But the more important consideration in the pursuit-of-happiness context is that many of the teacher's job satisfactions are hindered by a merit system. For example: It is more fun to teach in a collegial atmosphere. Merit pay gets in the way of that atmosphere. Or another example: Part of the fun of teaching is embedded in one's personal style. A merit review system is likely to include classroom observation of the teacher, which is very likely to put pressure on the teacher to conform to the style most likely to win the merit pay.

But the great (and ironic) argument against a merit pay system is that *any formal attempt to identify merit is going to be less precise than the informal system already in place*. In almost any school, the teachers and administrators know who the best teachers are. They know who the worst teachers are. And they know strengths and weaknesses at a much more detailed level than "good" and "bad." They know that Miss Jones's class is a good place to steer a youngster with behavior problems, that Mr. Smith is great with children who need drawing out, that Mrs. Jackson is a terror but the students learn a lot.

Because the natural level of knowledge about the teachers is so detailed and accurate, and because objectified merit reviews are necessarily so much less detailed and accurate, the formal rankings from the merit review process will create immense trouble. The people who are *wrongly* graded as undeserving of the merit bonus by a formal procedure (as some will be) will have been treated unfairly. And the people who are *correctly* graded as undeserving will have a ready-made legalistic argu-

---

teachers are in a completely different situation and may well want a performance review system. I am arguing that in a school where almost all of the teachers are already good, a formal merit system is not only unnecessary but actually damaging to the quality of professional life within the school.

ment that they have been treated unfairly—because the formal measures of performance are in fact known to be inaccurate.

Contrast these problems with the situation in the school which does not have a merit system but where the parents are paying the tuition directly to the school. The built-in knowledge about who is good and bad is used efficiently. The bad teacher is soon eased out—market forces are at work, after all, on the headmaster by parents who tend to switch schools if their children get stuck with too many bad teachers too often. Just as importantly—perhaps ultimately much more importantly—the best teachers in such an environment are recognized and rewarded. They do not get a higher salary than other teachers with the same seniority. But they are deferred to, consulted, applauded, and indulged in the small and large ways through which a valued teacher becomes a special part of a school.

Set 4: The GOA Wants to Make Sure Its Money Isn't Being Wasted. Finally there is this overriding, irresistible reason why the attempt to augment the teachers' salaries will backfire: The GOA is not going to be able to confine itself to giving the money and leaving the hundred parents alone. Let us transport ourselves five years into the future and look back on what happened after the GOA decided to help out the teachers.

During the first year, the GOA observed the original terms of the agreement: The money was turned over to the hundred parents and used to augment teachers' salaries as the hundred parents saw fit. No strings.

During the second year, the GOA decided it had to exert some oversight over the money to ensure that it wasn't being wasted—nothing onerous, just a few accounting forms.

During the third year, the GOA realized that it was necessary to determine that the money was being distributed *equitably*. The accounting information was supplemented by extensive questionnaires on which teachers got how much, for what reasons, and the reporting forms became a thick book.

During the fourth year, the GOA decided that the teachers needed more assistance not just in salaries but in doing their jobs correctly. The GOA set up an advisory office to develop ideas for how they might become better teachers. These ideas were so enchanting to the planners at the GOA that they decided to encourage schools to adopt them.

So during the fifth year, the GOA began to offer "incentives" to the hundred parents to implement the programs that the GOA had determined to be the Best Way to educate children. And if some of the guidelines were not agreeable to the hundred parents, the parents were of course free to ignore them. The GOA didn't have any power to *force* the hundred parents to do things its way. All the GOA would do was . . . withdraw the subsidy—which, by that time, the hundred parents found an intolerable prospect. After all, they could never run a school without financial assistance from the GOA.

And it was such a simple good thing that was being done. Just raise the salaries of some valuable and underpaid people, using some money from outside the community.

WE CAN PAY THE TEACHERS MORE, BUT IT'S NOT EASY

The epigraphs that opened this part of the book included Lao Tzu's observation that "governing a large state is like boiling a small fish," referring to the way that the flesh of a small fish is damaged by being handled.[3] The argumentation in this discussion tends toward the same conclusion. The dynamics of the process whereby the right people end up in classrooms will work if they are left alone, and will tend to break down if jostled by even the most helpful of hands. So it is with a wide variety of social processes that governments want to encourage.

Every moderate impulse makes me want to qualify this conclusion. And in the political arena, where there is no choice but to settle for half-loaves, I will continue to urge that using the pursuit of happiness as a framework for thinking about policy is better than not using it. But there is this troubling other half of the picture: If one of the merits of the pursuit-of-happiness approach to policy is to reveal the interconnectedness of dynamics, the same merit tends also to produce pessimism about the efficacy of moderate steps. For to consider how good effects may be brought about (as they seem to have been in the case of the hundred parents) is also to realize how easily they may be disrupted.

It is not a desire for purity that pushes me toward radical

conclusions, but the stubborn characteristic of human nature that used to lead Henry Stimson to say that "the only way you can make a man trustworthy is to trust him." It is the dilemma of the reality test: If humans *really are* making their own decisions and *really are* reliant on their own resources, then their behavior will be importantly guided by that reality. As soon as that reality is compromised, people know it. We observe this reaction in ourselves in dozens of trivial ways in everyday life (if my wife were to announce that from now on she will not turn down the thermostat before retiring then I would remember to do it, whereas now I tend to forget).

Moreover, the changes cannot be compartmentalized. As the example of the GOA and the teachers' salary supplement attempted to illustrate, they seep into attitudes and decisions that at first seem wholly unrelated to the salary subsidy. Solutions to many social problems are possible, but they have to be of a piece. Even minor alterations may cause them to fail altogether.

Would it be possible under *any* circumstances to augment from outside resources the salaries of teachers in a particular locale? Yes, but only once we understand why it is so difficult to do it as a general policy. And that leads to the paradoxical robustness of the policies that do in fact rely on the natural responses of people instead of trying to manipulate them.

HARD CASES AND ROBUST EFFECTS

An understandable reaction to the hundred-parents scenario is that it works fine for people with middle-class values and middle-class money, but fails for everyone else. I am arguing the opposite possibility. A solution that truly implements the hundred-parent scenario draws on such powerful and widely shared human motives that it will work across a very broad spectrum of social and economic classes. Furthermore, the power of the solution will produce not only the desired main effect, but a variety of other serendipitous side effects as well.

The specific driving force is the relationship of parents to their children. To recapitulate: Parents want good things for their children. In a society where education means opportunity for getting ahead, one of those good things is education. This is not just one of many goods, but a central one. Therefore, one of the things that parents in a free society want most intensely for their children is an education. This generally holds true across parents of widely varying backgrounds, incomes, and abilities. To that, I add the critical belief from the discussion of the idea of man that human beings are resourceful, and that this latent resourcefulness is not limited to just a few especially able human beings but is a general characteristic including everyone but the most mentally or emotionally disabled. To put it less formally: Give parents control over the education of their children, as I gave it to the hundred parents, and you will unleash enormous energy and imagination, all tending toward the excellent end of educated children.

Why wouldn't these observations apply to poor people? Several answers come to mind. Thinking about them argues for what I believe to be the general truth that the more natural the dynamics that produce good results, the more robust they will be under difficult circumstances.

A POLICY FRAMEWORK

To illustrate the argument I need to peg it to a policy prescription more broadly realistic than the hundred-parent scenario. At the same time, I want to avoid getting bogged down in arguments over procedural details, for all that is really needed to make my points is one indispensable feature of the hundred-parent scenario: that parents, teachers, and schools all have freedom of choice. Parents can apply for admission of their children to any school they wish. Teachers can apply to teach at any school they wish. A school can accept or reject any student or teaching applicant it wishes, teach any curriculum it wishes, enforce any school rules it wishes.

Three generic solutions accommodate this indispensable condition in varying degrees. One is to decentralize the public school system so that each school operates autonomously. Another is a voucher system that gives to each parent a chit worth an amount deemed sufficient to pay for an adequate education. The third is a tuition tax-credit system that maintains a public school system but permits parents to deduct the cost of tuition at a private school (or some portion of that cost) from their tax bills. For purposes of this discussion I will assume my own preference, a tuition tax-credit system. Specifically: Any parent who chooses to put his child in a private school may deduct from his taxes the amount of money the school system saves by not having to educate him. Let's say that this amounts to a maximum of $2,500 per pupil.* I will call it the "free-choice" system, because it does away with the sunk cost in public education that presently loads the economic dice in favor of public schools.† Now we are ready to ask: What might happen next

---

* Calculating the marginal cost of a child in a school system is a slippery process involving interactive factors. For example, the marginal cost of a single child could be construed as zero because one extra child can always be accommodated by the materials and staff already on hand. But of course children in larger numbers do involve major marginal costs. And, to make things more complicated yet, the calculation of marginal cost depends a great deal on the assumptions one makes about the baseline size of the system. Two extremes will illustrate the point: Suppose we could know in advance that under the tuition tax-credit scheme only one parent in the whole system would take advantage of it. In that case, the appropriate size of the tax credit—"the amount of money the school system saves by not having to educate him"—would be $0. Suppose in contrast that we could know in advance that *every* parent would withdraw his children from the public school system under a tuition tax-credit plan. In that case, the budget of the public school system could be devoted entirely to tax credits and the average tax credit (let alone the maximum) could be the entire per-pupil expenditure. To get a sense of the figures that led me to use a ballpark of $2,500 for a credit: In 1986, the average expenditure per pupil in elementary and secondary school (from federal, state, and local funds) was $3,677 if measured in average daily attendance and $3,491 if measured in average daily membership.[4] The $2,500 figure assumes a large but not complete exodus from the public school system.
† For those who question whether government should be involved in education at all, I share the view that education in a democracy is a classic public good. Milton Friedman has said it as well as anyone: "A stable and democratic society is impossible without a minimum degree of literacy and knowledge on the part of most citizens and without widespread acceptance of some common set of values. Education can contribute to both. In consequence, the gain from the education of a child accrues not only to the child or to his parents but also to other members of the society. . . . It is not feasible

to all those people who *aren't* like the hundred middle-class
parents of the thought experiment?

IMMEDIATE OUTCOMES

It seems certain that the immediate outcome of a free-choice
system will be a massive transfer to private schools and a mush-
rooming expansion in the number and variety of private schools.
This migration will be greatest in the urban areas among poor
parents whose children attend the worst schools.* The growth
in urban private schools for low-income parents even now, in
the face of punishing financial sacrifices, has been rapid. As of
1986, more than 220 private schools for blacks were operating
in the nation's largest cities, mostly for working-class and low-
income parents.[7] A 1983 study by the National Institute of
Education revealed that with only a $250 tax credit, 20 percent
of Hispanic parents and 18 percent of black parents with children in public schools would transfer them to private ones.[8]
The proposed system envisions a maximum of ten times that
$250, in the context of private school tuitions that in 1985 still
averaged only $1,218.[9]

The reason why so many low-income black parents have
fled the public school system is because they have observed
that the private schools do better than the public schools. The
teachers are better, the curriculum is better, the discipline is
better. From everything we know from recent research, these
anecdotal observations are correct. Inexpensive private schools

---

to identify the particular individuals (or families) benefited and so
to charge for the services rendered."[5] Or less formally but more
passionately, Thomas Jefferson, writing to George Wythe: "Preach,
my dear Sir, a crusade against ignorance; establish and improve the
law for educating the common people. Let our countrymen know
that the people alone can protect us against these evils, and that the
tax which will be paid for this purpose is not more than the thou-
sandth part of what will be paid to kings, priests and nobles who
will rise up among us if we leave the people in ignorance."[6]

* The least change is predicted to occur in suburbs and small towns
where the public school system is small enough to be responsive to
parental pressures—where, in effect, the public school system in the
1980s has the merits of a private system.

in low-income neighborhoods usually do far better than the public schools in educating their students.[10]

This improvement will be most conspicuous for one particular group of people, working low-income people in large urban areas. One of the tragically ironic commentaries on the current situation is that many low-income parents have higher standards for their children than the schools do. Low-income communities have plenty of hardworking parents who teach their children to study, be courteous, pay attention to the teacher, avoid the kids who are in gangs or use drugs—and then the children are sent into an environment that does not enforce the standards that the parents have tried to set. One of the major virtues of the free-choice system is that it will instantaneously permit those parents to put their children into schools that are run according to their rules. This in itself will constitute a huge success in social policy, the kind of dramatic main effect that social programs have so seldom achieved.

BUT WHAT ABOUT THE CHILDREN OF PARENTS WHO DON'T CARE?

But not all people are like the virtuous working-class parents I have just described. Along with the low-income parents who are deeply involved in their children's education are many others who do not socialize their children into values that will stand them in good stead as students. Their children skip school a lot, don't pay much attention to the teacher, don't study, and, as children will, encourage other children to do the same. Some of them "act out," as the jargon has it, meaning that they create disturbances in the classrooms and halls. A few are downright dangerous. Among low-income populations there exists a subclass of children who exhibit these behaviors, which in turn may often be traced to home environments in which parents do a very poor job of training their children to behave otherwise.* What will happen to these children?

---

* The use of "lower class" follows Edward C. Banfield's in *The Unheavenly City*.[11] But, yes, some children of middle-class parents behave the same way. The subsequent discussion applies to them as well.

Unintended Outcomes and the Public Schools. The quick answer is that the children of indifferent parents will still have the public schools. But what kind of schools will they be?

First, try to imagine what the educational situation will look like. We assume a massive exodus from urban public school systems by everyone from the working class on up. The size of the public school system shrinks to a fraction of its present size, let us say, and a high proportion of students in the public system are the children of parents who have no income that qualifies them for a tax credit. Will the quality of education in the remaining public schools be better or worse than it was before?

Leaving aside how little risk we are running (How much worse can education in the inner city get?), there are reasons for thinking that the public schools might improve. Let us think about what this reduced public school system will be like.*

The first important change we can confidently predict is that a system with only a fraction of its former size will have only a fraction of its former political importance. The school board will no longer be second only to the city council as a political plum and stepping-stone to higher office, but roughly equivalent to a medium-sized social service agency. It seems likely, then, that school administrators will be less in the limelight, their decisions less subject to political interference. If so, who will be defining their mission? Allocating their budgets?

One answer is professional educators, but educators in a very different situation from the educators who administer today's public schools. They will now be administering a much smaller system with a more homogeneous population of students. It is just possible that the educators who are attracted to the public school system under these circumstances will be ones who are attracted by the challenge of demonstrating that children with

---

* I concentrate on the school systems with a substantial poor population attending them. In large affluent suburbs where virtually everyone will be getting the maximum $2,500 tax credit, the residual public school population will consist of children who are being kept in the public system by the parents' choice, which means that they will be in effect a small network of private schools of a particular type that those parents find congenial.

great disadvantages *can* learn. What kinds of teachers will be attracted to the public schools? Perhaps the teachers' unions will remain as entrenched as ever, and nothing will change. But it is hard to imagine that a system so shrunk in size and having undergone such a dramatic change in mission will not also be able to get some more leeway in its use of teachers. If so, it will have one potential advantage going for it: Some of the best and most motivated teachers prefer to teach the most disadvantaged students, if only they can be given a reasonable working environment.

Another source of support and interest will be the public. Under the current system, large urban public school systems often are, for middle-class parents and voters, the enemy, seen as expensive, bungling, and destructive. A small public school system perceived as an institution for serving the most disadvantaged youngsters (not one perceived primarily as one that has expensively failed to serve our own children) is in a much different situation. Judging from historical experience, the reaction of citizens to such children and their needs is likely to be a very active solicitude.*[12] Part of this attention will take the form of public interest by influential people in the progress of the public schools. Another part of it will take the form of extensive private efforts to make sure that the poorest students have options. Foundations will fund scholarships for poor students to attend private schools. Churches will establish subsidized schools for the best students in poor neighborhoods.

Can one prove from such speculations that education for children who cannot take advantage of the tax credit will get better? No. But I suggest that it is much easier to make a plausible case that their education will get better than that it will get worse. Nor (as a final comment) is the situation of the youngsters who remain in the public schools necessarily unenviable. Some of the most effective schools can be those that can con-

---

* There is of course an easy way to ensure an active pressure group seeking not only adequate but perhaps even *greater* per-pupil funding for the public schools, by pegging the size of the maximum tuition tax-credit to the current per-pupil expenditures of the public school system. If per pupil expenditures fall, so will the maximum tax credit; if they rise, so will the maximum tax credit.

vincingly say to their students, "You are all in the same boat, everything is against you, and you've got to be twice as good as you think you can be. And we're here to show you how." The public schools have the potential to become that kind of prep school for escaping poverty.

UNINTENDED OUTCOMES AND THE RAISING OF CHILDREN

One common objection to voucher and tuition tax-credit systems is that many parents will be duped. Schools will be started that are schools in name only, run by charlatans. The parents will throw their money away and the children will not be educated. It is possible, the kind of unintended outcome that requires consideration. But the more one thinks about the likely course of events, the more (I suggest) a quite different possibility emerges: that the main effect on the least capable parents will not be that they are duped, but that they are exposed to powerful incentives to do better.*

Now we are considering the indifferent parent who has an income and pays taxes, so he can take advantage of a tax credit and send his child to a private school. But he is not like one of the hundred parents. He has not under the current system socialized his child to the world of studying and the school. So the youngster goes to school, does very poorly, graduates (if he gets that far) with little education and all the attendant problems that go with this sequence. What can a school do about this? Under the current system, the public schools can do little. They are supposed to educate everybody. Private schools, in contrast, can refuse to educate anyone they don't want to educate, and thereby can end up achieving much on behalf of the very students they refuse. To pursue this line of argument, I need three assumptions.

---

* A quick point in favor of a tax-credit system over vouchers: To get a meaningful tax credit, you have to have held a job for much of the year. Insofar as people who hold down jobs tend as a group to be more responsible than people who are chronically unemployed, and insofar as spending money one has earned is different than spending money one has been given, there are forces at work militating against thoughtlessness and gullibility.

Assumption #1 is that many of the parents who are not effective in socializing their youngsters nonetheless have ambitions for them and want them to do well. The intentions are right, even if the skills for achieving them are lacking.

Assumption #2 is that, in low-income neighborhoods as in affluent ones, the private schools will get reputations, with the better schools getting reputations as desirable places to send one's children. If each parent were kept in an isolation booth when deciding upon a school, the threat of widespread victimization by scams is real. But people talk to each other. They compare notes. They have opinions. Some people in the neighborhood are extremely gullible, yes; others are not. Some follow local opinion; others lead it.

Assumption #3 is that low-income parents want to keep up with the Joneses in their neighborhood, just as affluent parents do in theirs. They want to be able to boast about their children. They want to have things to take pride in.

If these assumptions are correct, then we can expect that many ineffectual parents who haven't the least understanding of what makes a good school will nonetheless want to get their children into locally popular schools *that are in fact good schools*. The attendant consequences are fascinating.

Such parents apply for admission for their children. And they get turned down. Or perhaps their child is admitted, but soon kicked out. This will happen *because the schools which are prospering on account of their reputation cannot afford to keep many disruptive children in their classrooms.* The other parents won't stand for it. Their teachers won't stand for it. And there is no better way to convey the message: If you want your child to go to one of the good schools, one that you can brag to your neighbor about, one that can make good on your aspirations for your child, you, the parent, have to do your part. It's no use saying to the school, "I'm paying you to educate him, so you better do it," because the school can say in return, "Your child is a net liability to us. Take your tuition money somewhere else." Best of all, the message will be sent quickly, when there may still be time to change the parents' behavior and the child's.

Under a free-choice system, there will be other places to go.

In addition to the public schools, some private schools will specifically cater to problem children. But these schools will have no social cachet (just as today the special private schools catering to affluent problem children have no cachet). The parents will continue to have aspirations to get their children into one of the locally fashionable schools.

How much effect will these dynamics have? It is hard to say, because we have not had a chance to observe a free-choice school system in operation in low-income neighborhoods. We have had a chance to observe affluent parents in such situations, however, and their efforts to make sure that their children get into the locally desirable schools fall barely short of groveling. If low-income parents behave more or less the same, then it seems reasonable to assume that some—not all, perhaps not most, but some—parents will do a better job of socializing their children for the school world. And "some" parents doing a better job may be all it will take to shift the prevailing norms in the neighborhood.

A CLASS SYSTEM?

One of the most persuasive arguments in favor of retaining the public school system is that it provides training in democracy by mixing students of different backgrounds. This is no small virtue. The prospect of a system in which all the rich folks send their children to one set of schools and all the poor folks send theirs to another is chilling, and it must be asked of a tuition tax-credit system whether this would not be the result.

I suggest that the opposite is true. It is the current public school system, especially as reformed in the last two decades, that conspires to produce segregation by race and economic class. The free-choice system will break down some of that segregation.

A high degree of socioeconomic stratification has always existed in the schools and always will, under any nontotalitarian system. In the old days of neighborhood schools, neighborhoods tended to be formed along socioeconomic lines and the schoolrooms followed suit. The calculations of parents were (and remain) concrete and explicit. Ask any real-estate agent about the difference in value between two houses in a middle-class suburb, across the street from each other, of equivalent size and condition, when they straddle a strictly enforced school district line and the school on one side of the street draws its students from a low-income neighborhood while the other one draws from middle-class neighborhoods. The perceived value of socioeconomic stratification can be calibrated in the market prices of the two houses.

So let us not deceive ourselves that there will ever be complete mixing under any system. Parents prefer that their children go to a school with an appropriate environment, an "appropriate environment" meaning one in which the predominant values are ones they share; and the parents who have money will resort to whatever is necessary to see that it happens in the face of virtually anything the government does. This is understood (I submit) by everyone who has both children and money.

But to say that parents want schools with an appropriate environment is not the same as saying that parents want their children to go to school *only* with other children of their own class. On the contrary, many parents who send their children to private school want a mix of children in the school, so that their children do not grow up as hothouse flowers unable to cope with the real world. Under the free-choice system a large proportion of middle- and upper-middle-class parents will be looking for schools that have diverse student bodies. How many parents are like that? Collect some data from yourself: Given a choice between two schools with similar curricula and teaching environments, which would you choose for your children? One with a racially and economically diverse student body or one with a racially homogeneous upper-middle-class student body? If you have answered, as I predict a majority of readers of this book will have answered, that you would choose the socially heterogeneous school, the question to consider is this: What makes you think that most people aren't as sensible and fair-minded as you are?

Under the current situation, it is impossible for many private schools to make good on this parental preference for diversity because of the economics of the situation. Among people who make $75,000 a year or more, the mean tuition for private school in 1985 was $2,483.[13] A school with that tuition cannot realistically hope to include many students from working-class homes; the cost is too great. Under the free-choice system, the potential range of applicants suddenly widens. Take, for example, a family of four with a gross annual income of $25,000 (these days, a working-class income) for whom a $2,500-per-year private school is out of the question. If these parents could deduct from their total tax bill all tuition up to $2,500, the out-of-pocket cost of the private school for that family would drop to something near zero, depending on which taxes are counted in calculating the tax credit (the average family of four with a $25,000 gross income pays about $2,700 a year in personal taxes).*[14] Suddenly it becomes possible for a wide range of working-class families to put their children in private schools that formerly were out of their reach; and a wide range of the better private schools will be actively seeking such children, not out of a sense of social justice but because to have such children will be an excellent selling point for filling their classrooms.

Will some schools cater to wealthy parents who don't want their sensitive youngsters to mix with riffraff? Of course. *Many do now*, in the private school system. Will some working-class schools be lily white and hostile toward applications by blacks (or any other kind of outsider)? Of course. *Many are now*, in suburban public school systems. The world would not be perfect; it would just be better. A large number of middle-class parents who would prefer a socioeconomically and racially mixed school for their children now can rarely find one that is also a good school. A large number of working-class parents, white and black, who want good teachers, demanding cur-

* Who is paying for the highways and health centers and other noneducational services that the parents' $2,500 would otherwise have helped pay for? Other citizens without children in school. The tuition tax-credit system, like the current public school system, is redistributionist. Under both systems, the taxpayer without children in school subsidizes the cost of education for the citizen with children whose taxes do not cover the cost of his children's education, justified by education's status as a public good. This is simply more obvious in the case of a tuition tax-credit scheme when a person paying $2,500 in federal, state and local taxes gets a credit of the full $2,500 to devote just to education.

ricula, and an orderly classroom for their children now can rarely find one that they can also afford. The free-choice system would permit those two sets of parents to send their children to the same schools. This represents progress. In fact, it represents progress considered so important for the last three decades that the public school systems of the nation were convulsed in order to bring it about. To suggest that this most fiercely struggled for and fiercely resisted outcome will occur naturally across a broad spectrum of Americans if only we let parents send their children to the schools they prefer seems close to blasphemy. Surely it's too easy.

In the last decade, at scattered places around the country, free-choice systems for education have occasionally been proposed. They have always been much more modest than the one proposed here, usually amounting to a few hundred dollars in vouchers, not tax credits. All have been laced with restrictions to protect the position of the public schools. None (to my knowledge) has passed. That experience suggests how little the preceding discussion has to do with political realities.

But political realities have not been my topic. The assertion underlying the discussion in these three chapters has been that applying the pursuit of happiness as a criterion for designing and evaluating social programs illuminates a variety of issues that otherwise tend to be obscured. Whether that is good enough depends on what problem one is trying to solve. If the problem in question is how to prepare youngsters to compete with Japan in a world economy, then there are many ways of increasing the numbers of well-educated high-school graduates. I will still doubt that any other way can achieve so much so quickly with so little new money as the system I have described, and I am quite confident that no other plan will have a fraction of the impact on the education of low-income urban families. But there *are* other ways of improving elementary and secondary education for the middle class, and that will be sufficient to help us compete better with Japan. There are also many ways to put roofs over the homeless, food into the bellies of the hungry, and money into the hands of the poor.

If, however, the problem is how to enable people in all classes and in all occupations to pursue happiness, then this limited example of applications to educational policy has simply been tantalizing. One might conduct similar thought experiments for a variety of other problems. For example, we could work through how *odd* it is that some urban neighborhoods have such high rates of violent crime. Under what strange circumstances would the people of that neighborhood, pursuing happiness, permit such a situation to exist? Or the problem of drugs: It is easy to understand how a given individual might become addicted, but how odd that a *widespread* problem of drug addiction *can continue over a long period of time*, when such powerful forces (economic and social) would naturally seem to dampen it. How do current policies manage to sustain a naturally self-limiting problem? And so on. I hope that the extended example of education has been sufficiently generalizable to make the lines of the arguments more or less self-evident; in any event, I will not try to produce a workbook of such experiments. Clearly, I have been alluding in the education example to some broader conclusions about the ways in which enabling people to pursue happiness should affect social policy. It is time to pull those strands together.

12

Little Platoons

STRONGLY BOUND communities, fulfilling complex public functions, are not creations of the state. They form because they must. Human beings have needs as individuals (never mind the "moral sense" or lack of it) that cannot be met except by cooperation with other human beings. To this degree, the often-lamented conflict between "individualism" and "community" is misleading. The pursuit of individual happiness cannot be an atomistic process; it will naturally and always occur in the context of communities. The state's role in enabling the pursuit of happiness depends ultimately on nurturing *not* individuals, but the associations they form.

The text for this discussion is one of Burke's best-known passages: "To be attached to the subdivision, to love the little platoon we belong to in society, is the first principle (the germ as it were) of public affections. It is the first link in the series by which we proceed towards a love to our country, and to mankind."[1] I will be using the image of the "little platoon" to represent the essential relationship of social organization to the pursuit of happiness and, by extension, the relationship of the state's social policy to the pursuit of happiness. We each belong to a few "little platoons." The great joys and sorrows, satisfactions and preoccupations, of our daily life are defined in terms of them. This observation, I will assert, applies to everyone, wherever his little platoons fall within the larger social framework.

Using a central government to enable people to pursue happiness becomes in this perspective a process of making sure that the little platoons work. The enabling conditions have to be met—in a properly constructed society, people must have access to material resources, safety, self-respect, and intrinsic rewards. But the little platoons of work, family, and community are the nexus within which these conditions are worked out and through which the satisfactions that happiness represents are obtained. That being the case, "good" social policy can be defined only after we have answered the questions:

How do little platoons form?
How are they sustained?
What makes them nourishing?

AFFILIATION AS THE MECHANISM FOR FORMING LITTLE PLATOONS

When in part 2 I began to explore enabling conditions for the pursuit of happiness via Abraham Maslow's needs hierarchy, I observed that the third of the needs, for intimacy and belongingness, was also a resource; in effect, it is the master resource whereby human beings in society go about seeing that the other needs are met. The label I will give to this mechanism is "affiliation." Here, too, Burke has distilled the essence of what I mean: "Men are not tied to one another by papers and seals. They are led to associate by resemblances, by conformities, by sympathies."[2]

The last two chapters presented an elaborated illustration of affiliation. Parents, teachers, and (in their turn) the children were engaged in a tacit, complex process. Each parent had certain individual interests. So did each prospective teacher. The result was not just the meeting of those particular interests, but something more. The little platoon called "community" had been enriched, with positive results that were more than the sum of the educational and professional outcomes. This was no accident, but a characteristic result when small groups of people have individual problems that can best be solved by gaining the voluntary cooperation of others—or in other words, when small groups engage in voluntary affiliations through the force of individual circumstance. We are now in a position to talk about affiliation more systematically.

AFFILIATIONS AS SMALL STEPS

An affiliation behavior may be one whereby one person forms new relationships with others (by marrying or moving to a particular town or neighborhood). It may consist of an effort to alter an existing environment (circulating a petition, or forming a neighborhood block watch). Sometimes it means leaving relationships that are unsatisfactory (getting a divorce or quitting a club). But the word "affiliation" probably tends to evoke too many of these formal types of affiliation and not enough of the small acts of affiliation that make up the larger ones. The places you shop, the friends you choose to see a lot of, the relationships you have with coworkers, the ways you spend your leisure time, all bespeak and define affiliations.

Affiliation behaviors, as I am using the term, are not contractual. I have a favorite delicatessen up the street. The prices sometimes aren't the best I could find, but I like the place for many little reasons. I can joke with the people behind the counter. They recognize my children when they come in. They let me buy a sandwich on credit when I have forgotten my wallet. And the food's pretty good. If once in a while my expectations are not met, I do not immediately start considering other options. If they were consistently not met, then sooner or later I would drift off. Technically, what I am doing could be construed and analyzed as a series of market decisions about where to shop (just as affiliations in the aggregate bear many similarities to the way that free markets work, through analogous dynamics). But in reality, the formation and sustenance of my affiliation with the delicatessen are much closer in their characteristics to the way that friendships form and are sustained.

I use this homely example to emphasize that people very rarely wake up one morning and "decide" to form a particular affiliation. They only rarely decide all at once to leave them.

Most commonly, the interactions embraced under the heading
of affiliation are small steps, taken for reasons having nothing to
do with any conscious interest in forming affiliations, that have
cumulative effects over time. As people go about their daily
life, affiliation behaviors occur.

Or fail to occur. For a second important point about affiliations is that they do not have to exist. It is possible to live in a
neighborhood, isolated and alone, and have no affiliations. It is
possible to have a job that consists of a purely contractual outlook ("I agree to be at this place, doing these tasks, for this
many hours per week, for this amount of money"), devoid of
affiliations. Affiliations may be many or few, strong or weak,
rich or bland. One of the chief determinants of their existence
and their nature is the extent to which they are used to live out
beliefs.

AFFILIATIONS AS A WAY
OF LIVING ACCORDING TO BELIEFS

The affiliation involving the delicatessen is one of many that
constitute my larger affiliation with a neighborhood, which in
turn is one component of the affiliations that constitute my still
larger affiliation with a community. Trivial as it is in itself, the
affiliation with the deli serves to illustrate a feature of affiliations that has tended to be lost in the recent and often romanticized rhetoric about people "relating" to other people. People
affiliate with other people because of *something about* other
people—in this case, the qualities of being friendly, helpful, and
amusing.

It may seem a distinction too obvious to mention. Of course
one is attracted to "something about" someone else, since there
there is no such thing as being attracted to someone as an abstract entity. But however obvious, the distinction is essential to
understanding why little platoons are rewarding or unreward-
ing, why they sustain themselves or fall apart: *Affiliation is a
means whereby people of common values are enabled to live
by those values.* "Values" in this case means your views about
how the world works or ought to work, ranging from religion
to childrearing to politics to table manners to standards of
public civility.

The reason why affiliation is so intimately linked to values is that, to have much use—or, in fact, to be truly held—values must be acted on. Furthermore, they are typically expressed not in a one-shot action but as patterned behaviors over a period of time. Still further, values can seldom be acted upon in isolation; to live by them requires that your standards be shared by a consensus of your neighbors. Unless most of your neighbors believe in calling the police when something suspicious is happening to a neighbor's house, you are not going to be able to practice community crime control. Unless most of your neighbors believe that stealing is wrong and that sex for fourteen-year-olds is bad, you are going to have a tough time making your norms stick with your own children. If you conduct your business on the assumption that one's word is one's bond, you are going to go broke unless the other businessmen you deal with operate by the same principle. In other words, to live according to many of your most important beliefs, it is essential that you be free to affiliate with fellow believers and that, together, you enjoy some control over that environment. To the extent that you are satisfied that you are "living according to your beliefs"—that anciently honored right of Americans—it is because of affiliations.

So far, presumably, no surprises: All I have done is impose some nomenclature on a familiar process. But it also remains true that in the everyday world some affiliations work much better than others. Some marriages are much richer affiliations than others, some neighborhoods are much more closely knit than others, and so on. Even a commonality of beliefs is obviously not enough—some local churches are much more vital than others. The question therefore becomes not only how affiliation occurs, but how it becomes infused with satisfying content.

RESPONSIBILITY AND EFFORT AS THE MECHANISMS FOR ACHIEVING SATISFACTION

Put aside the concept of affiliation for a moment (we shall return to it) and recall the earlier discussions of self-respect, locus of control, intrinsic rewards, autotelic activities, competence, and self-determination. In different ways, from different perspectives, they argue for the reality of this relationship: The satisfaction one takes from any activity is a complicated product of the degree of effort one puts into it, the degree of responsibility one has for the outcome, and the function it serves.

Effort. The importance of effort is perhaps self-evident—try to think of something from which you take great satisfaction (not just momentary pleasure) that involved no effort on your part. I need not belabor this. Any number of aphorisms make the same point: "Nothing worth having comes easily," for example, or "You take out of something what you put into it." The technical literature I discussed in part 2 provides scientifically respectable language for very old common wisdom.

Responsibility. It is the importance of responsibility that needs emphasis. To achieve satisfaction, there must be an element of "It was because of me!" in the accomplishment. Effort alone is not enough. Underlying this sense of responsibility are three crucial conditions: the sense of having made a choice (it was possible that you would *not* have done it); of following through, consummating an identifiable effect; and of having done this in the face of the possibility of failure. It is not necessary to be fully responsible for every aspect of an achievement, but it is necessary to be responsible for some identifiable and meaningful corner of it. Thus construction workers commonly report that one of the satisfactions of their job is to return to the completed skyscraper or bridge and say to themselves that they helped build it. They had an extremely high degree of what might be called "local responsibility" for their component of the effort.

The brunt of these remarks is that the relationship of effort and responsibility to satisfaction is not simply additive. If I were putting the relationship in the form of an equation, I would say that effort and responsibility have both an additive and a multiplicative effect. If either is zero, the multiplicative component of the effect is zero as well.*

---

* The relationship is still more complicated when the behaviors are not voluntary. For example, being *forced* to put forth great effort with no responsibility typically produces dissatisfaction (a negative

Function. The assertion here (and it is an assertion, not covered by the findings in part 2) is that the degree of satisfaction produced by the effort and responsibility depends on the function being served. Generally speaking, functions can be arrayed on a continuum in importance from "trivial" (e.g., passing the time) to "profound" (e.g., saving someone's life). In the absence of some highly unusual circumstances, it can be generalized that spending a great deal of effort and assuming great responsibility on a trivial function is not as satisfying as spending the same amount of effort and assuming equally great responsibility on a profound function.* This is an assertion, but not such an implausible one.

The point I wish to stress is that *the same conditions that shape individual satisfactions apply to the satisfactions gained from affiliations.* The affiliation called a friendship is decisively affected by the effort, responsibility, and functions it serves as well as by the personal attractiveness that the two friends see in each other. The affiliations that make up a community are much different if they are formed by dinner parties and encounters at the supermarket than if they are formed by barn-raisings and fighting off the locusts. Or to put it in terms of the little platoons through which we work out the pursuit of happiness: To exist and to be vital, little platoons must have something to do.

Let me now begin to put these considerations alongside the problem of making good social policy. I am no longer trying to formulate effective policies to deal with discrete social problems, but trying to characterize more broadly the shape that good social policy will take. The proposition is that the importance of affiliation—of *rich* affiliations, imbued with respon-

---

score, as it were). The main point in the text is that effort and responsibility interact in producing satisfactions.

* It is important not to confuse *activity* with *function.* The same superficial activity can serve quite different functions. Tennis, for example, "just a game" in itself, has escalating levels of potential satisfaction for the casual player, for whom tennis is a way to pass the time pleasurably; for the dedicated amateur, for whom tennis is a principal means of "expressing his realized capacities"; and for the professional, for whom tennis is both a principal means of self-expression and a way of making a living.

sibility and effort, used as a way of living according to one's beliefs—transcends any of these discrete social goods. Much of what we observe as rootlessness, emptiness, and plain unhappiness in contemporary life may ultimately be traced to the many ways, occasionally blatant, more often indirect and subtle, in which social policy has excised the option of taking responsibility, the need to make an effort, or both—the ways in which social policy has, in a phrase, taken the trouble out of things.

THE GENERAL RELATIONSHIP OF SOCIAL POLICY TO SATISFACTIONS

"Taking the trouble out of things" is the theme song of modernity. The very process of technological progress may be seen as an unending attempt to take the trouble out of things. Certainly "taking the trouble out of things" has driven the consumer economy. Electric can openers take the trouble out of opening cans. Garbage disposals take the trouble out of getting rid of the garbage. Automobiles take the trouble out of getting from one place to another. Such changes are, by and large, welcome. People naturally try to make life better, and "better" not unnaturally has tended to be identified with "easier."

"TAKING THE TROUBLE OUT OF THINGS" AS THE DE FACTO GOAL OF SOCIAL POLICY

Most changes in social policy over the last half century may be viewed as having served the same function. Social Security took some of the trouble out of preparing for retirement. Unemployment insurance took some of the trouble out of being unemployed. Aid to Families with Dependent Children (AFDC) took some of the trouble out of having a baby without a father. Alterations in the bankruptcy laws took some of the trouble out of failing at business.

A problem with such reforms, quite apart from anything having to do with their immediate effects, is that in every instance in which "taking the trouble out of things" works, there is a corresponding diminution in the potential satisfaction that might be obtained from the activity that has been affected. To be employed is not quite as satisfying if being unemployed doesn't cause hardship. To be a businessman who scrupulously pays his bills is not quite as satisfying if not-paying-bills is made less painful.

The carrots and sticks act at second hand. Theoretically, for the businessman to continue to take as much satisfaction in paying his bills, it is necessary only that his fellow businessmen continue to consider it disgraceful not to pay bills. In reality, to soften the tangible penalties of bankruptcy also, over a period of time, softens the degree of disgrace. To soften the tangible penalties for being unemployed also, over a period of time, diminishes the status associated with holding a job. To return to the running example of education, the reforms in education during the 1960s and 1970s may be seen as a series of steps that "took some of the trouble" out of educating one's child and to that degree attenuated this important source of satisfaction. Responsibility for decisions about nearly everything—curricula, textbooks, disciplinary standards, rules of attendance and suspension, selection of teachers, testing requirements, the amounts of money to be spent, guidelines for lunch menus—moved outward from the neighborhood to the state or federal government. The argument here is not about whether these changes were substantively good or bad; rather, it is that *even if* they had been good educationally, they were still bad for parents in that they constrained and depressed the ways in which a parent with a child in public school could take satisfaction from that component of life called "overseeing the education of one's child."

Adopting this viewpoint, one may also make the case that what really happened for any given reform was that some enrichment of satisfactions occurred further down the line. The United States has always avoided truly Draconian penalties for bankruptcy, to enable people to make a fresh start—certainly a plus in enabling people to pursue happiness. Social Security takes some of the trouble out of preparing for retirement, yes; but the existence of Social Security makes it possible for large numbers of people who otherwise would be destitute to have enough material resources—a critical enabling condition—to pursue happiness in their old age. The actual net of each trade-off has to be calculated on its merits.

THE NEED FOR A STOPPING POINT

The problem is not deciding whether good social policy ever means taking the trouble out of things, but rather finding where to stop. Almost everyone thinks it is good that the police take the trouble out of having to catch burglars. A large majority of Americans seem to be content with the more extensive transfer of burdens that has occurred. Judging from international experience, the process will continue. No democracy has yet said to its government, "Stop doing this for us." If we look to Western Europe for a picture of our future, and if in Europe the Scandinavian countries represent the cutting edge of social progress, then we may look forward to more and more trouble being taken out of more and more things.

The psychological reasons why people seem endlessly willing to accept such measures is no more complicated than the reason why any of us, given a choice, will often take the easy way out even when we know that we will derive more satisfaction from the more troublesome choice. It is the all-too-familiar problem of knowing that one "will have enjoyed" doing something (reading a fine novel) but lacking the will to get started on it (therefore picking up a magazine instead). This is not reprehensible, but it does raise two important points.

The first is that the process cannot ultimately be a healthy one. Taking the trouble out of things must eventually go too far. Somehow the mixture of things with which we fill up our time must give us long-term satisfaction with life as a whole. And satisfaction depends crucially on being left important things over which we take trouble.

The second observation is that we cannot expect legislatures to define a stopping point. If the decisions about what government may not do on our behalf is left to a majority vote of elected representatives, logrolling and shifting coalitions will mean a perpetually expanding domain of benefits.

Programs that provide benefits are triply vulnerable to this form of perpetual expansion. First and most obviously, perception of the benefit tends to dominate perception of the cost, for the same reason that the offer of a free lunch used to attract business to saloons. Second, a majority can easily be put together to vote for a wide variety of benefits if only a minority is taxed to pay for them. Third, even a *minority* can often pass a benefit because of the asymmetry in the incentives to support and oppose any given benefit. Specifically, when a minority within the population stands to benefit greatly from a particular good and the individuals who constitute the majority suffer only a minor cost, the highly motivated minority can get the "public good" that it wants.[3] In defining a proper stopping point for government services and benefits, trusting to the vote-by-vote behavior of the members of the United States Congress is a mistake. They will never define a stopping point on their own.

So the problem is set. Somehow the mix of somethings with which we fill up our time must give us happiness. And happiness depends crucially on taking trouble over things that matter. *There must be a stopping point, some rule by which governments limit what they do for people*—not just because of budget constraints, not just because of infringements on freedom (though either of these might be a sufficient reason in itself), but because happiness is impossible unless people are left alone to take trouble over important things.

Furthermore, the stopping point must leave untouched certain possibilities of failures, of losses, of pains. Recall Csikszentmihalyi's formulation: Enjoyment follows from the balance of challenge and skills. The word "challenge" has embedded in its meaning the element of "possibility of failure"; take away that possibility, and the possibility of enjoyment goes with it. Take away the possibility of failure, and the concept of "measuring up" that underpins self-respect is meaningless.

So we dare not make life as hazardless for ourselves as we have it in our power to do. The pursuit of happiness means making life deliberately difficult in certain ways—not so difficult that we *cannot* cope, but difficult enough, in certain important ways, that coping is an authentic accomplishment.

THE CURRENT STOPPING POINT: A SAFETY NET

The current stopping point for social welfare policy is supposed to be based on *who* is helped, not on the functions to be performed—the rationale of the safety net.* The statement of

---

* In reality, a very large proportion of income transfers violates the

the stopping point goes something like this: "A good social policy leaves individuals free to do as they wish. The government steps in only when an individual demonstrates that he is *not* able to cope, that the challenges have overmatched his skills. Any form of help may be provided, but only to those who need it." The underlying premise—the central government should act to help those who need help—is accepted by mainstream conservatives and liberals alike. Their differences lie in definitions of who needs help and what constitutes an appropriate level of help.

But social policy affects not only individuals. It also takes away functions from the little platoons, and therein lies a much more difficult set of trade-offs to be assessed. If it is true that most of the important satisfactions in life are rooted in, processed through, or enhanced by little platoons, we are left with the general (if still not very specific) conclusion that it is extremely important for social policy to leave the little platoons with the "somethings to do" that keep them vital.

AN ALTERNATIVE STOPPING POINT: PROSCRIBING FUNCTIONS

The alternative is to establish the stopping point according to functions. This might be defined in various ways. Curiously, those out of the political mainstream—libertarians and democratic socialists, for example—share this principle in common, just as conservatives and liberals share the safety-net rationale in common. Their differences lie in the lists of functions that are forbidden to government. The democratic socialists see the government as the provider of basic services, setting aside a few areas of noneconomic personal behavior as areas in which government may not intrude. Libertarians want a government forbidden from all except the most limited functions (national defense and the police function being the main ones). For purposes of discussion here, I propose a loosely stated stopping

---

rationale of the safety net. The rationale for farm subsidies has nothing to do with helping people in need. The Social Security system embraces everyone, not just those in need. But the rationale of the safety net nonetheless pervades the debate and is treated as if it were a self-limiting stopping point, even if it has not been in practice.

point: "Functions that people as individuals and as communities are *able* to carry out on their own should be left to them to do as individuals and communities." That the federal government thinks it could do a *better* job of carrying out those functions is not a sufficient justification for intervention.

The motivation for the rule is the logic of the teacher shortage writ large: Just as it is *odd* that too few people want to do something as satisfying as teach, it is above all else *odd* that satisfying affiliations fail to occur in other sectors of life, for everyone. For individuals of all classes and abilities, the activities associated with getting and holding a job, finding and holding a spouse, and raising a family all are, in the natural course of things, chock-full of challenge and satisfaction, and cause rich affiliations to occur. They are the stuff of which life is made. It is odd that so many people should see themselves as living lives in which they go through meaningless motions.

The same applies even more emphatically to community activities. There is no shortage of important tasks, requiring people to take responsibility and effort, everywhere that human beings congregate. There are hungry to be fed, children to be taught, the uncivil to be civilized, the sick to be cared for, failures to be commiserated with and successes to be celebrated. All the raw material is always there, in every collection of human beings. Modernity has not done away with a bit of it.

On the contrary, one of the virtues of modernity is that it has given larger and larger proportions of people the wherewithal to extend more and more help. When a society is living on the margins of subsistence, Maslow's formulation sets in and competition for limited goods can sweep away all other considerations.* But given contemporary American wealth, under what conditions does a person of ordinary goodwill—not a saint,

---

* Elsewhere, I have elaborated on this thought by comparing village cultures in what I call "subsistence" vs. "sufficiency" environments. My generalization is that behaviors associated with Edward Banfield's "amoral familism" and Oscar Lewis's "image of the limited good" are found in cultures where no one is far from the possibility of starvation. In cultures where subsistence can be taken for granted and with loose social structures (the anthropologist's phrase for substantial personal freedom), generosity and community cooperation are taken for granted.[4]

just average—*not* feed a hungry neighbor? Under what conditions does a sick person go untended? Under what conditions do adults not keep a benevolent watch over children playing nearby? Everybody doesn't always behave in helpful ways, true, but how is it that in an average collection of human beings there is not a sufficient quantity of such responses? In short, how is it that we have managed in recent decades to *prevent* vital little platoons called "communities" from forming?

Allow me to anticipate here one big question that my own questions will have raised: What about the inner cities? Hasn't recent history demonstrated that poor urban neighborhoods in America are too alienating and impersonal to permit community, that in places where people are so poor and victimized by discrimination, human affiliations of the type I have described break down? I am not so pessimistic, and can call upon considerable historical evidence in support (urban ethnic communities, including black urban communities, being the main source). Still, it is fair to say that under such circumstances affiliations are more difficult to sustain and more vulnerable to disruption—especially including disruption by government policy. Let me suggest two responses. First, to argue that such neighborhoods are lacking in community at this moment in history is not to prove that community is an irrelevant issue, or that anything else can take its place. The second response is that something less than 4 percent of Americans live in those most battered neighborhoods. If it should be decided (over my objections) that some different system is needed for that 4 percent, so be it. But as we try to develop a social policy that enables people to pursue satisfying lives, it must be a system that first of all works for the 96 percent, then deals with the other 4 percent—not the other way around.

THE TENDRILS OF COMMUNITY

Now, to repeat the question: Why, in a nation with the wealth of the United States, would there not be enough people to attend naturally and fully to the functions of community that I have been describing?

The answer I am proposing is indicated by the image in the

title, "tendrils" of community. To occur in the first place, then to develop, certain kinds of affiliations must have something to attach themselves to. Communities exist because they have a reason to exist, some core of functions around which the affiliations that constitute a vital community can form and grow. When the government takes away a core function, it depletes not only the source of vitality pertaining to that particular function, but also the vitality of a much larger family of responses. By hiring professional social workers to care for those most in need, it cuts off nourishment to secondary and tertiary behaviors that have nothing to do with formal social work. An illustration: In the logic of the social engineer, there is no causal connection between such apparently disparate events as (1) the establishment of a welfare bureaucracy and (2) the reduced likelihood (after a passage of some years) that, when someone dies, a neighbor will prepare a casserole for the bereaved family's dinner. In the logic I am using, there *is* a causal connection, and one of great importance.

I am arguing ultimately from two premises. One is again straight from Aristotle, that the practice of a virtue has the characteristics of a habit and of a skill. People may be born with the capacity of being generous, but become generous only by practicing generosity. People have the capacity for honesty, but become honest only by practicing honesty.[5] The second, for which I do not have a specific source, is the human response to which I have referred several times: People tend not to do a chore when someone else will do it for them. At the micro-level, the dialogue between the government and the citizen goes roughly like this:

> "Do you want to go out and feed the hungry or are you going to sit here and watch television?"
> "I'm tired. What'll happen if I don't go?"
> "Well, if you don't go I guess I'll just have to do it myself."
> "In that case, you go."

It shows up in the aggregate as well. In the normal course of events, the personal income that people and corporations contribute to philanthropies "ought" to increase not only in raw dollar amounts, but as a proportion of income, as wealth itself increases: If I can afford to give away 5 percent of my income when I make $10,000, then (ceteris paribus, as always) when I make $11,000 I can afford to give away a higher percentage and still have more money for my personal use than I had before. From the beginning of the 1940s through 1964, this expectation held true: the richer the United States got, the greater the proportion of its wealth that was given to philanthropy. Then, suddenly, sometime during 1964–65, in the middle of an economic boom, this consistent trend was reversed. The proportion of wealth being given away began to fall even though wealth continued to increase. This new and disturbing trend continued through the rest of the 1960s, throughout the 1970s, and then suddenly reversed itself again in 1981 (during a period of hard times), when a new administration came to office that once more seemed to be saying "If you don't do it, nobody will." Figure 14 shows this intriguing history from 1950 through 1985.

I use the graph to illustrate, not as proof. But the causal relationship—government spending crowds out private philanthropy—has been demonstrated in a number of technical analyses.*⁶ The causal explanation needn't be much more complicated than the private dialogue ("What'll happen if I don't do it?") played out on a national scale.†

---

* The displacement effect is both exaggerated and understated by the illustrative case shown in the figure. It is exaggerated in that comparatively little philanthropy during the period shown in the figure (1950–85) went to services for poor people—the trend line reflects changes in a more generalized "propensity to contribute income to public causes." It is understated in that the technical analyses demonstrate dramatically how efficiently government funding for the poor drives out private money: Whatever money is contributed is shifted from the poor to other causes. In other words, it is not just that people stopped increasing the proportion of income given to philanthropy, much more of the money they *did* give would have gone to helping the poor in the absence of governmental action.

† For those who are curious how much more money would be donated today if the trend of the 1950s had continued: If the relationship between real personal income and percentage given away had persisted, we would in 1985 have been donating 5.1 percent of personal income, or $88.2 billion dollars more than we actually donated. To get an idea of the comparative size of such numbers, the

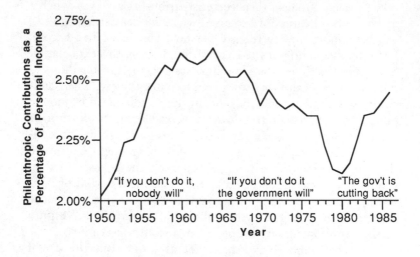

FIGURE 14
A COINCIDENCE OF POLICY RHETORIC
AND PRIVATE PHILANTHROPY . . .

SOURCES: Bureau of the Census, *Historical Statistics of the United States* (Washington, D.C.: Government Printing Office, 1975), Series F297–348 (for personal income), Series 398–411 (for philanthropic contributions), and Bureau of the Census, *Statistical Abstract of the United States 1987* (Washington, D.C.: Government Printing Office, 1987), table 713 and comparables in other volumes (for personal income), table 630 and comparables (for philanthropic contributions).

It seems to be inevitable. If the message is that if people don't do these things themselves then the state will hire people to do

---

cost of the entire federal "public aid" effort in 1985—comprising AFDC, Medicaid, social services, Supplemental Security Income, training programs, low-income energy assistance, surplus food for the needy, work-experience programs, refugee assistance, and a miscellany of other programs—came to $60 billion. The point is not a specific prediction, but a general statement: There is a whole lot of money that private individuals can, do, and would donate to public uses, depending on what the reality test tells them about who else will do what if they watch TV instead.

these things for them, that knowledge affects behavior. You may once again use yourself as a source of evidence.* Suppose, for example, that tomorrow you were told that every bit of government assistance to poor people—federal, state, and municipal—in your neighborhood had ended. If you are a physician, would this have any effect on your availability for pro bono services? If you are a member of a church board, would it have any effect on the agenda items for next week's meeting? If you are an unconnected member of the community, would you give any thought to what you might do to pick up needs that the government had so callously dropped? If you already do volunteer work, would you increase your efforts?

If you would be likely to function more actively as a member of your community under such circumstances, the puzzle to ponder is this: It is very probable that such activities will provide you with satisfactions. You can be fairly confident of this—so why is it that you are not behaving *now* as you would behave if the government stopped performing these functions? After all, the evening news is filled every night with stories of people who have fallen between the cracks of the existing social service system. Why not go out and take for yourself these satisfactions in the same full measure that you would take them if the government were no longer involved?

The correct answer is that "It just wouldn't be the same." If a child in the neighborhood will not be fed unless the neighborhood church feeds it, the church will feed that child. But if the church is merely a distribution point, if it is simply a choice of whether the church feeds the child or a Generous Outside Agency does it, the urgency is gone, and so is some of the response by the church members. And so is some of the vitality of that church.

Recall the formulation: Satisfactions are a product of responsibility, effort, and function. When the Generous Outside Agency has the action, the reality is that your level of responsibility is small and nebulous. Thus voluntary agencies are

---

* At the extremes are people who will be involved in community activities no matter what and misanthropes who will never be involved. I am referring to a wide middle range of people who can tip in either direction depending on circumstances.

faced with the problem of either finding something to do that does not have a government program competing with it, or of convincing prospective volunteers that they are doing something that is falling between the cracks. As government responsibilities expand, each of these cases becomes harder to make persuasively. Why donate $500 of your money (which represents a lot, to you) to a local agency when there is a bureaucracy in your city spending $20 million on the same function? Why give up an evening a week, when you're working a full day at your job, to do something for which the city has a full-time paid staff of several hundred people? If the job's not getting done, make them do what they're being paid to do.

None of this is meant to ignore the voluntary and philanthropic programs that exist; rather, I am suggesting that what we observe is the tip of what would exist otherwise, the behavior of a comparative few who are highly motivated. Nor am I at this particular moment making a case for the best way to feed hungry children. The welfare of the fed child is not the issue here; the issue is the vitality of the church as a community institution.* The church will be a satisfying institution of com-

---

* Another approach to such issues was developed by a research project at the American Enterprise Institute initiated by Peter L. Berger and Richard John Neuhaus. They explored the uses of what they termed "mediating structures," defined as "those institutions standing between the individual in his private life and the large institutions of public life"—local churches, for example. Their arguments anticipate many of the points made here, with the more sanguine conclusion that large-scale federal assistance can continue if channeled through the mediating structures. I am not optimistic, for the reasons that I explained in the discussion of what happens when the GOA provides the hundred parents with more money to pay teachers. It is quite possible that the use of mediating structures would result in more efficient and effective delivery of services than now exists, which is not a trivial benefit. But it is in my view unlikely that the benefits that I am most concerned with in this chapter will occur. It is not possible to get the benefits of a vital community on the cheap; the price *must* be authentic reliance on the community to do its job, because it is only authentic responsibility that will energize the response. Nonetheless, mediating structures is an intriguing concept that has gotten far too little attention from policy planners.[7]

munity life (not just religious life) to the extent that the members have something important to do; that institutional role will atrophy to the extent that it does not. Similarly for schools, clubs, chambers of commerce, and any other local institution. They have to have something to do, and their responsibility has to be real.

So I am proposing that there is nothing mysterious about why people become atomized in modern urban settings. Individuals are drawn to community affiliations and attach themselves to them in direct proportion to the functional value of those organizations. As people attach themselves to individual community institutions the aggregate intangible called "community" itself takes on a life and values that are greater than the sum of the parts. Take away the functions, and you take away the community. The cause of the problem is not a virus associated with modernity, it is a centralization of functions that shouldn't be centralized, and this is very much a matter of political choice, not ineluctable forces.

Is Anything Broken That Needs Fixing?

Even with the question put in those terms, one could ask, So what? Let us imagine an antagonist who has read faithfully to this point, and says:

"It is still not clear to me that we need any major reforms. I, for one, have a career that I enjoy. It both challenges me and interests me—it gives me a chance to 'exercise my realized capacities' just as the Aristotelian Principle prescribes. [Or: I do not have such a career, but nothing in social policy is preventing me from trying to find one.] I am deeply engaged in trying to be a good husband and father. [Or: I don't have a good marriage, or I have no marriage, but again, that's not the fault of social policy.] All the enabling conditions have been met for me—material resources, safety, self-respect, intrinsic rewards, friendships and intimate relationships with a few selected people.

"For me, there is nothing broken that needs fixing. I am, at this moment, under this system, living in very nearly the best of all possible worlds. Whatever the 'stopping point' for government must be, the government has so far not infringed upon it. On the contrary, I am quite busy enough already, and I prefer *not* to have to worry about all the things that contemporary social policy so conveniently takes care of for me. I want the poor and disadvantaged to be looked after and I am glad to pay taxes so that someone else will see that such things get done. It is precisely to escape from the demands of the old-fashioned community that I have moved to a housing division zoned in two-acre lots.

"The choice of a 'stopping point' is not such a difficult thing. It is to be solved pragmatically on the basis of costs and effectiveness. We are a rich enough country that we can make everybody comfortable and then let them pursue happiness as they see fit. If providing benefits to the less fortunate reaches a point that the work disincentives impair the nation's economy, then we should retrench. And costs must be kept within bounds. But these are practical economic calculations. As of now, I'm doing fine, the poor and disadvantaged don't seem to be complaining that they've got too many benefits, so what's the problem?"

In thinking about the position of this imaginary antagonist, I shift between two different responses, with different valences and implications. The first is to assume that he is right: He is living in the best of all possible worlds, for him. But such a world is not best for everyone, because of what I will call the problem of the upside-down pyramid. My second response is to argue that he is wrong. He doesn't know what he is missing. I will take up each response in turn.

The Pursuit of Happiness and the Problem of the Upside-Down Pyramid

Privilege, like poverty, is often first imagined in terms of money. The distribution of the population in terms of privilege is symbolically imagined as a pyramid with a broad base of ordinary folk at the bottom and then successively narrow strata of more privileged people at the higher levels rising to a narrow peak at the top peopled by Rockefellers and Mellons.

But it takes only a little thought to realize how little money has to do with leading a privileged life, just as income has only a little to do with living an impoverished life. Money buys access to things and possibilities but not to the capacity to enjoy them. In that sense, the privileged are not those with the most money but those with other gifts—natural abilities, curiosity and interests, realized through education—and enough money (which is not necessarily a lot) to exercise them.

Conceived in this way, the most privileged people are those with the largest number of options for finding satisfying ways of filling up the hours of their lives. The more privileged you are, the more options you have for pursuing happiness. In terms of the Aristotelian Principle ("Other things equal, human beings enjoy the exercise of their realized capacities . . . and this enjoyment increases the more the capacity is realized, or the greater its complexity"), you have both more capacities to choose from and higher levels of complexity within your reach.

You also have latitude for "wastage." It is possible that you would have found great satisfaction in becoming an engineer, but no matter. You fell in love with biology in college and ended up being a biologist, in which you also find great satisfaction. And if it hadn't been engineering or biology, it could have been one of the many other satisfying vocations that your level of cognitive skills would have permitted you to follow.

Now, suppose that you have no gifts. You are not particularly smart, nor especially well-coordinated, nor musical. You are not beautiful or witty or charismatic. How, in the best of all possible worlds, will it come to pass that you reach the end of your life happy? It is not a rhetorical question. I begin from the assumption that in a good society, *everyone* may pursue happiness, not just the smart or the rich or the gifted. But the pyramid of options for achieving happiness narrows rapidly as gifts narrow, and the people at the bottom of the socioeconomic ladder are often not only the poorest people and the least educated, but also those with the fewest *options* for achieving happiness. Whence the upside-down pyramid.*

---

* I had better say explicitly what should be obvious: The socioeconomic relationship is a statistical tendency. Money and social status have very little inherent causal role. There are plenty of people

This logic admits of an ideological objection. We may decide that there is no such thing as the individual without special gifts; all that is required is a social system that liberates them. A revolution succeeded in Russia on just such expectations—in the best of all possible Soviet worlds "the average human type will rise to the heights of an Aristotle, a Goethe, or a Marx,"[8] as Leon Trotsky told us.

Against that, I propose this formulation: Yes, there are hidden resources in just about everyone, resources that can make just about everyone a self-determining, self-respecting, competent human being. But the medians in the many assets which humans possess are going to remain about where they are now. And now and forever more, half of the human race will at any moment be below the median on any given measure. Only a comparatively few will ever have any one asset that is so far above average that they can compete for the peaks in any field, whether the peak is defined as Nobel Laureate or California's top Chevrolet salesman. A system founded on the assumption that the only successful lives are the visibly brilliant ones is bound to define the bulk of the population as unsuccessful. Or to remain within the vocabulary of the pursuit of happiness, very large proportions of the population are not going to be achieving happiness by "the exercise of their realized capacities" in the sense that they excel in some specific vocational (or avocational) skill.

So how are we to construct society so that anyone, no matter what his gifts, can reach the age of seventy, look back on his life, and be able to say it has been a happy life, filled with deep and justified satisfactions? The answer is that, no matter what his gifts, he will in a properly run society be able to say things such as,

"I was a good parent to my children,"
"I was a good neighbor,"
"I always pulled my own weight,"

---

high on the economic ladder who watch TV all day, plenty of people with less money who pursue varied and complex interests. Usually, however, people with greater gifts do better economically.

and that he lived among people who respected those achievements.

These are excellent things to be able to say of a life. They are probably the best there are. The point of the upside-down pyramid is that, for many people, these are the *only* options. There is no possibility of having been famous to offset having been a poor parent, no consolation of an absorbing career to compensate for having had too few friends. We are forced to this question: If we assume a man of no special skills, under what circumstances will society enable him to achieve these goals? And the answer centers on one particular little platoon of immense importance, the immediate physical neighborhood in which he lives.

This is not a bad thing, but it is to some extent a *necessary* thing. Consider the situation of a man who works hard at a low-skill, low-responsibility job—he is a baggage handler, let's say. He is not a potential surgeon just needing a chance to reveal his potential, he is not a prospective supervisor. He is an ordinary working stiff, as millions are. Consider first the surgeon's situation, then compare it with the baggage handler's.

The surgeon's world of affiliations (as the lawyer's or businessman's) may consist of many little islands: old school friends, golfing friends, fishing friends, doctor friends; professional affiliations at the clinic and the hospital; memberships in clubs and fashionable charities; seasons' tickets for whatever is locally chic. His world doesn't have to include all of these islands, but it may if he so wishes. He has options. One of the reasons the surgeon buys the house with the two-acre lot is to have a refuge, to get away from the demands of the geographic community.

The surgeon's wider world also offers him protections against onslaughts on his self-esteem. He can be a failure at home, he can be inactive in his geographic community, and still see himself as "measuring up" in terms of his contribution to society. And as far as the esteem of others is concerned, *of course* he is esteemed by society at large—that's a given.

For the baggage handler, the immediate geographic community is much more his entire world. The baggage handler's friends are likely to come from the neighborhood, not across town, from a bar down the street, not the country club five miles away. A night out is likely to be at a local movie theater, not the Civic Arts Center. Equally importantly, the baggage handler's sense of who he is, both his self-respect and self-esteem, are rooted much more deeply in the immediate neighborhood than are the self-esteem and self-respect of the surgeon. No underlings scurry to assist him. No patients tell him how wonderful he is. If he gets respect, it is primarily from his family and neighbors. If he is appreciated, it is primarily by his family and neighbors.

And where are his satisfactions to come from? What are going to be for him the activities serving important functions for which he has responsibility? He is not going to save a life or develop a new procedure for arterial bypass or "exercise his realized capacities" in any other way that depends on unusual personal assets. What remains to him, however, is the one resource that he *can* contribute and that *will* be highly valued, if the circumstances are right. He can be a good neighbor.

He can help feed the hungry—especially if his neighborhood is enough of a functioning community not to be overwhelmed with them. He can comfort the bereaved. He can be a source of support to people who are having a hard time, just as they can help him. And in these most important of all possible "things to take trouble over," he can do as well as anyone.

This point needs emphasis. Throughout the discussion of the upside-down pyramid, I have been in one sense relentlessly elitist. Some people have more options than others, the reason they have more options is that they have more "realized capacities," and this difference in options is not going to disappear no matter what social system is in place. It cannot disappear because the latent capacities themselves differ. People vary in such things as cognitive skills, interpersonal skills, small motor skills, ambition, industriousness, and the rest. With this view of the situation goes an acceptance of such conclusions as: If we give the baggage handler the same income as the surgeon, he will not then acquire the same satisfactions that the surgeon enjoys. Having adopted this elitist argument, there is another that I must make at least as forcefully: The socioeconomically advantaged people in my hierarchical view have *more* options, but not *better* ones for achieving happiness.

I am trying to focus attention on one aspect of the situation facing the baggage handler: If it is true that the little platoon constituting the immediate geographic neighborhood is extremely important to the lives of many people—probably most—and *if there are few other alternatives,* especially to those at the bottom of the socioeconomic pyramid—then it becomes extremely important to consider how a neighborhood becomes a functioning little platoon that provides such sources of satisfaction.

First, because affiliations are both the basis for living according to one's values and the building blocks of a vital little platoon, it *becomes extremely important to let the low-income person affiliate with people who think as he does.* No effort is required to get him to do so, if he is given the choice. When he rents an apartment, he will choose a neighborhood where people share his values over a neighborhood where they don't, *if* he is given the choice. No effort is required to get landlords to give preference to tenants like the baggage handler over someone with the same amount of money who is less respectable. If the choice is left undistorted, neighborhoods of low-income working people, sharing common values, will form. All that social policy has to do is make sure that it doesn't interfere.

Second, because the important satisfactions are so bound up with the functions of community, social policy must be designed to leave those functions in the community. Or to bring the question back to my antagonist who prefers to pay other people to take care of such things for him: I concede his right to set up a system in which *he* pays other people to do these things but that does not mean it is appropriate to run the whole country that way.

Having worked through that argument, however, it must also be acknowledged that my imaginary antagonist has an excellent response. He says:

"You are really playing Lady Bountiful in reverse. I am satisfied with my life the way it is, including an arrangement whereby the government has the responsibility for taking care of all sorts of human needs I don't want to have to worry about. You seem to be saying that such a system impedes others from pursuing happiness. If that's the case, why don't you go out and find some of these people at the bottom of your up-side-down pyramid who agree with you? You will fail to come close to a majority. Most people on the lower levels of the pyramid don't want fewer benefits; they want more. They don't want government to leave their communities on their own; they want more things done for them. Ultimately, isn't the argument of the upside-down pyramid just another instance of trying to tell other people what's good for them?"

My answer is: Yes and no. If the country is to be run by a sequence of national legislative decisions in which a majority may pass any law it pleases, then yes. Put it to an up-and-down vote, and a majority of people given the chance to get something from the government will take that chance more often than not, and over time the result will be similar to the process we have witnessed in modern Western democracies—indeed, in every democracy everywhere, throughout history.

But on another level I am arguing for a world in which no one is at the mercy of strangers' opinions about how he should live, neither mine nor anyone else's. I am arguing for a system in which we stop making ad hoc judgments about what other people "really" need, and obliging those others to live by them. I am arguing that we must try to step outside the exigencies of day-to-day politics and lay down a way of running society that will protect us from ourselves, and from each other, in years to come. This is why any nation needs a constitution, and why I believe that we should return to a more literal implementation of ours.

Let me leave the problem of the upside-down pyramid at that, and proceed to my other reason for thinking that all is not well with the current state of affairs, even for the privileged person who perceives no need for the little platoon called community.

COMMUNITY AS THE THIRD DIMENSION IN TWO-DIMENSIONAL LIVES

The story so far is that my imaginary antagonist on his two-acre lot has asked to opt out of becoming involved in his community. If the government stops doing certain things, let us say that he will respond by contributing more than he does now, in money and perhaps in personal time and effort. But even conceding this, he argues that for him the world will have changed for the worse. He *wants* the government to take the trouble out of the community functions I have described, so he can concentrate on the other little platoons through which he pursues happiness—work, and family.

Now I argue that he is ignoring the reverberations that a vital community has for the things that he does value in his life. Even for those who want to pay people to do the work of the community for them, there are good reasons to want to be paying that money to people nearby, not to people far away. It is the same problem of interconnectedness that was discussed in the case of school systems. Let me take as an example the little platoon known as the family, and try to trace just a few of the paths that interconnect the satisfactions of family with the satisfactions obtained by leaving communities with something to do.

A FUNCTIONING COMMUNITY AND A FUNCTIONING FAMILY

Marriage, like other affiliations, acquires content over time. On the wedding day the two people are already attracted to each other and they have aspirations for what the marriage will become, but the things that constitute a good marriage are in embryonic form. The clichés are once again true: Marriage and family become satisfying cumulatively through years of shared experiences. Mutual reliance, respect, and trust are essential. And so on.

The question then becomes, What shared experiences? Mutual reliance for what purposes? Mutual respect for what accomplishments? Mutual trust based on what? For a comparatively few people, the answer might be something like, "Our shared love of opera," or "Mutual respect based on our accomplishments in our respective careers"; but commonly the raw materials center on paying the mortgage, raising the children, and the things that happen in the immediate physical vicinity of the home and work.

Specifically, one extremely important source of mutual respect, reliance, and trust involves *the way that the married couple interact with the people around them.* To gain the respect of a virtuous spouse, one must act virtuously, and to practice the habit of virtue requires an environment in which one has opportunities. A functioning community—which is to say, a community with functions to fulfill—provides an extremely important venue for practicing virtue. It is a stage upon which the partners in a marriage may reveal themselves to each other. It also provides a marriage with the room it needs to flourish: Husbands and wives who are everything to each other are in peril of one day being not nearly enough. Yet if their "communities" are entirely separate ones, they are likely to be pulled apart.

The same dynamics impinge on another of the central functions of marriage, the "passing on" of values from parent to child. It is one of the most satisfying of the roles of parenthood. It happens both through the parents' example and by having available for the child an environment in which the child can develop the habits of virtue that the parents have taught. In both cases, the existence of a community is important, for the process of passing things on once again involves the reality test. Suppose, for example, that you want to pass on to your children the virtue of compassion. Under what circumstances will this be a heritage that can be passed on? How does one bequeath a habit of helping others, of giving, of generosity, if this has not been part of one's own life? Once again, the activities immediately surrounding the home—the functions of the community—provide raw material. It is not necessary that the parent be engaged in every possible community activity. On the contrary, most of what is involved in being a "good neighbor" as I am using the term does not involve organized activity at all. It seems necessary, however, that there be an environment in which the child observes these things happening, knows people who are engaged in them, and comes to understand the concept of social obligation by observing other people living according to that concept. Watching parents support compassionate politicians just isn't the same.

These comments apply as well to parents who prefer to pay other people to perform the functions of community. If such parents are engaged in directly paying other people *in the community*—supporting local institutions—they at least must do such things as choose whom they will pay and how much. And even these actions provide a richer basis for instruction than signing a 1040 Form and then trying to explain compassion to the child in the abstract.

A FUNCTIONING COMMUNITY AND
THE SINGLE-PARENT FAMILY

The interconnections linking functioning communities with functioning families go far beyond these. Many are self-evident (functioning communities tend to have low crime and good schools, which makes it much easier to have functioning families, for example). I will end the discussion of the interconnections with a less obvious example involving the single woman without a job, without education, without the support of a male, and with children to raise. She is receiving assistance. How is that assistance to be given so that it gives the woman and her children alike their best chance to live satisfying lives?

One answer is: in whatever way gives her the best chance to become self-determining and self-respecting by becoming economically self-sufficient. But that does not happen naturally no matter how much material support is provided during the process. To move from dependence to precarious independence to secure independence is an intimidating and exhausting experience, and *there has to be a reason to do it.* Functioning communities can provide that reason, both in the form of encouragement, holding out to the woman the prospect of something-worth-having (full-fledged membership in a community she wants to be a part of), and in the form of prodding, holding up to the woman the reasons why failing to become self-sufficient is a drain on the community.* And when the assistance itself is being provided by people in the locality, the pressures on her to become a self-determining, self-respecting person are going to be much greater than if the money comes from a bureaucracy. This is the reason for observing earlier that the fed

---

* Functioning communities are also effective in discouraging males from making single mothers out of single women in the first place.

child will be better off if fed by the church instead of by a social service bureaucracy. The goal is not just to feed the family and keep them in shelter, but to provide that family with the enabling conditions for pursuing happiness, and the more short-term encouragement *and* pressure on them to become self-sufficient in the long term, the better for the family.

But in some ways the more provocative case involves the single woman with children who for some reason cannot be expected to become self-sufficient, or for whom it is especially difficult. There are many reasons why this might be the case, and it raises intriguing questions. How can she still "measure up" to community norms and thereby achieve self-respect? How does she pass on to her children, by her example, a good way to live in the world? The options are few and forced. One of the most obvious and best is that *she has herself been a contributor to the community*, by being a good neighbor in all the ways that she indeed can be, economically self-supporting or not, if she lives in a vital community. One of the important reasons for leaving the functions of a community in the community is that doing so increases the chances for the recipients of help to be givers of help as well. The same institutions that are providing the dependent with help have some things they will be asking in return, and through that lies a possibility for authentic self-respect. The only way to "take the stigma out of welfare" is to provide a means of paying it back.

Perhaps I have used too many formal social service examples of community (feeding the hungry) and not enough informal ones (taking a casserole to the bereaved family). I should emphasize, therefore, that I am not envisioning an ideal society in which everyone is a social worker, but one in which the full dimensions of being a neighbor are played out in full view of everyone, on the local stage. The motivation underlying the vision is not to construct a more efficient way of delivering social services, but to permit communities to be communities.

The Gain

A summing-up: The ways in which people pursue happiness are rooted in, processed through, and enhanced by little platoons. Little platoons are vital insofar as they consist of people voluntarily doing important things together. To enable people to pursue happiness, good social policy consists of leaving the important things in life for people to do for themselves, and protecting them from coercion by others as they go about their lives.

The policy principle may be stated as simply as this: No one has to teach people how to pursue happiness. Unless impeded, people form communities that allow them to get the most satisfaction from the material resources they have. Unless impeded, they enforce norms of safety that they find adequate. Unless impeded, they develop norms of self-respect that are satisfying and realistic for the members of that community. Unless impeded, people engage in activities that they find to be intrinsically rewarding, and they know (without being taught) how to invest uninteresting activities with intrinsic rewards.

The behaviors that lead to these happy results do not have to be prompted by or mandated for anyone, neither for people with wealth and education nor for people with little money and little education. Does everyone always act in every way to achieve these positive results? No. My assertion rather is that these behaviors reach a maximum on their own. Unless impeded, people continually make small, incremental changes in their lives that facilitate their pursuit of happiness, and the mechanism whereby they accomplish this is voluntary affiliations with other people. To encourage, nourish, and protect vital little platoons, the government's main task is to make sure that no one interferes with people coming together in these voluntary acts of mutual benefit.

But aren't my fears after all more theoretical than real? Aren't we muddling through, most of us, reasonably well? What, finally, is to be gained?

My sense of the present state of affairs is captured by one of Adam Smith's thought experiments in *The Theory of Moral Sentiments*, and it provides a fitting conclusion to this discussion. In this passage, Smith begins by asking his readers to "suppose that the great empire of China, with all its myriads of inhabitants, was suddenly swallowed up by an earthquake." How would a humane man in Europe be affected upon hearing the dreadful news? Smith sketches the predictable reactions. This humane gentleman would express his great sorrow. He would reflect upon the precariousness of life. He might then speculate upon the economic effects this catastrophe would have on the rest of the world. And then he would go about his business "with the same ease and tranquility as if no such accident had happened."[9] This, Smith continues, is the understandable consequence of distance and disconnection, and he continues by discussing the very different response of the same man to people whose happiness he *does* affect. This is what Smith, the emblem of uncaring laissez-faire self-interest, has to say:

> When the happiness or misery of others depends in any respect upon our conduct, we dare not, as self-love might suggest to us, prefer the interest of one to that of many. The man within immediately calls to us, that we value ourselves too much and other people too little, and that, by doing so, we render ourselves the proper object of the contempt and indignation of our brethren.[10]

Human nature has not changed since the eighteenth century. I am arguing that when we are disconnected from the elemental functions of community and "the happiness or misery of others" around us no longer depends in any meaningful way upon our conduct, we consign even our neighbors to a kind of China from which we become as detached as Smith's humane and otherwise compassionate gentleman. The loss this represents is not redeemed by satisfactions from career nor wholly compensated even by the satisfactions of family. No matter how much satisfaction we may derive from work and family, they are only two dimensions of life in a three-dimensional world.

13

"To Close the Circle of Our Felicities"

In the Best of All Possible Worlds, How Would You Know?

Sometimes openly, sometimes in the subtext, this has been a book about attainable utopia, the best of all possible worlds. But it has been therefore an imperfect utopia. In my best of all possible worlds, some people still are poor, some children still grow up badly educated, criminals still commit crimes, and human beings still do foolish and hurtful things to themselves and to other human beings. But upon reflection, this thought should temper our ambitions: That's what the best of all possible worlds would really be like.

Imagine a time centuries hence when some nation, somewhere, has reached the best of all possible political worlds. The laws and institutions of the country have been so arranged that day-to-day life is as good (however you choose to define the word) as possibly can be, so good that the legislature has nearly put itself out of business. Minor modifications to the existing arrangements are made from time to time to adjust to changing external conditions, but these are only refinements to basic laws and structures of government that have produced a situation in which all good things within the control of government are maximized and all bad things within the control of government are minimized. Trying to improve on any one aspect of life by changing the law or starting a new program will create enough problems elsewhere that, on balance, things will be worse than before.

What would that world look like *to the people living in it at the time?*

One possibility, of course, is that humans are perfectible, in which case we may imagine a thoroughgoing utopia in which everyone is prosperous, a good citizen, and happy. But if you are any less optimistic, assuming that humans are and always will be infinitely variegated, then a curious implication follows: *If you were living in that best of all possible worlds, you would be unaware of it.* Omniscient bystanders observing from outside the system, armed with a social science calculus that can tell them the first derivative for a culture, would know that any attempt to reduce the bad things still further would be futile, only increasing the net amount of bad things. But you, living in the attainable utopia, would have no way of knowing that any additional effort would move you from the-best-that-can-be to some inferior alternative.

You would see around you what would look like clear proof of your government's imperfection. Perhaps everyone would have access to good food—but some would be malnourished nonetheless. Everyone might have it within his power to have decent shelter—but some would live in squalor anyway. In the best of all political worlds, some parents would still abuse their children, for human beings sometimes behave terribly. All of these things would happen, because it is inconceivable that in the best of all possible worlds people will be force-fed, or made to be tidy, or put under twenty-four-hour-a-day surveillance.

In the best of all possible worlds, the incidence of such problems would be much smaller than it is now, let us assume. But the incidence would be nontrivially greater than zero, and the existence of such bad things would inevitably raise cries for their alleviation. The smaller the amounts of the bad things, the more vocal the cries ("In a society as rich as ours, it is intolerable that a single person should . . . ," etc.). And if enough people in the society measured progress by counting the number of abused children and hungry people, *they would succeed in their campaign*. They would legislate new steps to reduce the observed problems, and thereby move past the best-that-can-be, down the slope on the far side of the peak, and begin to realize it only many years later when it finally became apparent that they had been using the wrong measures of success.

We in the United States at this point in history are very far from the best of all possible worlds. But we do have to worry about whether we are making progress toward it, and the generic problem we face is the same as that faced by the people living unknowingly in utopia. The bad-thing-to-be-reduced is malnourished children, let us say. We have different ways to try to reduce it. Plan A promises to get food into the hands of every one of the needy children within a week from now. Plan B promises to get food to some of those children within a year from now. Plan C has nothing at all to do with the distribution of food but rather with the circumstances under which people become parents, and promises that the number of malnourished children will get steadily smaller over the years. No one who is trying to decide among these options is under the illusion that reducing the number of malnourished children is the *only* good to be fostered. Hardly anyone who has lived through the last few decades is under the illusion that just because a program promises to do something, it will happen. So the question remains: Which options will work? Which options will do more harm than good? How can we know how to make progress?

Knowing That We Are Making Progress

In the preceding chapters, I have argued for two answers. The more pragmatic one is that policymakers tackling discrete social problems will be well served if they use the concept of human happiness as a backdrop against which to assess results and to design solutions. In part, this is as simple as spending more time thinking about the effects of policies on individuals rather than aggregating results. In part, it is as simple as spending more time articulating what the goal of a policy really is, asking ourselves more rigorously, What are we really trying to accomplish? The key to making these efforts productive is to apply them to an understanding of the enabling conditions for the pursuit of happiness. The more accurately we understand what gives people lasting and justified satisfaction with their lives, the more accurately we will discern whether we are gaining or losing ground.

This quest for understanding is one in which the social sciences may participate and indeed already have, much more than has been recognized. By all the evidence that science has been able to muster, people *need* to be self-determining, accountable, and absorbed in stretching their capacities, just as they need food and shelter. The crucial question that must decisively affect policy is whether it is possible to make people *feel as if* they are self-determining, accountable, and realizing their capacities when they are not.

Social programs have been designed as if it were enough to get people to "feel as if," designed seemingly on the assumption that there can be challenge without risks, accountability without penalties, self-determination without the assumption that every person—*everyone* not mentally deranged—possesses freedom of will. I have suggested that smoke and mirrors don't work, that these fundamental wellsprings of human satisfaction must rest on reality. The test that any proposed program must meet is that it *really does* contribute to them.

Still within the realm of pragmatic possibilities, I have argued that the design of programs will also become much more productive when we step back from the problem and ask how it can be that the problem exists in the first place, given what we know about the pursuit of happiness. It is only when we come to realize of many social problems that it is above all *odd* that they should exist that we will begin to think of natural solutions. Only then will we stop trying to channel behavior and instead identify the ways in which people are being prevented from behaving in the ordinary ways that would mitigate the problem. Many important improvements can be made in social policy by using this framework, without having to restructure government from the ground up.

My second response to the problem leads me to the not-at-all-pragmatic conclusion that we can be most confident we are making progress when people are as free as possible to make the thousands of small choices that nudge them toward environments in which they are better able to pursue happiness. I have argued that policymakers who try to manage and guide those choices into outcomes that are more fair, or just, or generous than those which would occur otherwise, are deluding themselves. The billions of microtransactions that make up the *actuality* of the most carefully engineered social program are beyond the comprehension or control of planners, and the aggregate impact of the program, especially in the long-term, is not only beyond their control but beyond their prediction. In contrast, two built-in safety devices limit the damage done by individual voluntary transactions. One is that mistakes affect fewer people. The second is that, for a transaction to occur, all parties must at least believe that the outcome is an improvement over the existing situation. The great virtue of the voluntary transaction is that they are usually right.

Furthermore, I have argued, the longer one explores the constituent elements of the pursuit of happiness, the more apparent it becomes that it is *the act of making those choices* that constitutes the stuff of the process called "pursuing happiness." I have not meant by that a series of relentlessly precise and detached calculations of one's own self-interest, but engagement in the multiple, complicated sets of pressures, inducements, supplications, penalties, manipulations, fortuities—and, yes, unfairnesses and inequalities—that make up life within little platoons.

And all this being the case, much of what central government must do first of all is to leave people alone, and then make sure that they are left alone by others—that people are restrained from the use of force against each other.

This line of thinking, however, leads to the abyss. For one response is, Yes, by all means the government must make sure that people are protected from the use of force—it must protect car buyers from being forced by General Motors to buy cars without air bags, protect tenants from being forced to pay whatever the landlord wants to charge, protect businesswomen from being forced not to belong to men-only business clubs. . . . And all these protections require the government to intervene on behalf of some citizens to redress inequalities of power and influence.

I stand on the other side of that abyss, saying to such responses, No, they miss the point. But that's why I call it an abyss. It is deep, wide, and hard to bridge. To try to do so would require another book within this one. Since from the beginning I have asserted that this is a practical book for dealing with real social problems, let me therefore conclude with some propositions about why perhaps "leaving people alone," while not *realistic* in terms of political realities, is more *practical* than one might think—which is to say, it might actually work if we gave it a chance. Further: The chances of it working increase, not diminish, with each advance in technology and each increase in national wealth.

The first proposition is that humans acting in a private capacity *if restrained from the use of force* have a remarkably good history. To test this, pick your favorite image of private people acting oppressively—a slumlord, perhaps, or white oligarchs in a southern town in Jim Crow days, or some rapacious nineteenth-century monopoly. Now ask: Under what conditions are or were they able to do bad things for a long time without the connivance of the state? Without special laws and regulations being passed on their behalf? Without being allowed by the state to use coercion? I suggest that the longer you consider each specific instance that comes to mind, the more plausible you will find this rule of thumb: It is really very difficult for people—including large associations of people and huge corporations—to do anything very bad, for very long, when they are not buttressed by the threat of physical coercion. Private oppression deprived of access to force withers away rather rapidly.

The second proposition is that modern technology has made it more practical than ever before for governments to leave people alone. Small tyrannies in which private groups co-opt the police power have historically been a problem—the white oligarchs I mentioned above, the company that runs a violence-enforced company town, the union that runs a violence-enforced closed shop, or more informal arrangements in which illicit power is lodged in small places. But such small tyrannies rely on captive audiences and safety from exposure, and one of the serendipitous results of modernity is that both conditions have become increasingly difficult to meet. For one thing, it is simply much easier for most people to move around today than it was a hundred years ago—financially, logistically, psychologically. Easier to acquire information about alternatives. Easier to change their physical locations, their jobs, their spouses, their style of life, their political allegiances—you name it. The repertoire of responses that technology has made available to the ordinary person, including poor people, has tended to expand enormously with modernity.

At least as important, however, is the ombudsman's role of the modern communications media—not just the networks, but the role of the six o'clock news in covering any conceivable story in which the big guys have been picking on the little guys. Throughout American history, the role of the newspapers in exposing abuses has been large, but with the advent of television, the scope and resources for uncovering these mushroomed. It may be said of the civil rights movement, for example, that it both required and was made inevitable by television. But we need not limit the examples to great national issues. The exposure of small local instances of malfeasance, sharp practice, and fraud are all wonderful human-interest stories and hence very good business. Television has found a lucrative market that is eternally self-sustaining—and in the process, has made decentralization of government more practical.

The third proposition is that contemporary levels of aggregate wealth open up possibilities for leaving people alone that did not formerly exist. Much of our thinking about "meeting the needs of the poor" continues to be based on an assumption of scarcity, as if the system for helping poor people must tap every last remnant of human generosity and a little bit more in order to get enough, as if the prodigious growth of American wealth has no bearing on the flexibility the nation has in choosing ways to deal with poverty and disadvantage. As each year goes by, it becomes possible for us to employ a more and more "inefficient" system—a system that does not need to extract the maximum from everyone, and indeed leaves many free riders—and still have plenty of dollar resources to meet problems. Indeed, if this book has tried to say anything, it is that dollars are a trivial part of the problem. The question is not whether everybody would behave generously if the central government quit acting as the alms collector and alms distributor, but whether a fair-sized segment of the population would behave generously—not an outlandish possibility.

INVENTING UTOPIA: A FANTASY

All this is radical stuff, in the sense that, taken seriously, it implies a radically more decentralized and limited government than any that is seriously contemplated. And yet we Americans are a people with a radical heritage. Just how radical is brought home by considering the form of government we once had in light of the most extreme philosophical versions of limited government.

In 1974, a professor in the Harvard philosophy department named Robert Nozick nailed down that extreme in a book entitled *Anarchy, State, and Utopia*, a brilliant and wacky book in which mathematical logic sits side by side with thought experiments involving Wilt Chamberlain and a moose named Thidwick. Nozick eventually takes up the subject of utopia and a thought experiment for imagining what it might be like.

Nozick asks you to imagine utopia first by making up the one you like best. Imagine for yourself, he asks, the ideal world for *you*. It may be any kind of world you happen to find most desirable, and you may people it with whomever you wish. Before you proceed to concoct an imaginary world filled with beautiful and amusing people who are devoted utterly to your pleasure, however, Nozick adds one stipulation. It so happens that *every other person* in this imaginary world of yours must be given the same "imagining rights" that you have. Thus if they can imagine a better world for themselves than you have created for them (as they surely can if you have given them only the option of being an adoring subject), they are free to emigrate from your world and no longer be part of your dream.

You, not desiring to be king of a depopulated world, are then to imagine a new utopia that is more likely to keep the inhabitants whose company you desire. Obviously, you have to give them something of value. A good income. A nice place to live. Some job prestige, maybe. You won't be able to be a dictator; you will have to share power with them. Then you stop and consider this new version of your utopia, no longer quite so loaded in your favor as the previous version but still the next-best-thing, and ask whether the people you want to be with you in this world will consent to remain. If they won't, you have to imagine a new world, making more concessions.

And so the process goes on. The iterations come to rest when you have finally imagined a world in which, Nozick writes, "*none* of the inhabitants of the world can *imagine* an alternative world they would rather live in, which (they believe) would continue to exist if all of its rational inhabitants had the same rights of imagining and emigrating."[1]

What might such a world be like? Abbreviated, Nozick's logic is that you cannot expect anyone to stay in your world if you are able to extract from the others something that they value more highly than whatever you contribute by your presence. By the same token, you need not consent to live in a world in which you receive less than you contribute, for you can always find some other world that will offer you more. But this doesn't mean narrowly defined transactions of payment for delivery of goods and services. Nozick's utopia is fascinating in large part because it does *not* depend on a narrowly stipulated set of goods that are being valued and exchanged.

Now, for "worlds," substitute "associations," and imagine a society composed of thousands of such associations. The values that are held by the members of different associations may vary infinitely.* An Amish religious community may exist in utopia, for those who find it the most desirable world for them to live in. An association may be run by the precepts of John Locke or of John Rawls, as it sees fit. To be utopia, it is necessary only that there be numerous associations, freely formed. It is forbidden only that any association force anyone to be a member.

---

* I am drastically condensing Nozick's discussion of utopia, which is much more detailed and precise than I indicate here, and extrapolating my own examples, of which Nozick might or might not approve.

INVENTING UTOPIA: A REALITY

Nozick's utopia, like all utopias, is a fantasy. But suppose, for the fun of it, that a people decided to translate it into reality. What would be the closest they could approach the ideal, given the constraints of the real world?

The central authority would have to provide basic protections so that the associations could not override the ability of people to come and go freely. The best way to do that would be to invest individuals with certain absolute rights and to invest the central authority with certain limited powers to prevent associations from putting up barriers to the free exercise of those rights. Apart from vigorously enforcing the basic protections (in effect, making sure that associations played according to the original rules), the central government wouldn't be permitted to do much. People would be left alone to structure the lives of their communities as they saw fit.

Because it is the real world we are talking about, no longer a fantasy, the "associations" would be towns, and they would have to possess taxing power and the right to pass laws by majority vote—which means there would be somewhat less than the constant unanimous consent of an "association." But these laws would be constrained by the basic rules of the game adopted at the outset, enforced by the central government. And (still being practical about it), the existence of a great many towns in some proximity to one another would at once provide the easiest remedy to bad government and also restrain the worst features of government: foolish laws drive out good citizens.

Or in other words, translating Nozick's utopia into reality would produce a structure eerily similar to the one produced in Philadelphia in 1787. Not perfectly, of course. The original vision left more room for little tyrannies than it should have (not to mention the great tyranny of slavery). But we came very close once, and for a long while we seemed to be on a path that was taking us still closer. And it had nothing to do with abstract utopias. This is how Thomas Jefferson put it, not when he was philosophizing, not when he was contemplating fanciful hopes and idealistic dreams, but in his first inaugural speech, on the day he undertook to govern a working republic:

Entertaining a due sense of our equal right to the use of our own faculties, to the acquisitions of our industry, to honor and confidence from our fellow citizens . . . , what more is necessary to make us a happy and prosperous people? Still one thing more, fellow citizens—a wise and frugal government, which shall restrain men from injuring one another, which shall leave them otherwise free to regulate their own pursuits of industry and improvement, and shall not take from the mouth of labor the bread it has earned. This is the sum of good government, and this is necessary to close the circle of our felicities.[2]

I am asking that we take more seriously the proposition that Jefferson's was a vision suitable not only for a struggling agricultural nation at the outset of the nineteenth century but also for a wealthy, postindustrial nation at the close of the twentieth.

Acknowledgments

I wrote *In Pursuit* while continuing to enjoy the gift of time to read, think, and write that the Manhattan Institute for Policy Research has afforded me for almost six years now. My special thanks go to William Hammett, president of the Manhattan Institute, who not only believes that ideas should drive the debate about policy but acts on that belief. My thanks go as well to the Bradley Foundation, which for the last two years has funded a fellowship to help support my work.

Leslee Spoor took time from her other responsibilities at the Manhattan Institute to make my life much more trouble-free than I deserve. David Shipley was endlessly patient as he ran interference for me at Simon and Schuster. Joan Kennedy Taylor watched the book develop and, as in the old days, told me how to make numerous improvements. Walter Olsen read an early draft and suggested a far better way of opening the book—which also finally went by the wayside, but had pointed me in the right direction. Michael Novak brought his unique combination of erudition and humanity to my discussion of Aristotle's concept of happiness and thereby improved it immeasurably. I thank each of them.

Part 3 of *In Pursuit* draws with little formal citation from one intellectual tradition that is commonly identified with John Locke and Adam Smith and another commonly identified with Edmund Burke. (Some will find these traditions incom-

304

patible. I do not. My feeling is, if Burke could admire Smith, why can't I admire both?) There are so few citations because often I haven't any idea which of the many people who said the same thing in different ways over the last three centuries should get the credit. I will take this opportunity to acknowledge my great, if diffuse, debt to two contemporary exponents of classical liberalism, Friedrich Hayek and Milton Friedman, and of conservatism, Russell Kirk and Robert Nisbet.

This has been an intimidating book to write, with many moments when I was sure it was a rotten idea. James Q. Wilson probably doesn't even remember, but a few words of his no-nonsense encouragement in the early days stayed with me throughout the effort. Others whose interest and encouragement at critical moments were appreciated include Michael Joyce, Edward Crane, Richard Vigilante, and Miles Hoffman.

This has also been a difficult book to write. Now that it's over, I cannot imagine having done it without my editor, Alice Mayhew, and her commitment to getting the best that her authors have in them no matter how peculiar their ideas. To Alice, thanks and admiration.

And Catherine. This time, she was busy with a book of her own, not to mention a baby, so it wasn't until the penultimate version—or what we thought at the time was the penultimate version—that she began working on *In Pursuit*, finding the lapses that so obviously need attention after she points them out. Until then, all she contributed was happiness itself.

Notes

PROLOGUE

1. Alexis de Tocqueville, *Democracy in America*, ed. J. P. Mayer, trans. George Lawrence (New York: Doubleday, 1969), 62.
2. Ibid., 69.
3. Ibid., 62.
4. Ibid.
5. Ibid., 68–69.
6. Quoted in Richard Hofstadter, *The American Political Tradition and the Men Who Made It* (New York: Knopf, 1948), 43.

CHAPTER ONE
MEASURING SUCCESS IN SOCIAL POLICY

1. The Federalist No. 62, in *The Federalist Papers* (New York: Bantam, 1982), 316.
2. James Wilson, "Considerations on the Nature and the Extent of Legislative Authority of the British Parliament," in *Works of James Wilson* (1804 ed.), III, quoted in Carl L. Becker, *The Declaration of Independence: A Study in the History of Political Ideas* (New York: Vintage Books, 1958 ed.), 108.
3. John Adams, letter to George Wythe, "Thoughts on Government," 1776, quoted in Morton White, *Philosophy of the American Revolution* (New York: Oxford University Press, 1978), 233.
4. See the Farewell Address, *An American Primer*, ed. Daniel J.

Boorstin (Chicago: University of Chicago Press, 1966), 214–15. See also Washington's Circular Letter of 1783, quoted in Henry Steele Commager, *Jefferson, Nationalism and the Enlightenment* (New York: Braziller, 1975), p. 109.

5. For example, Jonathan Mayhew, *A Sermon Preach'd in the Audience of His Excellency William Shirley Esq.* (Boston, 1754), 7; James Otis, *The Rights of the British Colonies Asserted and Proved* (Boston, 1764), 14; Josiah Quincy, Jr., *Observations on the Act of Parliament Commonly Called the Boston Port-Bill* (Boston, 1774), 28. See also Charles S. Hyneman and Donald S. Lutz, eds., *American Political Writing During the Founding Era* (Indianapolis: Liberty Press, 1983).

6. "Enable" might mean either "not impede" or "assist." In an intriguing piece of close textual analysis, Morton White argues that the changes from the rough draft of the Declaration to the final version reflect a shift from an optimistic view (that government can enlarge the freedom to pursue happiness) to the pessimistic view (that government should at least do no harm). See White, *Philosophy of the American Revolution*, 244–53. For other recent discussions of the use of "pursuit of happiness" in the Declaration, see Garry Wills, *Inventing America: Jefferson's Declaration of Independence* (New York: Vintage Books 1978), 240–58, and John P. Diggins, *The Lost Soul of American Politics: Virtue, Self-Interest, and the Foundations of Liberalism* (New York: Basic Books, 1984), 32–42.

7. William James, *Psychology, Briefer Course*, from John K. Roth, ed., *The Moral Philosophy of William James* (New York: Crowell, 1969), 52.

CHAPTER TWO

COMING TO TERMS WITH HAPPINESS

1. Barrington Moore, Jr., *Reflections on the Causes of Human Misery and upon Certain Proposals to Eliminate Them* (Boston: Beacon Press, 1970), 1.

2. Ibid., 1.

3. V. J. McGill, in *The Idea of Happiness* (New York: Praeger, 1967), 4.

4. *Nicomachean Ethics*, bk. 1, chap. 7. The quotations in the text use Martin Ostwald's translation (Indianapolis: Bobbs-Merrill, 1962).

5. Ibid.

6. Ibid.

7. *Ethics*, bk. 6, chap. 5(c).

8. Alasdair MacIntyre, *After Virtue: A Study in Moral Theory*,

2d ed. (Notre Dame, Ind.: University of Notre Dame Press, 1984), 161.

9. *Ethics,* bk. 1, chap. 7.

10. Ibid., bk. 1, chap. 8.

11. Ibid., bk. 1, chap. 9.

12. Ibid., bk. 1, chap. 10.

13. Bertrand Russell, *A History of Western Philosophy* (New York: Simon and Schuster, 1945), 173.

14. Peter Gay, *The Enlightenment: The Rise of Modern Paganism* (New York: Knopf, 1966), 11.

15. John Locke, *Essay on Human Understanding,* bk. 2, chap. 21, par. 42.

16. MacIntyre, *After Virtue,* 1–5 and passim.

17. Francis Hutcheson, *An Inquiry into the Original of Our Ideas of Beauty and Virtue* (1725), quoted in Wills, *Inventing America,* 251–52.

18. David Hume, *Enquiry Concerning the Principles of Morals,* 9, ii, quoted in Wills, *Inventing America,* 252–53.

19. Locke, *Essay,* bk. 2, chap. 21, par. 52. See also Howard Mumford Jones, *The Pursuit of Happiness* (Cambridge, Mass.: Harvard University Press, 1953), 93. For a discussion of Locke's Calvinism, see John Dunn, *The Political Thought of John Locke: An Historical Account of the "Two Treatises of Government"* (New York: Cambridge University Press, 1969), 165–99.

20. Jeremy Bentham, *A Fragment on Government and the Principles of Morals and Legislation* (Oxford: Basil Blackwell, 1948), 125.

21. For a fuller discussion of the utilitarian concept of happiness, see McGill, *Idea of Happiness,* 119–43.

22. John Stuart Mill, "Utilitarianism," in *Utilitarianism, Liberty and Representative Government* (New York: Dutton, 1944), 7, 8.

23. Ibid., 9.

24. McGill, *Idea of Happiness,* 126.

25. In this, Jefferson was drawing from Jean-Jacques Burlamaqui. For the distinction between Locke and Burlamaqui on this issue and an analysis of Founders' views, see White, *Philosophy of the American Revolution,* 230–39.

26. Thomas Jefferson to John Adams, October 14, 1816, in *The Adams-Jefferson Letters,* ed. Lester J. Cappon (New York: Simon and Schuster, 1971), 492.

27. Diggins, *Lost Soul of American Politics,* 42.

28. Ibid., 41.

29. Jones, *Pursuit of Happiness,* 123.

30. Ibid., 146–47.

31. Daniel P. Moynihan, "Social Policy: From the Utilitarian Ethic to the Therapeutic Ethic," in *The Americans, 1976: An Inquiry into Fundamental Concepts of Man Underlying Various U.S.*

Institutions, ed. Irving Kristol and Paul Weaver (Lexington, Mass.: Lexington Books, 1976), 25–50. Moynihan attributes the term to Philip Rieff (29).

32. Norman M. Bradburn and D. B. Caplovitz, *Reports on Happiness: A Pilot Study of Behavior Related to Mental Health* (Chicago: Aldine, 1965). The item was originally developed by Gerald Gurin and his associates and used in G. Gurin, J. Veroff, and S. Feld, *Americans View Their Mental Health: A Nationwide Interview Survey* (New York: Basic Books, 1960).

33. Frank M. Andrews and Stephen B. Withey, *Social Indicators of Well-Being: Americans' Perceptions of Life Quality* (Ann Arbor: Institute for Social Research, University of Michigan, 1976).

34. Hadley Cantril, *The Pattern of Human Concerns* (New Brunswick, N.J.: Rutgers University Press, 1965).

35. Angus Campbell, Philip E. Converse, and Willard L. Rodgers, *The Quality of American Life* (New York: Russell Sage Foundation, 1976).

36. A recent and encyclopedic review of the literature is Ruut Veenhoven, *Conditions of Happiness* (Boston: D. Reidel, 1984).

37. See Alex C. Michalos, "Satisfaction and Happiness," *Social Indicators Research* 8 (1980): 385–422.

38. It is taken most directly from Wladyslaw Tatarkiewicz, *Analysis of Happiness* (The Hague: Martinus Nijhoff, 1976 ed.), chap. 2. Tatarkiewicz himself, who was trying to develop a definition "which corresponds to the meaning actually attached to happiness in ordinary discourse," (ibid., 8) in turn uses a quotation from H. Rashdall's *The Theory of Good and Evil* for the chapter's epigraph: "Happiness represents satisfaction with one's existence as a whole."

39. Tatarkiewicz, *Analysis of Happiness,* 12.

40. Robert Nozick, *Anarchy, State, and Utopia* (New York: Basic Books, 1974), 42–45.

CHAPTER THREE
ENABLING CONDITIONS AND THRESHOLDS

1. Abraham H. Maslow, "A Theory of Human Motivation," *Psychological Review* 50 (July 1943): 371–96.

2. Ibid., 374.

3. Ibid., 375.

4. Ibid., 383.

CHAPTER FOUR
MATERIAL RESOURCES

1. Gertrude Himmelfarb, *The Idea of Poverty: England in the Early Industrial Age* (New York: Knopf, 1984), 533–34.

2. Both studies used Cantril's approach (Cantril, *Pattern of Human Concerns*, 22ff.). The Gallup organization conducted the global study for the Kettering Foundation. The question Gallup used (No. 36A) was: "To indicate how you feel about your life at this time, would you use this card? Suppose the top of the mountain represents the best life you can imagine, and the bottom step of the mountain represents the worst possible life you can imagine. On which step of the mountain would you say you personally feel you stand at this time?—assuming that the higher the step the better you feel about your life, and the lower the step the worse you feel about it. Just point to the step that comes closest to how you feel." George H. Gallup, "Human Needs and Satisfactions: A Global Survey," *Public Opinion Quarterly* 41 (1976): 459–67.

3. Richard A. Easterlin, "Does Money Buy Happiness?" *The Public Interest*, no. 30 (1973): 7. For a more complete account, see Easterlin, "Does Economic Growth Improve the Human Lot?" in *Nations and Households in Economic Growth*, ed. P. A. David and M. W. Reder (New York: Academic Press, 1974), 89–125. See also Cantril, *Pattern of Human Concerns*.

4. Easterlin, "Does Money Buy Happiness?" 10.

5. "Hedonic treadmill" is the invention of Philip Brickman and Donald T. Campbell, "Hedonic Relativism and Planning the Good Society," in *Adaptation-Level Theory: A Symposium*, ed. Mortimer H. Appley (London: Academic Press, 1971).

6. Moses Abramovitz, "The Retreat from Economic Advance: Changing Ideas about Economic Progress," in *Progress and Its Discontents*, ed. Gabriel A. Almond, Marvin Chodorow, and Roy Harvey Pearce (Berkeley: University of California Press, 1982), 253–80.

7. See Fred Hirsch, *The Social Limits to Growth* (Cambridge, Mass.: Harvard University Press, 1978).

8. Stefan Linder, *The Harried Leisure Class* (New York: Columbia University Press, 1970).

9. Thomas Babington Macaulay, *The History of England from the Accession of James II*, quoted in Himmelfarb, *Idea of Poverty*, 533.

10. Bureau of the Census, *Historical Statistics of the United States, Colonial Times to 1970* (Washington, D.C.: Government Printing Office, 1975), table D779–793.

11. An earlier version of this thought experiment appeared in Charles Murray, *Losing Ground: American Social Policy 1950–1980* (New York: Basic Books, 1984), 233.

12. John Rawls, *A Theory of Justice* (Cambridge, Mass.: Belknap Press of Harvard University Press, 1971), 14-15.

CHAPTER FIVE
SAFETY

1. For a discussion of safety from these perspectives, see Aaron Wildavsky, *Searching for Safety* (New Brunswick, N.J.: Transaction Books, 1988).

2. Based on crimes reported to the police. "Violent crimes" as defined by the Federal Bureau of Investigation include homicides, robbery, aggravated assault, and forcible rape. "Property crimes" include burglary, larceny-theft, motor vehicle theft, and, in recent years, arson. Data on crime rates are taken from the Federal Bureau of Investigation, *Uniform Crime Reports for the United States,* published annually (Washington, D.C.: Government Printing Office).

3. Claude Brown, in "Images of Fear," *Harper's* 270 (May 1985): 44.

4. U.S. Bureau of the Census, *Statistical Abstract of the United States 1987* (Washington, D.C.: Government Printing Office, 1987), computed for the resident population from tables 1 and 35.

5. Ron Rosenbaum, "Crack Murder: A Detective Story," *The New York Times Magazine,* February 15, 1987, 60.

6. William Tucker, *Vigilante: The Backlash Against Crime in America* (New York: Stein and Day, 1985), 33, 34.

7. Anyone who doubts this intuitive sense of "seriousness" of the offense is referred to an extensive national survey of how people view the seriousness of crimes. The role of physical injury or the threat of physical injury is decisive. Marvin E. Wolfgang, Robert M. Figlio, Paul E. Tracy, and Simon I. Singer, *The National Survey of Crime Severity* (Washington, D.C.: Government Printing Office), 1985.

8. For an accessible technical discussion of these topics, see Peter Huber, *Liability: The Legal Revolution and Its Consequences* (New York: Basic Books, 1988).

9. Nathan Glazer, "On Subway Graffiti in New York," *The Public Interest* (Winter 1979), 4.

10. James Q. Wilson and George Kelling, "Broken Windows: Police and Neighborhood Safety," *Atlantic Monthly,* March 1982, 29-38. A subsequent version now constitutes chap. 5 of James Q. Wilson, *Thinking About Crime,* rev. ed. (New York: Basic Books, 1983), from which the following quotations are taken.

11. Wilson, *Thinking About Crime,* 78.

12. Ibid., 79.

13. Ibid., 77.

14. Ibid., 77.

CHAPTER SIX
DIGNITY, SELF-ESTEEM, AND SELF-RESPECT

1. G. W. Allport, *Pattern and Growth in Personality* (New York: Holt, Rinehart and Winston, 1961), 10. The concept of self-esteem is among the oldest in psychology, first appearing in William James, *Principles of Psychology*, 1890. The references here are drawn from John K. Roth, ed., *The Moral Philosophy of William James* (New York: Crowell, 1969).

2. Morris Rosenberg, *Conceiving the Self* (New York: Basic Books, 1979), 260. See also Gardner Murphy, *Personality* (New York: Harper, 1947); E. R. Hilgard, "Human Motives and the Concept of the Self," *American Psychologist* 4 (1949): 374–82; and Allport, *Pattern and Growth*.

3. See, for example, Morris Rosenberg, *Society and the Adolescent Self-Image* (Princeton, N.J.: Princeton University Press, 1965), and H. B. Kaplan and A. D. Pokorny, "Self-Derogation and Psycho-Social Adjustment," *Journal of Nervous and Mental Disease* 149 (1969): 41–65.

4. J. G. Bachman, *Youth in Transition*, vol. 2, *The Impact of Family Background and Intelligence on Tenth-Grade Boys* (Ann Arbor, Mich.: Survey Research Center, Institute for Social Research, 1970), 122.

5. P. W. Luck and J. Heiss, "Social Determinants of Self-Esteem in Adult Males," *Sociology and Social Research* 57 (1972): 69–84.

6. H. Linton and E. Graham, "Personality Correlates of Persuasibility," in *Personality and Persuasibility*, ed. C. I. Hovland and I. L. Janis (New Haven, Conn.: Yale University Press, 1959), 69–101.

7. Rosenberg, *Society*.

8. Stanley Coopersmith, *The Antecedents of Self-Esteem* (San Francisco: Freeman, 1967).

9. R. Boshier, "A Study of the Relationship between Self-Concept and Conservatism," *Journal of Social Psychology* 77 (1969): 139–40.

10. A. Kardinar and Ovesy, *The Mark of Oppression* (New York: Norton, 1951).

11. M. Jahoda, *Current Concepts of Positive Mental Health* (New York: Basic Books, 1958).

12. R. Crandall, "The Measurement of Self-Esteem and Related Constructs," *Measures of Social Psychological Attitudes*, rev. ed., ed. J. P. Robinson and P. R. Shaver (Ann Arbor, Mich.: Institute for Social Research, 1973), 45–168.

13. Bachman, *Impact of Family Background*, 122.

14. Rosenberg, *Conceiving the Self*, 260.

15. Arthur O. Lovejoy, *Reflections on Human Nature* (Baltimore: Johns Hopkins University Press, 1961), 100. Lectures III–V of that book contain an excellent discussion of self-esteem as it related to eighteenth-century thought.

16. Rawls, *Theory of Justice*, 433, 440.
17. Ibid., 440.
18. James, in Roth, ed., *Moral Philosophy*, 53.
19. Rosenberg, *Society*, 5.
20. Coopersmith, *Antecedents of Self-Esteem*, 5.
21. This is not to say that the study of self-esteem has been adequately systematized. A recent review of the methodology was scathing: "Self-esteem is a central focus of research examining human personality, and yet the conceptualization and operationalization of this variable have been both haphazard and inconclusive. There is little consensus on a definition; there is a diverse range of measurement procedures; and in many cases, there are weak or nonexistent correlations among indicators." David H. Demo, "The Measurement of Self-Esteem: Refining Our Methods," *Journal of Personality and Social Psychology* 48 (1985): 1490.
22. The test is the Rosenberg Self-Esteem Scale (RSE). See Rosenberg, *Conceiving the Self*, 291.
23. David Sachs, "How to Distinguish Self-Respect from Self-Esteem," *Philosophy and Public Affairs* 10 (1981): 346–60.
24. Michael Walzer, *Spheres of Justice: A Defense of Pluralism and Equality* (New York: Basic Books, 1983), 278–79.
25. Ibid., 279.
26. Norman M. Bradburn, *The Structure of Psychological Well-Being* (Chicago: Aldine, 1965); Campbell et al., *Quality of American Life*.
27. See, for example, E. M. Stafford, P. R. Jackson, and M. H. Banks, "Employment, Work Involvement and Mental Health in Less Qualified Young People," *Journal of Occupational Psychology* 53 (1980): 291–304; P. B. Warr, "A Study of Psychological Well-Being," *British Handbook of Work and Organizational Psychology* (London: Wiley, 1983); M. H. Banks and P. R. Jackson, "Unemployment and Risk of Minor Psychiatric Disorder in Young People," *Psychological Medicine* 12 (1981).
28. Paul R. Jackson, Elizabeth M. Stafford, Michael H. Banks, and Peter B. Warr, "Unemployment and Psychological Distress in Young People: The Moderating Role of Employment Commitment," *Journal of Applied Psychology* 68 (1983): 525–35. This article was the first to apply longitudinal data to the relationship between distress and commitment to the labor market. Previous cross-sectional work on the topic includes Milton R. Blood, "Work Values and Job Satisfaction," *Journal of Applied Psychology* 53 (1969): 456–59; Elizabeth M. Stafford, "The Impact of the Youth Opportunities Programme on Young People's Employment Prospects and Psychological Well-Being," *British Journal of Guidance and Counselling* 10 (1982): 10–21; and S. Wollack, J. G. Goodale, J. P. Wijting, and P. C. Smith, "Development of the Survey of Work Values," *Journal of Applied Psychology* 55 (1971): 331–38.
29. J. B. Rotter, "Generalized Expectancies for Internal Versus

External Control of Reinforcement," *Psychological Monographs* 80 (1966): 2–28.

30. R. Carlson, "Personality," *Annual Review of Psychology*, 1975 26 (1976), 396.

31. Taken from the "Internal, Powerful Others, and Chance Locus of Control Scales," H. Levenson and J. Muller, "Multidimensional Locus of Control in Sociopolitical Activists of Conservative and Liberal Ideologies," *Journal of Personality and Social Psychology* 33 (1976): 199–208. Internals tend to be politically conservative; externals tend to be liberal.

32. Bonnie R. Strickland, "Internal-External Control of Reinforcement," in *Personality Variables in Social Behavior*, ed. Thomas Blass (New York: John Wiley, 1977), 264.

33. E. Palmore and C. Luikart, "Health and Social Factors Relating to Life Satisfaction," *Journal of Health and Social Behavior* 13 (1972): 68–80.

34. M. P. Naditch, M. Gargan, and L. B. Michael, "Denial, Anxiety, Locus of Control, and the Discrepancy between Aspirations and Achievements as Components of Depression," *Journal of Abnormal Psychology* 84 (1975): 1–9.

35. E. J. Langer and J. Rodin, "The Effects of Choice and Enhanced Personal Responsibility for the Aged: A Field Experiment in an Institutional Setting," *Journal of Personality and Social Psychology* 34 (1976): 191–98; R. J. Bulman and C. Wortman, "Attributions of Blame and Coping in the 'Real World,': Severe Accident Victims React to Their Lot," *Journal of Personality and Social Psychology* 35 (1977): 351–63.

36. Among the diseases for which this has been demonstrated are hypertension. See M. P. Naditch, "Locus of Control, Relative Discontent, and Hypertension," *Social Psychiatry* 9 (1974): 111–17. Studies of the relationship of internality to health-related behavior include J. E. Johnson, H. Leventhal, and J. M. Dabbs, "Contribution of Emotional and Instrumental Response Processes in Adaptation to Survey," *Journal of Personality and Social Psychology* 20 (1971): 65–70; R. E. Ireland, "Locus of Control Among Hospitalized Pulmonary Emphysema Patients," *Dissertation Abstracts International* 33 (1973): 6091; and T. F. Garrity, "Vocational Adjustment after First Myocardial Infarction: Comparative Assessment of Several Variables Suggested in Literature," *Social Science and Medicine* 7 (1973): 705–17.

37. For example, see J. Biondo and A. P. MacDonald, "Internal-External Locus of Control and Response to Influence Attempts," *Journal of Personality* 39 (1971): 407–19, and R. M. Ryckman, W. C. Rodda, and M. F. Sherman, "Locus of Control and Expertise Relevance as Determinants of Changes in Opinion about Student Activism," *Journal of Social Psychology* 88 (1972): 107–14.

38. For example, H. A. Pines and J. W. Julian, "Effects of Task

and Social Demands on Locus of Control Differences in Information Processing," *Journal of Personality* 40 (1972): 407–16; M. Seeman and J. W. Evans, "Alienation and Learning in a Hospital Setting," *American Sociological Review* 27 (1962): 772–83.

39. H. Gozali, T. A. Cleary, G. W. Walster, and J. Gozali, "Relationship between the Internal-External Control Construct and Achievement," *Journal of Educational Psychology* 64 (1973): 9–14; H. M. Lefcourt, L. Lewis, and I. W. Silverman, "Internal versus External Control of Reinforcement and Alteration in a Decision Making Task," *Journal of Personality* 36 (1968): 663–82.

40. The literature on this topic is particularly extensive; see Strickland, "Internal-External Control of Reinforcement," 236–40, for the major titles.

41. M. P. Duke and S. Nowicki, "Personality Correlates of the Nowicki-Strickland Locus of Control Scale for Adults," *Psychological Reports* 33 (1973): 267–70.

42. B. E. Goodstadt and L. A. Hjelle, "Power to the Powerless: Locus of Control and the Use of Power," *Journal of Personality and Social Psychology* 27 (1973): 190–96; E. J. Phares, "Internal-External Control as a Determinant of Amount of Social Influence Exerted," *Journal of Personality and Social Psychology* 2 (1965): 642–47.

43. S. Nowicki and N. Blumberg, "The Role of Locus of Control of Reinforcement in Interpersonal Attraction," *Journal of Research in Personality* 9 (1975): 48–56.

44. G. Kimmons and S. J. Greenhaus, "Relationship between Locus of Control and Reactions of Employees to Work Characteristics," *Psychological Reports* 39 (1976): 815–20; G. R. Gemmill and W. J. Heisler, "Fatalism as a Factor in Managerial Job Satisfaction, Job Strain, and Mobility," *Personnel Psychology* 25 (1972): 241–50; D. W. Organ and C. N. Green, "Role Ambiguity, Locus of Control and Work Satisfaction," *Journal of Applied Psychology* 59 (1974): 101–2; and H. P. Sims and R. T. Keller, "Role Dynamics, Locus of Control, and Employer Attitudes and Behavior," *Academy of Management Journal* 19 (1976): 259–76.

45. P. Gurin, G. Gurin, R. C. Lao, and M. Beattie, "Internal-External Control in the Motivational Dynamics of Negro Youth," *Journal of Social Issues* 25 (1969): 25–53. See also E. E. Lessing, "Racial Differences in Indices of Ego Functioning Relevant to Academic Achievement," *Journal of Genetic Psychology* 115 (1969): 153–67; and A. Zytkoskee, B. R. Strickland, and J. Watson, "Delay of Gratification and Internal Versus External Control Among Adolescents of Low Socioeconomic Status," *Developmental Psychology* 4 (1971): 93–98.

46. Renee G. Rabinowitz, "Internal-External Control Expectancies in Black Children of Differing Socioeconomic Status," *Psychological Reports* 42 (1978): 1339–45.

CHAPTER SEVEN
ENJOYMENT, SELF-ACTUALIZATION, AND INTRINSIC REWARDS

1. John Stuart Mill, *Autobiography*, ed. Jack Stillinger (Boston: Houghton Mifflin, 1969), 81.
2. Ibid., 85–86.
3. William Faulkner, quoted in Studs Turkel, *Working* (New York: Pantheon, 1972), xi.
4. Thomas Carlyle, *Sartor Resartus*, quoted in Steven Marcus, "Conceptions of the Self in an Age of Progress," in Almond, Chodorow, and Pearce, *Progress and Its Discontents*, 435.
5. Karl Marx, quoted in E. Fromm, *Marx's Concept of Man* (New York: Ungar, 1961).
6. Turkel, *Working*, xiii.
7. N. D. Glenn and C. N. Weaver, "Enjoyment of Work by Full-Time Workers in the U.S., 1955 and 1980," *Public Opinion Quarterly* 46 (1982): 463.
8. Ibid., 465.
9. Robert Nisbet, *The History of the Idea of Progress* (New York: Basic Books, 1980), 354 ff. See also Gertrude Himmelfarb, "In Defense of Progress," *Commentary* (June 1980): 53 ff.
10. Daniel Bell, "The Return of the Sacred," in Almond, Chodorow, and Pearce, *Progress and Its Discontents*, 522.
11. See especially bks. 7 and 10 of the *Ethics*.
12. Rawls, *Theory of Justice*, 426.
13. MacIntyre, *After Virtue*, 160.
14. Sigmund Freud, *A General Introduction to Psycho-Analysis* (1915).
15. C. L. Hull, *Principles of Behavior: An Introduction to Behavior Theory* (New York: Appleton-Century-Crofts, 1943).
16. For example, E. L. Thorndike, *The Psychology of Learning* (New York: Teachers' College, Columbia University, 1913); B. F. Skinner, *Science and Human Behavior* (New York: Macmillan, 1953).
17. The discussion of the Wundt Curve and the experimental evidence supporting it is taken primarily from Tibor Scitovsky, *The Joyless Economy: An Inquiry into Human Satisfaction and Consumer Dissatisfaction* (New York: Oxford University Press, 1976), chap. 3.
18. Tibor Scitovsky points out that the Wundt Curve is essentially a graphic representation of Aristotle's Doctrine of the Mean. Scitovsky, *Joyless Economy*, 35.
19. W. N. Dember, "Response by the Rat to Environmental Change," *Journal of Comparative Physiological Psychology* 49 (1956): 93–95.
20. Scitovsky, *Joyless Economy*, 38–39. Scitovsky's source for these experiments is D. E. Berlyne, *Conflict, Arousal, and Curiosity*

(New York: McGraw-Hill, 1960), and D. E. Berlyne, *Aesthetics and Psychobiology* (New York: Appleton-Century-Crofts, 1971).

21. R. L. White, "Motivation Reconsidered: The Concept of Competence," *Psychological Review* 66 (1959): 297–333.

22. Maslow, "Theory of Human Motivation," 383.

23. Mihaly Csikszentmihalyi, *Beyond Boredom and Anxiety: The Experience of Play in Work and Games* (San Francisco: Jossey-Bass, 1982), 9.

24. Ibid., 37–38.

25. Ibid., 47–48.

26. Ibid. The discussion of characteristics of flow is adapted from 38–48.

27. Ibid., 43.

28. Ibid., 46.

29. Ibid., 47.

30. Ibid., 182.

31. The examples are based on Tom Wolfe, *The Kandy-Kolored Tangerine-Flake Streamline Baby* (New York: Farrar, Straus, and Giroux, 1965), William A. Nolen, *The Making of a Surgeon* (New York: Random House, 1968), Mike Cherry, *On High Steel: The Education of an Ironworker* (New York: Ballantine Books, 1974), and Dennis Smith, *Report from Engine Co. 82* (New York: Saturday Review Press, 1972), respectively. See also (from among a vast selection) Joseph Wambaugh's novels and his nonfiction *The Onion Field* on police work; Tracy Kidder, *The Soul of a New Machine* (Boston: Little, Brown, 1981), and Steven Levy, *Hackers: Heroes of the Computer Revolution* (New York: Dell, 1984), on computer work; Tom Wolfe, *The Right Stuff* (New York: Farrar, Straus, and Giroux, 1979), on test pilots; and Herman Melville, *Moby-Dick* (1851), on whaling.

32. Fred Hapgood, "At 411, It's Simply a Matter of Keeping in Tune with the Numbers," *Smithsonian*, November 1986, 74.

33. Turkel, *Working*, 393–94.

34. Csikszentmihalyi, *Beyond Boredom and Anxiety*, 181.

35. Ibid., 49.

36. Edward L. Deci and Richard M. Ryan, *Intrinsic Motivation and Self-Determination in Human Behavior* (New York: Plenum Press, 1985), 43.

37. B. J. Calder and B. M. Staw, "Self-Perception of Intrinsic and Extrinsic Motivation," *Journal of Personality and Social Psychology* 31 (1975): 599–605.

38. R. D. Pritchard, K. M. Campbell, and D. J. Campbell, "Effects of Extrinsic Financial Rewards on Intrinsic Motivation," *Journal of Applied Psychology* 62 (1977): 9–15.

39. J. Harackiewicz, "The Effects of Reward Contingency and Performance Feedback on Intrinsic Motivation," *Journal of Personality and Social Psychology* 37 (1979): 1352–63.

40. For example, D. Green, B. Sternberg, and M. R. Lepper,

"Overjustification in a Token Economy," *Journal of Personality and Social Psychology* 34 (1976): 1219–34.

41. For example, R. Anderson, S. T. Manoogian, and J. S. Reznick, "The Undermining and Enhancing of Intrinsic Motivation in Preschool Children," *Journal of Personality and Social Psychology* 34 (1976): 915–22.

42. D. Y. Lee, R. Syrnyk, and C. Hallschmid, "Self-Perception of Intrinsic and Extrinsic Motivation: Effects on Institutionalized Mentally Retarded Adolescents," *American Journal of Mental Deficiency* 81 (1977): 331–37.

43. M. Yoshimura, "The Effects of Verbal Reinforcement and Monetary Reward on Intrinsic Motivation," manuscript, Kyoto University Psychology Laboratory, Kyoto, Japan, 1979; D. Eden, "Intrinsic and Extrinsic Rewards and Motives: Replication and Extension with Kibbutz Workers," *Journal of Applied Social Psychology* 50 (1982): 360–73.

44. T. S. Pittman, J. Emery, and A. K. Boggiano, "Intrinsic and Extrinsic Motivational Orientations: Reward-Induced Changes in Preference for Complexity," *Journal of Personality and Social Psychology* 42 (1982): 791.

45. Z. Shapira, "Expectancy Determinants of Intrinsically Motivated Behavior," *Journal of Personality and Social Psychology* 34 (1976): 1235–44.

46. The original identification of the informational and controlling categories was in Richard M. Ryan, V. Mims, and R. Koestner, "Relation of Reward Contingency and Interpersonal Context to Intrinsic Motivation: A Review and Test Using Cognitive Evaluation Theory," *Journal of Personality and Social Psychology* 45 (1983): 736–50.

47. The first experiments were on dogs (O. H. Mowrer, "Learning Theory and the Neurotic Paradox," *American Journal of Orthopsychiatry* 18 [1948]: 571–610. Subsequent landmark studies with humans include: D. S. Hiroto and M. E. P. Seligman, "Generality of Learned Helplessness in Man," *Journal of Personality and Social Psychology* 31 (1975): 311–27; and S. Roth and L. Kubal, "Effects of Noncontingent Reinforcement on Tasks of Differing Importance: Facilitation and Learned Helplessness," *Journal of Personality and Social Psychology* 32 (1975): 680–91.

48. For example, J. Harackiewicz, "The Effects of Reward Contingency"; Ryan, Mims, and Koestner, "Relation of Reward Contingency."

49. For example, M. E. Enzle and J. M. Ross, "Increasing and Decreasing Intrinsic Interest with Contingent Rewards: A Test of Cognitive Evaluation Theory," *Journal of Experimental Social Psychology* 14 (1978): 588–97; and Ryan, Mims, and Koestner, "Relation of Reward Contingency."

50. For a summary of the interrelationships among reward struc-

tures and feedback modes, see Deci and Ryan, *Intrinsic Motivation and Self-Determination*, table 2, 82.

51. A fourth proposition added for purposes of restating the first three propositions in terms of intrapersonal dynamics, reads: "Intrapersonal events differ in their qualitative aspects and, like external events, can have varied functional significances. Internally informational events facilitate self-determined functioning and maintain or enhance intrinsic motivation. Internally controlling events are experienced as pressure toward specific outcomes and undermine intrinsic motivation. Internally amotivating events make salient one's incompetence and also undermine intrinsic motivation" (Deci and Ryan, *Intrinsic Motivation and Self-Determination*, 107).

52. Deci and Ryan, *Intrinsic Motivation and Self-Determination*, 107. "The first proposition is related to people's intrinsic need to be self-determining. . . . External events relevant to the initiation or regulation of behavior will affect a person's intrinsic motivation to the extent that they influence the perceived locus of causality for that behavior. Events that promote a more external perceived locus of causality will undermine intrinsic motivation, whereas those that promote a more internal perceived locus of causality will enhance intrinsic enjoyment. The perceived locus of causality is theorized to be a cognitive construct representing the degree to which one is self-determining with respect to one's behavior" (Deci and Ryan, *Intrinsic Motivation and Self-Determination*, 62).

53. R. de Charms, *Personal Causation: The Internal Determinants of Behavior* (New York: Academic Press, 1968); F. Heider, *The Psychology of Interpersonal Relations* (New York: Wiley, 1958).

54. Deci and Ryan review the pertinent literature on pp. 52–57 of *Intrinsic Motivation and Self-Determination*.

55. "The second proposition relates to people's intrinsic need to be competent and to master optimal challenges. . . . External events will affect a person's intrinsic motivation for an optimally challenging activity to the extent that they influence the person's perceived competence, within the context of some self-determination. Events that promote greater perceived competence will enhance intrinsic motivation, whereas those that diminish perceived competence will decrease intrinsic motivation" (Deci and Ryan, *Intrinsic Motivation and Self-Determination*, 63).

56. D. J. McMullin and J. J. Steffen, "Intrinsic Motivation and Performance Standards," *Social Behavior and Personality* 10 (1982): 47–56.

57. See Deci and Ryan, *Intrinsic Motivation and Self-Determination*, 59.

58. For example, P. D. Blanck, H. T. Reis, and L. Jackson, "The Effects of Verbal Reinforcements on Intrinsic Motivation for Sex-Linked Tasks," *Sex Roles* 10 (1984): 369–87; J. C. Russell, O. L. Studstill, and R. M. Grant, "The Effect of Expectancies on Intrinsic Motivation" (Paper presented at the American Psychological Asso-

ciation, New York, September 1979); and C. D. Fisher, "The Effects of Personal Control, Competence, and Extrinsic Reward Systems on Intrinsic Motivation," *Organizational Behavior and Human Performance* 21 (1978): 273–88.

59. R. J. Vallerand and G. Reid, "On the Causal Effects of Perceived Competence on Intrinsic Motivation: A Test of Cognitive Evaluation Theory," *Journal of Sport Psychology* 6 (1984): 94–102.

60. "The third proposition relates to the fact that events relevant to the initiation and regulation of behavior have three aspects that may be differentially salient to different people or to the same person at different times. These aspects are labeled the informational, the controlling, and the amotivating aspects; and it is the relative salience of the three aspects to a person that effects changes in perceived causality and perceived competence, and that alters the person's intrinsic motivation. . . . Events relevant to the initiation and regulation of behavior have three potential aspects, each with a functional significance. The informational aspect facilitates an internal perceived locus of causality and perceived competence, thus enhancing intrinsic motivation. The controlling aspect facilitates an external perceived locus of causality, thus undermining intrinsic motivation and promoting extrinsic compliance or defiance. The amotivating aspect facilitates perceived incompetence, thus undermining intrinsic motivation and promoting amotivation. The relative salience of these three aspects to a person determines the functional significance of the events" (Deci and Ryan, *Intrinsic Motivation and Self-Determination,* 63–64).

61. The most ambitious of these other theoretical perspectives is Albert Bandura's. See, for example, Bandura, "Self-Efficacy: Toward a Unifying Theory of Behavioral Change," *Psychological Review* 84 (1977): 191–215.

CHAPTER EIGHT
POLICY AND AN IDEA OF MAN

1. Martin Diamond, "The American Idea of Man: The View from the Founding," in Kristol and Weaver, eds., *Americans,* 2.

2. Ibid., 2.

3. Ibid., 2–3.

4. The wording for these two aspects of the idea of man is taken from MacIntyre, *After Virtue,* 52 ff.

5. George Gilder, *Visible Man: A True Story of Post-Racist America* (New York: Basic Books, 1978).

6. Thomas Sowell, *A Conflict of Visions* (New York: Morrow, 1987), 14.

7. Diggins, *Lost Soul,* 33.

8. Until a few years ago, this statement would have hardly re-

quired a footnote. But in the 1970s a revisionist interpretation of the Declaration grew up around the proposition that Jefferson was a proto-social-democrat. This dissident minority is best represented by Garry Wills in *Inventing America*, which appeared in 1978. Wills argued that Locke's influence on Jefferson was minor and that Jefferson's chief philosophical mentor was actually the Scottish moral philosopher Francis Hutcheson. Wills's thesis about Jefferson's debt to Hutcheson and his indifference to Locke has not found widespread support among scholars of Revolutionary intellectual thought. (Diggins, referring obliquely to Wills, begins his comparison of Hutcheson and Jefferson by remarking that "It would be interesting to try to rewrite the Declaration of Independence in the language of Scottish philosophy" and concludes that ". . . Jeffersonian individualism and Scottish moralism seem more like a study in immiscibility." Diggins, *Lost Soul*, 33, 34.) This is not to discourage readers from *Inventing America*, which is a fascinating and useful work, but it should be read alongside philosopher Morton White's work published the same year, *The Philosophy of the American Revolution*, just as Wills's subsequent book, *Explaining America: The Federalist* (Garden City, N.Y.: Doubleday, 1981) should be read alongside White's *Philosophy, The Federalist, and the Constitution* (New York: Oxford University Press, 1987). For specifics about Jefferson's debt to Locke, see White, *American Revolution*, 64–78; for White's analysis of Jefferson's understanding of the moral sense, 97–127.

9. Thomas Jefferson, Letter to Peter Carr, August 10, 1787, in *The Portable Thomas Jefferson*, ed. Merrill D. Peterson (New York: Penguin, 1975), 425.

10. Thomas Jefferson, quoted in Diggins, *Lost Soul*, 40.

11. Diggins, *Lost Soul*, 40–41.

12. For a detailed description of the properties of approbativeness as Lovejoy uses it, see Lovejoy, *Reflections on Human Nature*, 88–99.

13. Adam Smith, *The Theory of Moral Sentiments*, ed. A. L. Macfie and D. D. Raphael (New York: Oxford University Press ed., 1976). See especially part 3.

14. Ibid., 110.

15. Adam Smith, *Moral Sentiments*, quoted in Lovejoy, *Reflections*, 190–91.

16. Ibid., 195.

17. John Adams, *Discourses on Davila*, quoted in Lovejoy, *Reflections on Human Nature*, 200.

18. The opinions of the Founders about inborn inequalities (what is now known as the "nature versus nurture" debate) varied. Jefferson believed that all men (including his black slaves) had the instinctive moral sense, which Wills uses to substantiate his contention that Jefferson's "political beliefs grew directly from the philosophy

of moral sense, which had egalitarianism as an essential ingredient"
(Wills, *Inventing America*, 228; see 224–28 for the argument). On
the other hand, Jefferson was as explicit about his belief in the inherent intellectual and aesthetic inferiority of blacks as he was egalitarian in his attitude toward their moral parity. See Thomas Jefferson, *Notes on the State of Virginia* in *Portable Jefferson*, 186–92.
Others were more thoroughgoing believers in underlying equality.
Adam Smith, a contemporary of the Founders, thought that "[t]he
difference of natural talents in different men is, in reality, much less
than we are aware of." A philosopher and a common street porter,
he wrote, differ "not so much from nature, as from habit, custom,
and education" (Adam Smith, *An Inquiry into the Nature and
Causes of the Wealth of Nations* [Chicago: University of Chicago
Press, ed., 1976], 19–20). For an historical treatment of the issue of
equality, see Sowell, *Visions*, chap. 6.

19. Letter to John Adams, *Portable Thomas Jefferson*, 534.

20. The reference is to Madison's statement before the Virginia
convention that ratified the Constitution: "But I go on this great
republican principle, that the people will have virtue and intelligence to select men of virtue and wisdom." Quoted in Diamond,
"American Idea of Man," 16. Diamond expounds on the meanings
of "virtue" and "intelligence" as Madison used them—roughly,
"public-spiritedness" and "mutual conveyance of information" (as
in the continuing usage in "intelligence agencies") respectively.

21. Lovejoy is characteristically pithy: "There appears to be a
still widely prevalent belief among Americans that the Founding
Fathers were animated by a 'faith in the people,' a confidence in the
wisdom of 'the common man.' This belief, to use the terminology
of the logic books, is a grandiose example of the fallacy of division"
(Lovejoy, *Reflections on Human Nature*, 51).

22. Richard Hofstadter, *The American Political Tradition and
the Men Who Made It* (New York: Vintage Books, 1954), 4.

23. Ibid., 4.

24. Alexander Hamilton, *Selected Speeches and Writings*, quoted
in Sowell, *Visions*, 134.

25. Diamond, "American Idea of Man," 7–8.

26. Edmund Burke, *Reflections on the Revolution in France*
(New York: Dutton ed., 1960), 56.

27. Sowell, *Visions*, 121.

28. From *Works of John Adams*, quoted in Carl Becker, *The
Declaration of Independence* (New York: Vintage Books ed., 1958),
24.

29. From *The Writings of Thomas Jefferson*, quoted in ibid.,
25–26.

30. Bernard Bailyn, *The Ideological Origins of the American
Revolution* (Cambridge, Mass.: Belknap Press of Harvard University Press, 1967), 319.

31. Thomas Jefferson, letter to T. M. Randolph, Jr., May 30,

1790, quoted in White, *Philosophy*, The Federalist, *and the Constitution*, 3.

32. The Federalist No. 10, p. 43. The page numbers for this and other citations from *The Federalist* are taken from the Bantam edition (New York, 1982). I have altered spelling in that text to conform to modern usage.

33. Ibid., 44.

34. The Federalist No. 6, 24.

35. See, for example, the transcript of the "60 Minutes" segment on this topic, "Not to My Kid, You Don't!" *60 Minutes Verbatim* (New York, Arno Press, 1980).

36. David Hume, *Essays: Moral, Political, and Literary*, quoted in White, *Philosophy*, The Federalist, *and the Constitution*, 98. For documentation of the specific link between Hume and Madison, see Adair, *Fame and the Founding Fathers*, 102.

37. The Federalist No. 10, 45.

38. Ibid., 45.

39. Brutus has been identified as Robert Yates on the authority of Paul Leicester Ford, ed., *Pamphlets on the Constitution of the United States, Published during Its Discussion by the People, 1787–1788* (Brooklyn, N.Y.: 1888), 117. Thomas Treadwell is another candidate. See Herbert J. Storing, ed., *The Anti-Federalist: Writings by the Opponents of the Constitution* (Chicago: University of Chicago Press, 1985), 103.

40. Essays of Brutus, no. 1, 2.9.9, in Storing, ed., *Anti-Federalist*, 112–13.

41. Ibid., 2.9.189, 195.

42. The Federalist No. 10, 45.

43. The Federalist No. 51, 262.

44. Hofstadter, *American Political Tradition*, 16–17.

CHAPTER NINE

ASKING A NEW QUESTION,
GETTING NEW ANSWERS: EVALUATING RESULTS

1. This happens to be the result of one study, but is not atypical. Charles Maller et al., "The Short-Term Economic Impact of the Job Corps Program," in *Evaluation Studies Review Annual 5*, ed. Ernst Stromsdorfer and G. Farkas (Beverly Hills, Calif.: Sage Publications, 1980), 334.

2. "Most Favor 55 mph Limit but Few Obey," *Gallup Report*, March 1981, 37–39. It goes without saying that the estimate of "supporters who disobey" in such a poll is bound to be an underestimate.

3. Thomas H. Forester, Robert F. McNown, and Larry D. Singell, "A Cost-Benefit Analysis of the 55 mph Speed Limit," *Southern Economic Journal* 50 (1984): 635.

4. Ibid., 631.

5. I am not objecting to these procedures for the purposes for which they are employed; rather, I am suggesting they are beside the point when it comes to such things as "liking to get the trip over with because it's boring to sit in the car." For examples of the ways that economists have dealt with the valuation-of-time problem, see A. J. Harrison and D. A. Quarmby, "The Value of Time," in R. Layard, ed., *Cost-Benefit Analysis* (Baltimore: Penguin, 1972), 173–208. For explorations in valuing a human life, especially with regard to traffic accidents, see M. W. Jones-Lee, *The Value of Life: An Economic Analysis* (Chicago: University of Chicago Press, 1976), and G. Blomquist, "Value of Life Saving: Implications of Consumption Activity," *Journal of Political Economy* (1979): 540–58.

6. See U.S. Bureau of the Census, *Statistical Abstract of the United States, 1986* (Washington, D.C.: Government Printing Office, 1985), table 1049.

7. I am indebted to Christopher Jencks for suggesting this rationale to me.

8. The estimate of lives-saved must be adjusted to take into account two implications of the way I have defined the added safety of the 55-mph speed limit. The first implication is that the 7,901 people killed in single-vehicle accidents should be discounted when evaluating the safety value of the speed limit. (For simplicity's sake, I am including the passengers in these statements, which begs a very complicated argument, but including them or excluding them changes the results only at the eighth decimal place.) The reason for discounting fatalities in single-vehicle accidents is obvious in cases in which the car was going less than 55 mph anyway. But it is also true in the case of drivers of cars when speed *was* the cause and the driver *was* going faster than 55 mph. If a driver going at 80 mph loses control on a turn at three o'clock in the morning without another car in sight, his death is irrelevant to the calculation of the added safety of a speed limit to other drivers.

It's not as simple as that, of course. If the result of removing the speed limit is that a much higher proportion of drivers are weaving all over the road at high speeds, then all drivers run a higher degree of risk. This is one of the reasons why an actual calculation would take us far afield. But it remains true: *Any driver can at any time guarantee that he is not involved in a single-vehicle-accident-caused-by-going-faster-than-55-mph*, just by choosing not to go faster than 55 mph.

The second implication is that the 11,712 fatalities among people in multivehicle accidents must also be treated differently, depending on the circumstances. Such accidents fall into four basic categories: (1) fatalities in which speed was not a significant cause (all of these must be discounted), (2) accidents in which speed was a significant cause, but both cars were going 55 mph or less (all of these must be discounted), (3) accidents in which speed was the cause, but only because *both* cars were going more than 55 mph (all of these must be discounted), and (4) accidents in which speed was the cause and only one car was going more than 55 mph. For the accidents falling into category 4, the question is whether the fatalities would have occurred if both drivers had been driving at 55 mph or less. If the answer is no, then the fatalities that occurred to the occupants of the car traveling at 55 mph or less are pertinent. The fatalities among the drivers of the speeding car must once again be discounted (if they unilaterally had chosen to drive at 55 or less, they would still be alive).

For the rough estimate I am making, I assume that a quarter of the fatalities in multivehicle accidents fall into category 4, and that those fatalities are evenly divided between people in the guilty car (the one exceeding 55 mph) and the innocent car. This produces the estimate that in 1983, 1,464 persons driving at or below 55 mph were killed because another car was driving at speeds greater than 55 mph.

Now I repeat the calculation for the conditions if there were no 55-mph speed limit (Estimated Fatalities = Actual Fatalities + 7,466), using the same proportional breakdown of single- and multivehicle accidents. The result is an estimate that, without the law, 2,021 persons driving at 55 mph or less would have been killed because another car was driving at speeds greater than 55 mph.

9. I am not painting an unrealistically bleak picture of job training programs. In addition to the Job Corps evaluation cited above, readers interested in the results of the Manpower Development and Training Act are referred to Orley Ashenfelter, "Estimating the Effects of Training Programs on Earnings," *Review of Economics and Statistics* 60 (1978): 47–57. For a recent one-source synthesis of what is known about the effects of the Comprehensive Employment and Training Act see the August 1987 issue of the journal, *Evaluation Review*. For the results of the Supported Work Demonstration Program, see Manpower Demonstration Research Corporation, *Summary and Findings of the National Supported Work Demonstration* (Cambridge, Mass.: Ballinger, 1980).

CHAPTER TEN

ASKING A NEW QUESTION,
GETTING NEW ANSWERS: DESIGNING SOLUTIONS

1. Math was even worse. The mean math score of intended education majors was at the 34th percentile. See The College Board, *Profiles, College-Bound Seniors, 1985* (New York: College Entrance Examination Board, 1986). Percentiles were computed from data in tables 9 and 10, pp. 101 and 102.

2. Again, it was even worse for the nonverbal subtests. The mean for prospective graduate majors in education on the GRE-Quantitative test put them at the 29th percentile; for the GRE-Analytic, at the 32nd percentile. Henry Roy Smith III, *A Summary of Data Collected from Graduate Record Examinations Test Takers During 1984-1985*, Data Summary Report #10, April 1986 (Princeton, N.J.: Educational Testing Service, 1986). Percentiles computed from data in tables 59-61, pp. 79-81.

3. *A Nation Prepared: Teachers for the 21st Century: Report of the Task Force on Teaching as a Profession* (New York: The Carnegie Corporation, 1986).

4. Ibid., 39.

5. Ibid., 55-56.

6. Peter Rossi, "The Iron Law of Evaluation and Other Metallic Rules," in *Research in Social Problems and Public Policy*, vol. 4, ed. Joanne Miller and Michael Lewis (Greenwich, Conn.: JAI Press, 1987), 4.

7. Ibid., 5.

8. "Fairfax Teachers Back Away from Merit Plan," *The Washington Post*, May 1, 1987.

9. See, for example, the profiles of successful public schools in *Schools that Work: Educating Disadvantaged Children* (Washington, D.C.: Government Printing Office, 1987).

10. These ballpark figures (and that is all they are) are computed on the basis of the salary distributions by occupation given in the annual publication by the U.S. Bureau of the Census, *Money Income of Households, Families, and Persons in the United States*, various editions (Washington, D.C.: Government Printing Office).

11. This is a straight-line calculation based on a $23,500 mean salary in 1985 for 2,146,000 elementary and secondary public school teachers. Figures are taken from U.S. Bureau of the Census, *Statistical Abstract of the United States 1986* (Washington, D.C.: U.S. Bureau of the Census, 1985), table 227.

12. Colony Laws, chap. 78, quoted in James G. Carter, *Letters on the Free Schools of New England* (New York: Arno Press, 1969 ed.).

13. Tocqueville, *Democracy in America*, 302 ff., 92.

14. For a history of early American education, see Lawrence A. Cremin's monumental two-volume work, *American Education: The Colonial Experience 1607-1783* (New York: Harper & Row, 1970), and *American Education: The National Experience 1783-1876* (New York: Harper & Row, 1980); also Bernard Bailyn, *Education in the Forming of American Society* (New York: Norton, 1960). For a concise history of the common school movement, see Frederick M. Binder, *The Age of the Common School 1830-1865* (New York: John Wiley, 1974). For those who want the flavor of the New Englanders' fervor for free schools, James G. Carter's *Letters on the*

Free Schools of New England has been reprinted in a modern edition (New York: Arno Press, 1969).

CHAPTER ELEVEN

SEARCHING FOR SOLUTIONS THAT WORK:
CHANGING THE METAPHOR

1. Ironically (as I am indebted to Robert Nisbet for pointing out to me), Burke, who is so widely identified with the organic metaphor, never actually uses the word "organic" to describe his vision.

2. For the most persuasive argument that I am wrong on this point, see Peter L. Berger and Richard John Neuhaus, *To Empower People: The Role of Mediating Structures in Public Policy* (Washington, D.C.: American Enterprise Institute, 1977). Another useful opposing discussion is Stuart Butler and Anna Kondratas, *Out of the Poverty Trap* (New York: The Free Press, 1987).

3. The quotation and the explanation are taken from Lao Tzu, *Tao Te Ching*, intro. and trans. D. C. Lau (Baltimore: Penguin, 1963), 121.

4. Bureau of the Census, *Statistical Abstract of the United States 1987* (Washington, D.C.: Government Printing Office, 1986), table 202.

5. Milton Friedman, *Capitalism and Freedom* (Chicago: University of Chicago Press, 1982 ed.), 85, 86.

6. Letter to George Wythe, *Portable Thomas Jefferson*, 399–400.

7. Survey conducted by the Institute for Independent Education, cited in "Private Schools for Blacks," *The New York Times*, October 26, 1986.

8. Cited in Andrew Oldenquist, *The Non-Suicidal Society* (Bloomington: University of Indiana Press, 1986), 42.

9. U.S. Bureau of the Census, *Statistical Abstract of the United States 1987* (Washington, D.C.: Government Printing Office, 1986), table 222.

10. See, for example, James S. Coleman et al., *High School Achievement: Public Schools, Catholic Schools, and Private Schools Compared* (New York: Basic Books, 1982), and James S. Coleman and Thomas Hoffer, *Public and Private High Schools: The Impact of Communities* (New York: Basic Books, 1987).

11. The most recent and extensively rewritten version is Edward Banfield, *The Unheavenly City Revisited* (Boston: Little, Brown, 1974).

12. Consider for example the education of the black urban population of Philadelphia as described by W. E. B. Du Bois in his pioneering sociological study, *The Philadelphia Negro*. In 1847 more than a thousand black children, representing 53 percent of black children attending school, were attending one of twenty-nine char-

ity and private schools for blacks. In 1856, there were thirty-eight such schools, enrolling 56 percent of the black children in school. W. E. B. Du Bois, *The Philadelphia Negro* (Millwood, N.J.: Kraus-Thomson, 1973), 73–96.

13. As noted, the mean tuition for all private schools in 1985 was $1,218 ($985 for church-related private schools). Among families with incomes of $75,000 and over, the mean tuition was $2,483. U.S. Bureau of the Census, *Abstract 1987*, table 222.

14. In 1984, the average household, with an income of $24,578, spent $2,670 in personal taxes. Ibid., table 718.

CHAPTER TWELVE

LITTLE PLATOONS

1. Edmund Burke, *Reflections on the Revolution in France* (London: J. M. Dent, 1960), 44.

2. Edmund Burke, *First Letter on a Regicide Peace* (1796), in *The Philosophy of Edmund Burke*, ed. Louis I. Bredvold and Ralph G. Ross (Ann Arbor, Mich.: Ann Arbor Paperbacks, 1967), 102.

3. One of the plentiful examples: the ability of a small number of American sugarcane and sugar beet growers to get the government to require 250 million Americans to pay far more for sugar than the rest of the world does. I am touching very lightly on the topic of collective decision-making. Two titles that are especially relevant to these points are James M. Buchanan and Gordon Tullock, *The Calculus of Consent: Logical Foundations of Constitutional Democracy* (Ann Arbor, Mich.: University of Michigan Press, 1962), and Manour Olsen, *The Logic of Collective Action: Public Goods and the Theory of Groups* (Cambridge, Mass.: Harvard University Press, 1965).

4. See Charles A. Murray, *A Behavioral Study of Rural Modernization: Social and Economic Change in Thai Villages* (New York: Praeger, 1977). The descriptions of "amoral familism" and "image of the limited good" may be found in Edward C. Banfield, *The Moral Basis of a Backward Society* (Glencoe, Ill.: Free Press, 1958), and Oscar Lewis, *Life in a Mexican Village: Topoztlan Restudied* (Urbana, Ill.: University of Illinois Press, 1951), respectively.

5. See especially Aristotle's *Ethics*, bk. 2, chaps. 1–5. As he points out, even the word ethics is derived from the word for habit, *ethos*.

6. See, for example, Russell D. Roberts, "A Positive Model of Private Charity and Public Transfers," *Journal of Political Economy* 92 (1984): 136–48. See also B. A. Abrams and M. D. Schmitz, "The 'Crowding-Out' Effect of Governmental Transfers on Private Charitable Contributions," *Public Choice*, no. 1 (1978): 28–40.

7. Berger and Neuhaus, *To Empower People*. David Kennett makes another type of case for the efficiency of private institutions,

arguing that they become more, not less, advantageous compared to state redistribution as society becomes more complex. See David A. Kennett, "Altruism and Economic Behavior, I: Developments in the Theory of Public and Private Redistributions," *American Journal of Economics and Sociology* 39 (1980): 193–98, and Kennett, "Altruism and Economic Behavior, II: Private Charity and Public Policy," *American Journal of Economics and Sociology* 39 (1980): 337–53. Another intriguing discussion, focusing on the "free rider" problem, is Robert Sugden, "Reciprocity: The Supply of Public Goods Through Voluntary Contributions," *Economic Journal* 94 (1984): 772–87.

8. Leon Trotsky, *Literature and Revolution*, quoted in Nozick, *Anarchy, State, and Utopia*, 241.

9. Smith, *Moral Sentiments*, III.3.4, 136. I am indebted to Sowell, *Visions*, for bringing this passage to my attention.

10. Ibid., 237–38.

CHAPTER THIRTEEN
"To Close the Circle of Our Felicities"

1. Nozick, *Anarchy, State, and Utopia*, 299.
2. Thomas Jefferson, the first inaugural address, in *Portable Thomas Jefferson*, 292–93.

Index

Abramovitz, Moses, 68
Adams, John, 24, 168
  on Declaration, 171
Affiliations. *See also* Community
  and common beliefs and
    values, 263–64
  and community resolutions of
    problems, 261–62
  in neighborhoods, 262–63
Aggregation, unit of, 184n, 184–
  185
Aid to Families with Dependent
  Children (AFDC), 267,
  276n
Alienation, 134–35
Allport, Gordon, 113
Anomie, 134
Anti-Federalists, 175–76
"Approbativeness," 167–68
Aquinas, Saint Thomas, 25, 36
Aristotelian Principle, 114n, 137,
  161, 279, 281. *See also*
  Aristotle
  and effect of money payment
    on intrinsic rewards, 150–51

graph representing challenges
  vis-à-vis skills, 146–47
Aristotle, 25, 98, 171, 274. *See
  also* Aristotelian Principle
  on enjoyment and self-
    fulfillment, 136–37
  on happiness and wisdom,
    32–36, 41
  on human capacities and
    enjoyment, 50
Autonomy
  of man, and Founding
    Fathers, 166–68, 179
  and professionalization for
    teachers, 204–5, 213–14, 288
  at work, and enjoyment,
    151–57
Autotelic experiences, 142,
  264

Bailyn, Bernard, 171
Banfield, Edward C., 250n
  "amoral familism" concept,
    272n